Entrepreneurship and Innovation in Second Tier Regions

Entrepreneurship and Innovation in Second Tier Regions

Heike Mayer

University of Bern, Switzerland

Edward Elgar

Cheltenham, UK • Northampton, MA, USA

Published by
Edward Elgar Publishing Limited
The Lypiatts
15 Lansdown Road
Cheltenham
Glos GL50 2JA
UK

Edward Elgar Publishing, Inc.
William Pratt House
9 Dewey Court
Northampton
Massachusetts 01060
USA

A catalogue record for this book
is available from the British Library

Library of Congress Control Number: 2011930991

MIX
Paper from
responsible sources
FSC® C018575

ISBN 978 1 84720 359 5

Typeset by Servis Filmsetting Ltd, Stockport, Cheshire
Printed and bound by MPG Books Group, UK

Contents

Acknowledgements

This book is about two of my favourite questions in economic geography: why do certain regions develop entrepreneurial and innovative economies, and how can policymakers support knowledge-based economic development? In order to answer these questions, one needs to develop an in-depth understanding about a region's peculiar strengths and weaknesses. Through this study of three second tier high-tech regions in the United States, I had the opportunity to gain such an understanding. I do not know whether the answers I give in this book shed the right light on the questions and whether they are sufficiently developed to help policymakers understand the complex dynamics of regional economic development. However, I continue to be fascinated by the ability of certain regions in the world to capture entrepreneurial and innovative dynamics.

I grew up near Stuttgart, Germany, and I spent many summers working for small and medium-sized firms that were part of Baden-Württemberg's industrial districts. I became intrigued by the region's economic development and during a seminar at the University of Konstanz as an undergraduate I developed a keen interest in understanding the drivers of economically successful regions like this. I continued my studies as a Masters and Ph.D. student in the US, and as a graduate research assistant at Portland State University's Institute of Metropolitan Studies I had the good fortune to work on several applied research projects about Portland's economy. Through this work, I gained insights into regional economic development which culminated in a dissertation about the evolution of the high-tech economy in the Portland region. While working at Virginia Polytechnic Institute and State University (Virginia Tech), I had the opportunity to expand this research and examine two more regions (Boise, Idaho, and Kansas City, which straddles the Kansas-Missouri state border). Through these comparisons I was able to reflect on each region's growth. I am now working as a Professor of Economic Geography at the University of Bern in Switzerland and I continue to study regional development issues in the US. Writing this book has given me the opportunity to develop some preliminary answers to my initial questions and discover additional questions that I look forward to exploring in the future.

Researching and writing this book would not have been possible without the help of many colleagues and friends. My advisers at Portland State University deserve many thanks: Professors Carl Abbott, Sy Adler, Robert Daasch, Robert Liebman, Ethan Seltzer, and the late Craig Wollner supported me during the dissertation. I also had the privilege of working with economist Joe Cortright on a variety of research projects about Portland's regional economy. During my time at Virginia Tech, colleagues such as Paul Knox and Robert E. Lang shared with me invaluable insights about metropolitan growth patterns in the US. My graduate research assistants at Virginia Tech provided much needed research support: David Bieri, Shana Johnson, Seth Peery, and Roger Zalneraitis – you rock! A special thank you goes to David Bieri, who was instrumental in developing the quantitative analysis presented in Chapter 3. I also owe thanks to Stuart Armstrong who visualized the spin-off activities presented in Chapters 4 and 5. Other friends and colleagues offered valuable comments, including Ron Boschma, Jennifer Clark, Maryann Feldman, Ed Feser, Darrene Hackler, Ned Hill, Chris Hoene, Britta Klagge, Nicola Lowe, Ann Markusen, Sheila Martin, Philip McCann, Max-Peter Menzel, John Provo, and Greg Schrock. I would also like to thank Bruce Katz, Jennifer Vey, and Howard Wial at the Brookings Institution. They allowed me to develop the Kansas City case study and the comparative study of all three regions for two publications with the Brookings Metropolitan Policy Program (Mayer, 2006, 2009a). Special thanks to Hilary Russell who edited the book and to Alan Sturmer, who as Executive Editor at Edward Elgar Publishing supported this book project. I would also like to thank the numerous experts who took the time to meet with me and share their knowledge and experiences about their firms, industries, and regions.

Heike Mayer
March 2010
Bern, Switzerland

1. Introduction

'Starting a cluster involves, first, building the economic fundamentals for an industry or technology, and second, finding the spark of entrepreneurship to get going.'

Bresnahan, Gambardella, and Saxenian (2001: 842)

'In a world of dramatically improved communications systems and increasingly internationally mobile corporations, it is puzzling why certain places are able to grow relatively rapidly as well as sustain their attractiveness to both capital and labor. Movement is, of course, costly and disruptive to both. Harvey's (1982) work on capital's need for "spatial fix" and Storper and Walker's (1989) work on labor and reproduction suggest generic reasons why hypermobility cannot completely obliterate production ensembles in space. But neither account explains why certain places manage to generate, attract, and anchor productive activity while others do not. Why, in other words, do some cities achieve "second tier" status and successfully challenge primate cities while others do not?'

Markusen, Lee, and DiGiovanna (1999: 21)

For much of the twentieth century, the rise and subsequent success of Silicon Valley as the world's leading high-technology centre has captured the attention of researchers and policymakers. Indeed the region's prowess is obvious: Silicon Valley boasts the highest concentration of high-tech workers of any metropolitan area in the US and captures the largest share of risk capital invested in new business ventures. Silicon Valley evolved as a network-based industrial system that allowed its regional economy to adjust to economic downturns. As a result, numerous Silicon Valley-based entrepreneurs create revolutionary technologies, and the region's industries continuously evolve and reinvent themselves. Yet, high-tech development has spread beyond Silicon Valley, and other regions are emerging as vibrant, innovative and entrepreneurial high-technology locations. These regions represent second tier high-tech regions. While they often lack a nearby world-class research university – which is often thought necessary for high-tech development by policymakers and academics alike – or large amounts of venture capital, they do host large firms that take on the role of 'surrogate universities'. In this function, they attract and develop highly specialized and skilled *talent*, they create and commercialize cutting-edge *innovations*, and they function as incubators for *spin-off* firms. Second tier high-tech regions develop unique specializations and competitive advantages.

1

This book illustrates how three metropolitan areas in the US – Portland, Oregon; Kansas City, Kansas-Missouri; and Boise, Idaho – have emerged as second tier high-tech regions without the presence of a major research university. These three regions have significant concentrations of high-tech industry activity. Relative to their size and location, they are highly innovative and entrepreneurial. In each region, large firms that functioned as 'surrogate universities' built critical corporate assets that led to the development of unique industry specializations. Intel, for example, opened its first branch manufacturing facility in Portland in 1976 and has since then expanded it into a state-of-the-art manufacturing process development facility for semiconductor production. Consequently most of Intel's innovations are 'made in Oregon'. During the 1990s, the majority of Intel's patents were assigned to Oregon-based inventors. Hewlett-Packard relocated its printer division to Boise in 1973. Its trademark product, the laser printer, was developed in Idaho, not in Silicon Valley. Kansas City is a highly specialized life sciences centre that hosts a cluster of contract research organizations and firms in the animal health industry which, combined, capture major parts of the world's leading animal health market. The three regions stand out because in addition to building these corporate assets, state and local policymakers are developing unique policies to link universities with industry, facilitate entrepreneurship, and support the commercialization of knowledge.

Portland, Boise, and Kansas City are different in several ways from such large, well-known high-technology centres as Silicon Valley and Boston. Smaller and somewhat less specialized in high-tech industries, their businesses do not attract large amounts of venture capital and spend less on research and development. Each second tier region is uniquely specialized in a subset of high-tech industries. Portland is known for its concentration in high-tech manufacturing, particularly test and measurement equipment, semiconductors, and computers. Boise specializes in computer peripherals and semiconductors, and Kansas City specializes in pharmaceutical manufacturing and development, contract research and animal health sciences. Table 1.1 compares the three case study regions with two prominent high-tech centres, Silicon Valley and Boston's Route 128. While all three second tier high-tech regions are significantly smaller in terms of high-tech employment, they do specialize in high-tech as indicated by the location quotient measure. Relative to their size and extent to which they have a high-tech employment base, they do show positive measures in terms of entrepreneurship. In addition, Portland and Boise are about as inventive as Boston, measured by patenting activity (Table 1.1).

What is responsible for the success of these second tier high-tech regions? Case studies reveal a model of high-tech regional development

Table 1.1   Comparison of high-tech regions

High-tech activity indicator	Portland	Boise	Kansas City	San Francisco-San Jose (combined)	Boston
High-tech industry					
High-tech employment, 2005	58646	18969	49918	375413	218392
Number of high-tech firms, 2005	5614	1335	4850	23003	14357
High-tech location quotient, 2005[1]	1.35	1.76	1.14	3.27	1.96
Entrepreneurship					
Total number of high-tech firm births, 1998–2000	24	23	71	622	297
Venture capital deals per 1000 people, 2000–5	6.2	1.0	2.2	58.1	35.5
Innovation and research					
Total industry R&D funding, 2000–5 (millions of dollars)	$2087	$506	$662	$44862	$26422
Total university R&D funding, 2000–5 (millions of dollars)	$123	$42	$163	$10480	$7930
Patents per 1000 people, 1990–99	260	24	40	2126	223

Notes: 1. The high-tech location quotient, a measure of the extent to which a metropolitan area is specialized in high-tech industries, is the ratio of the percentage of a metropolitan area's employment that is in high-tech industries to the percentage of nationwide employment in those industries. A location quotient above 1.00 indicates some degree of high-tech specialization, and the higher the location quotient the greater the metropolitan area's high-tech specialization. I define high-tech industries as those that Daniel Hecker of the Bureau of Labor Statistics classified as 'Level I' high-tech industries, that have the highest percentages of their nationwide employment in such technology-oriented occupations as engineers, technicians, life and physical scientists, engineering and natural science managers. In general these industries group broadly into biotechnology, information technology, high-tech manufacturing, high-tech services, and research and development (R&D) (see Hecker, 2005).

Source: Author's analysis of data from County Business Patterns, US Census, Small Business Administration, National Science Foundation, and US Patent and Trademark Office.

that is fundamentally different from Silicon Valley. By serving as 'surrogate universities', their firms were able to develop leadership and market dominance in their respective industries. Their research and development efforts sometimes spilled over to the region through spin-off activities by former employees, fostering a supportive environment in which a network of spin-offs, competitors, suppliers and support firms flourished. Public policy efforts respond to this successful development and are mostly focused on linking existing higher education assets to industry. The second tier regions reviewed in this book literally bootstrapped their high-tech economies. Their successful emergence illustrates that the presence of a university is neither necessary nor sufficient for regional development. The analysis highlights the importance of businesses – particularly large and dominant industry players – in regional economic growth.

CONCEPTS AND PREMISES

The book explores four premises regarding the emergence of second tier high-tech regions. The first premise advances the idea that the Silicon Valley model may represent the exception and not the norm, especially when we consider the role of the university in high-tech development. Silicon Valley may represent one mode of development, but it is not clear whether this mode can be generalized to other regions. Efforts to imitate this model have mostly failed and are testament to the Valley's uniqueness. The Silicon Valley model highlights the role of the major research university as an engine of growth, spawning a theory of sorts that such a university is necessary to grow a high-tech economy. Contrary to this common assumption, the literature on the evolution of high-tech regions is characterized by a lively debate regarding a university's role in catalysing economic growth. The debate can be structured into three models that explain high-tech growth. The first model is characterized by successful high-tech development in regions where such a university is present. Regions like California's Silicon Valley or Boston's Route 128 represent this model. The second model describes regions that host research institutions, such as a world-class university that is extremely active in research and development, but have failed to leverage these institutions for high-tech economic development. These regions suggest that the presence of a research university is not sufficient for high-tech industry to thrive. The third model focuses on regions that do not have a major research university, but have successfully developed a high-tech industry base. This book focuses on this model and provides an alternative explanation of high-tech regional development. From this debate, the notion emerges that a research university is not necessary to spur high-tech industries and that the lessons Silicon Valley appears to provide us may be misleading.

The second premise highlights the role of firms as 'surrogate universities'. Regions that lack a major higher education infrastructure but have managed to grow a vibrant high-tech economy have leveraged the presence of large and dominant high-tech firms. It is firms and not universities that drive the growth of second tier high-tech regions. These firms have catalysed entrepreneurial spin-off processes that resulted in the formation of dynamic cluster economies. Clusters can be defined as regional groupings of similar and related firms that display strong and dynamic inter-firm relationships, an entrepreneurial environment, or a set of specific location factors that support the cluster's growth (Martin and Sunley, 2003; Porter, 2000a). Second tier high-tech regions grow and evolve primarily through spin-off processes, so we can also call them spin-off regions. A spin-off region is characterized by dynamic new firm formation, which in turn leads to cluster development. Spin-off regions grow a specialized set of industries through entrepreneurial activities. It is through these spin-off processes that skills, capabilities, and capacities are transferred and converted by entrepreneurial individuals who carry routines and institutions learned in their prior jobs.

Conceptualizing second tier high-tech regions as spin-off regions allows us to consider the question of how specialized regional economies evolve in the first place. Considering this question puts us in the middle of a debate that is characterized by two competing explanations. On the one hand, scholars argue that industry clusters grow because of agglomeration economies. In this view, agglomeration economies represent advantages that occur to the firm due to the location in an urban environment (urbanization economies) or in a cluster (localization economies). Linking clusters to entrepreneurship, Porter argues that 'new business ideas will tend to bubble up within clusters because of the concentration of firms, ideas, skills, technology, and needs there. Once an idea is perceived, the barriers to entry and growth are lower at cluster locations' (Porter, 2000b: 269). This perspective assumes that agglomeration economies give rise to entrepreneurial activities and implies that a certain level of economic activity has to be present for a cluster to emerge. The concept is rather imprecise, especially regarding the dynamic aspects of cluster formation and growth, as it is unclear how agglomeration economies evolve in the first place and what factors spur their emergence (Lorenzen, 2005; Martin and Sunley, 2003). Yet this perspective represents the dominant view about high-tech regional development. Common explanations about Silicon Valley's growth focus on the importance of the network-based regional industrial system that gives rise to entrepreneurial activities. Trying to explain the emergence of clusters from the perspective of agglomeration economies is limiting not only because of the lack of precision but also because the perspective does not incorporate an explanation of why regions that do not possess these dynamic agglomeration economies in the first place do (or do not) develop clusters. The second tier high-tech regions discussed in this book are a case in point, as their economies evolved despite the lack of agglomeration economies. A competing explanation highlights the role of spin-off processes in the creation of agglomeration economies (Klepper, 2001b, 2008). In this view, firms are the source of entrepreneurship because they function as incubators, and their employees exploit knowledge and experiences they gained there and carry these insights over to their subsequent ventures. This results in new industries or clusters, with the characteristics of these firms influencing the extent and nature of entrepreneurial evolution.

The third premise links back to the previous discussion and focuses on the role of firm building and entrepreneurship in regional economic development. It posits that second tier high-tech regions emerged because firms that acted as 'surrogate universities' influenced regional growth. Firm building activities such as linkages with other firms inside and outside the region, connections to markets, the type and nature of products and services the firms produce, the nature of production, corporate policies and culture, human and capital assets, innovation models, and corporate changes in general, shape the ways in which firms influence the regions in which they operate. Firm building is a dynamic process because corporate strategies change in response to market opportunities, demand, and competition (Berger, 2005). The regions examined in this book leveraged the presence of large firms that took the lead in their respective markets – Tektronix, Intel, Hewlett-Packard, Micron Technology, and Marion Laboratories – and these lead firms have undergone major restructuring processes in response to changes in national and global markets. Entrepreneurial activities helped spur growth in the second tier high-tech regions and these activities were influenced by the nature and evolution of the lead firms.

The fourth premise leads to a discussion about policy implications. Even though second tier high-tech regions managed to grow without the presence of a major research university, they have developed policies that link existing higher education institutions and research institutions with industries. While I am arguing that research universities are neither necessary nor sufficient for the emergence of a high-tech region, I am also arguing that universities have become more important over time in these regions and they have become important partners with local industry. The three regions discussed in this book have developed interesting models for linking universities with industry.

METHODOLOGY

This study examines the emergence of second tier high-tech regions in the US. Emerging high-tech regions are sometimes referred to as 'second tier cities'. Markusen et al. analysed second tier cities and defined them as 'spatially distinct areas of economic activity where a specialized set of trade-oriented industries takes root and flourishes, establishing employment and population growth trajectories that are the envy of many other places' (1999: 3). These second tier cities represent fast-growing medium-sized metropolitan areas, and their emergence is seen as a consequence of industrial restructuring and economic transformation. Markusen et al. (1999), however, define second tier cities based on population rather than the nature and extent of their high-tech economies. As a result, they discuss Silicon Valley alongside Colorado Springs. This approach fails to recognize that there are substantive differences between emerging second tier high-tech regions like Portland, Boise, and Kansas City and pioneering high-tech regions like Silicon Valley. Second tier high-tech regions, as defined in this book, specialize in certain sub-sectors of the high-tech economy and take advantage of the presence of lead high-tech firms. Collectively, these emerging high-tech regions have performed better than regions that represent so-called high-tech centres in recent years. They were able to recover more quickly from the bursting of the dot.com bubble in 2001 and they have shown stronger growth rates between 1998 and 2005 than the regions that are typically considered as pioneers. Understanding the dynamics of growth in second tier high-tech regions is important because these regions may offer more realistic scenarios for how to grow and transform a regional economy than Silicon Valley or Boston.

This book explores several fundamental questions about second tier high-tech regions. First, I ask which regions in the US have emerged as second tier high-tech regions, and to what extent they differ from their more prominent counterparts like California's Silicon Valley, Boston's Route 128, or North Carolina's Research Triangle Park? I answer this question in Chapter 3 through an in-depth analysis of economic data regarding employment, talent, innovation, and entrepreneurship for all metropolitan areas in the US. Second, I ask how did these second tier high-tech regions emerge and in what ways have they been able to develop knowledge-based economies even though they lack important prerequisites such as a major research university and large amounts of venture capital? The answer to this question is explored through in-depth case studies of three US metropolitan regions, Portland, Boise, and Kansas City. Within the case studies, I examine the ways in which firms function as 'surrogate universities' and how processes of firm building and entrepreneurship contribute to regional development. The last set of questions focuses on public policy: what kind of policies did the regions' economic developers and planners develop to support the growth of their knowledge-based industries?

The research involved two related inquiries: a broad quantitative overview of high-tech development in all metropolitan areas in the US and in-depth case studies of three second tier high-tech regions. The quantitative perspective involved an assessment of high-tech growth in the US and specifically an analysis of high-tech economic activity in the metropolitan statistical areas (MSAs). The procedure used an employment-based definition of high-tech industries and followed Hecker's approach (Hecker, 2005). In developing the typology, we used a wide range of data that reflect the economic performance of the MSAs and their associated degrees of industrial specialization, as well as input-based characteristics such as quality of the labour force, R&D funding, and employment concentration. To examine the ways in which metropolitan areas differ in their high-tech development, we employed a principal component and model-based cluster analysis to create typologies of high-tech regions. (For a detailed discussion of the methodology, including the 20 individual variables used for the cluster analysis, see Appendix.) The data can broadly be grouped into four thematic categories: economic performance, talent, innovation, and entrepreneurship. The analysis yielded a typology of high-tech regions that describes five distinct types:

1.   High-tech centres
2.   High-tech challenger regions
3.   High-tech hidden gem regions
4.   Old economy regions in transition
5.   Regions with no significant high-tech activity

High-tech challenger regions and high-tech hidden gem regions represent second tier high-tech regions. They differ in terms of their development dynamics, not only from each other but also from high-tech centres, old economy regions in transition, and regions with no significant high-tech activity.

In a second step, three metropolitan areas representing emerging high-tech regions were selected for in-depth case studies. Unlike regions that are in advantageous positions because of hosting military facilities, major research universities, federal research laboratories, proximity to large metropolitan areas, or because they can build on old economy industries, these cases represent regions that 'bootstrapped' their high-tech economies. Regions that bootstrap their high-tech economies manage to foster such knowledge-based industries in the absence of large amounts of venture capital or the presence of world-class universities. By using the word 'bootstrap' I imply that their economies manage to thrive economically without help from the outside, or to put it simply, they manage to pull themselves up by their own bootstraps. I chose to examine Portland (Oregon), Boise (Idaho), and Kansas City (Kansas-Missouri). Portland and Kansas City represent high-tech challenger regions, while Boise belongs to the hidden gem region category.

For the case studies, I decided to focus on three emerging high-tech regions that bootstrapped by leveraging corporate assets or other types of anchor institutions. These regions were chosen because they have above average high-tech employment concentration as measured by the location quotient (Boise with a location quotient of 1.76, Portland with 1.35, and Kansas City with 1.14) and because they represent different sizes (ranging from about 500 000 to 2 million residents). More importantly, they were able to grow a significant concentration of high-tech firms without factors often considered critical in the growth of a technology region: a world-class research university and large amounts of venture capital. In addition, each region can be considered a peripherally located area that has been overshadowed by other more prominent cities. For example, Seattle has always trumped Portland and Boise in the Pacific Northwest as a location for important business activities, and Kansas City always stood in the shadow of St Louis, Missouri, even though both were considered important urban centres in the heartland. How did these regions compensate for these missing ingredients? How did they overcome their location disadvantages and develop high-tech economies?

The case study research was informed by key informant interviews, secondary sources such as academic studies, newspaper articles, and corporate reports. In total, 104 semi-structured interviews were held with key experts in the three regions (see Appendix 1). In addition, I conducted online surveys of high-tech firms in Portland and Boise that included questions about the entrepreneur(s), the spin-off, and regional development factors. The surveys were conducted between July and December 2007 and followed a snowball sampling technique. The Kansas City case study did not include a survey. Here the motivation for inquiry was on differences and similarities between regions specializing in high-tech manufacturing (Portland and Boise) and regions specializing in life sciences (Kansas City). The chapter on Kansas City highlights how the second tier development model applies to the pharmaceutical and biotechnology industry.

Throughout, the study was guided by Markusen's approach to 'studying regions by studying firms' (Markusen, 1994: 477). The broad areas of inquiry included the notions of firm building, entrepreneurial firm formation, and the formation of a regional innovation milieu or networked economy. I conceptualized the lead firms as 'surrogate universities' that develop talent, engage in innovation and knowledge creation, and function as incubators of spin-offs. To assess their impact on the region's entrepreneurial economy, I used a corporate genealogy approach, in which entrepreneurial firms and their parents are of interest (Cooper, 1971; Klepper, 2001a, 2001b, 2008; Neck, Meyer, Cohen, and Corbett, 2004).

SYNOPSIS OF CHAPTERS

This book intends to stimulate scholars of regional development and economic developers to think about alternative models of high-tech regional growth. Policymakers and planning practitioners will find the book instructive because it provides a viable and – most of all – feasible alternative to the Silicon Valley model. The study also contributes to questions about regional economic evolution and the emergence of industrial clusters. The book highlights the role of firm building and entrepreneurship in the evolution of regional economies. More specifically, the research highlights the evolution of regions that are traditionally not regarded as pioneers in high-tech development and therefore have not received much scholarly attention.

Chapter 2 offers insights into an evolutionary theory of the emergence of high-tech regions. These insights encompass the deconstruction of several myths that resulted from the overemphasis on Silicon Valley as the model for high-tech development. I outline three alternative models of high-tech development and qualify the role of universities as neither necessary nor sufficient for high-tech growth. In a second step, I outline a theory of cluster emergence that rests on the role of firm building and entrepreneurship. Through the lens of firm building I am able to conceptualize the role of firms as 'surrogate universities'.

Chapter 3 presents a quantitative analysis of the metropolitan geography of high-tech development. The analysis does not simply rank metropolitan areas by the number of high-tech jobs, a method that would favour large urban places and historically established high-tech centres (Chapple, Markusen, Schrock, Yamamoto, and Yu, 2004; Cortright and Mayer, 2004). Instead I employ a substantively different approach that focuses on the degree to which different metropolitan areas share similar innovation, human capital, and entrepreneurship dynamics. This approach yields a typology of high-tech regions that distinguishes established high-tech centres from second tier regions, which can be further distinguished into challenger regions and hidden gem regions. In addition, the analysis identifies old economy regions in transition and regions with no significant high-tech activity.

Chapters 4, 5, and 6 present case studies of emerging second tier high-tech regions. Each provides a detailed historical account of the evolution of a specific second tier high-tech region. Chapter 4 discusses the case of Portland, Oregon. This region, also known as the Silicon Forest, hosts a variety of high-tech firms that specialize in manufacturing semiconductors and test and measurement instruments. These include companies with a world-class reputation, including Intel and Tektronix. Intel, one of the most prominent computer chip makers, employs about 15 000 workers in the Portland region, and the company's Oregon facilities host Intel's most important R&D functions. The presence of Intel has attracted a variety of competitors, and the region produces about 10 per cent of the world's semiconductors. Tektronix is internationally known for its high quality oscilloscopes. Intel and Tektronix played the role of incubators for many well-known high-tech start-ups such as Sequent Computer Systems (now IBM), Mentor Graphics, Triquint Semiconductors, and InFocus Systems, among others. In this chapter I argue that Intel and Tektronix attracted a talented workforce, functioned as incubators for start-up companies, and engaged in research that spilled over to the region. In addition, Portland was able to develop an innovation milieu in which new companies – both homegrown and from the outside – flourish. I also discuss the ways in which Oregon's universities are building unique partnerships among themselves and with industry to address critical issues of innovation and knowledge creation. The Oregon Nanoscience and Microtechnologies Institute (ONAMI) could serve as a model for how other regions could leverage synergies from various higher education institutions.

Chapter 5 discusses the case of Boise, Idaho, another fast-growing metropolitan region in the Pacific Northwest. Like Portland, Boise benefited from the expansion of California-based companies such as Hewlett-Packard (HP). It also is home to a successful home-grown semiconductor manufacturing company, Micron Technology. Micron employs about 10 000 workers in Boise, of which an estimated 1300 are involved with R&D. Boise is also an important location for Hewlett-Packard. Even though HP's employment in Boise has declined, the remaining jobs are more concentrated in R&D. Both Micron and HP serve the region as 'surrogate universities', as the local higher education infrastructure is not as developed and has only improved slightly in recent years. Even though Boise has seen its economy transform into a knowledge-based regional economy, local and state policymakers are reluctant to embrace this new type of economy. Regional economic development policies are fragmented and underfinanced and efforts are often stifled by politics.

Chapter 6 discusses the case of Kansas City, a region in the heartland of the US that has managed to grow a vibrant life sciences economy. I argue that Kansas City shows underdeveloped capacity on a variety of indicators, such as top-tier research universities, patent registrations, and venture capital investments that could support an innovative economy. These deficiencies would lead a pessimist to assume that the region faces a daunting challenge in trying to establish a vibrant life sciences or high-tech industry cluster. However, I argue against that pessimism and show that Kansas City's economy possesses an array of assets that sets the city apart from its competitors. For example, Kansas City has been home to locally grown firms (especially the pharmaceutical company Marion Laboratories) that have functioned as anchors and entrepreneurial seedbeds for a budding life sciences economy. Marion Laboratories' impact on the Kansas City economy has been similar to that of Tektronix and Intel on the Portland region. The firm contributed to the creation of a talented labour pool (employees who were especially familiar with drug development and marketing) and entrepreneurship in the form of new locally based spin-off companies. In addition, major investments have been made in life sciences research over the past five years, with the Stowers Institute for Medical Research being the linchpin in this endeavour. Stowers' $2 billion endowment is the largest endowment for a medical research organization in the US and holds much promise for the Kansas City life sciences economy. I discuss how policymakers, business representatives, and higher education officials are facing their biggest challenge: to keep the economic benefits of commercialization of innovation in Kansas City and to grow entrepreneurial companies.

Finally, in Chapter 7, I review the implications of the growth of second tier high-tech regions and their significance. I discuss the opportunities and challenges these regions face and highlight their limitations in comparison to established high-tech centres. I also discuss policy implications for practitioners interested in fostering innovative and entrepreneurial high-tech economies.

NOTE

1. Flexibly specialized businesses can be defined as 'small, innovative firms, embedded within a regionally cooperative system of industrial governance which enables them to adapt and flourish despite globalizing tendencies' (A. R. Markusen, et al., 1999, p. 22). Other authors, particularly in the field of economic geography, have written about the concept and used it to explain the rise of specialized regional economies (Amin, 1994; Piore and Sabel, 1984; A. J. Scott, 2004; Storper and Christopherson, 1987).

2. The evolution of high-technology regions

'Our understanding of the origins of industrial clusters needs to move beyond suggestions of a list of ingredients that, once in place, result in economic development. It is as if in the current conceptualization clusters emerge full grown, like Athena from the head of Zeus, without passage through defining developmental stages.'

Feldmann and Braunerhjelm (2006: 1)

In this chapter I outline a conceptual approach to understanding the evolution of high-tech regions. In particular, I contest the conventional wisdom which suggests that a world-class research university (Levin, Jeong, and Ou, 2006) is necessary to seed and grow a high-tech cluster. Compared to regions like Silicon Valley or Boston, most second tier regions do not have a world-class, or even strong, higher education infrastructure. Yet some of them have managed to grow vibrant technology economies. In contrast, many regions with strong universities (for example Baltimore in Maryland) have not managed to leverage their higher education institutions. Thus universities are *neither necessary nor sufficient* for the emergence of a regional high-tech economy. If universities do not seed high-tech growth, how do such industry clusters emerge? My theory of cluster emergence posits that high-tech firms of a certain nature can function as *surrogate universities* which act as incubators of start-ups. They attract and develop talent and through their innovation activities they contribute to knowledge spillovers. Not every firm, however, can perform this function. Corporate strategies related to innovation, production, human resources policies, and market linkages influence the creation, growth, maintenance, and decline of high-tech industry clusters.

To support this argument, I examine the emergence of Silicon Valley and the ways in which this region has shaped our understanding of regional economic development. I then deconstruct several myths about Silicon Valley. For example, Stanford University is often credited with the emergence of the high-tech industry in that region, a notion that is too limited and does not consider the Valley's rich and varied history. Next I highlight three models of high-tech growth. I then focus on the emergence of second tier high-tech regions in relation to Silicon Valley,

Finally, I focus on the role of lead firms and entrepreneurship in cluster emergence.

THE SILICON VALLEY MYTH REVISITED

Second tier high-tech regions have not received much attention in the literature. Most discussions of high-tech regional development centre on the evolution of Silicon Valley and focus on the unique aspects of that region's growth. Yet second tier high-tech regions like Portland, Boise, and Kansas City have emerged in spite of Silicon Valley's dominance. Their emergence must be seen within the context of different models of regional economic development – including those that describe peripheral locations.

Silicon Valley is probably the most prominent high-tech region in the world. With more than 200 000 people employed in high-tech industries as of 2006, the region ranks highest in the US in the concentration of high-tech jobs. Silicon Valley-based high-tech start-ups consistently attract a majority of the venture capital available in the US. Its inventors are pioneers in developing cutting edge products and services. In sum, Silicon Valley is considered a pioneer high-tech region that many policymakers envy and try to imitate.

Numerous scholars have studied Silicon Valley and tried to explain its growth dynamics (such as Bresnahan, et al., 2001; Kenney, 2000; Lecuyer, 2005; Rogers and Larsen, 1984; Saxenian, 1994b; Sturgeon, 2000). The most widely accepted accounts emphasize cultural and organizational aspects and a set of prerequisites necessary for growing an entrepreneurial and innovative high-tech economy. Together these studies helped create a commonly accepted myth about what makes high-tech regions successful. This mythical formula resembles a simple recipe: take a network of small and medium-sized firms that cooperate extensively but compete fiercely with each other, put a world-class research university (like Stanford or MIT) at the centre of this network, and sprinkle large amounts of venture capital over the mixture.

Many studies have bolstered this view: Saxenian (1994a, 1994b, 2000) describes Silicon Valley as a network-based industrial district guided by high levels of trust, cooperation, labour mobility, and a culture of risk taking and entrepreneurship. She contrasts the California region with Boston's Route 128 corridor, a regional high-tech centre that stagnated in the 1970s and 1980s due to a completely different industrial organization – one that emphasized vertical integration, self-contained firms, and a culture of secrecy. Other studies, including some conducted by Saxenian (1994b), have emphasized the role played by Stanford University. These accounts credit Stanford with fostering entrepreneurial firms and spin-off companies, contributing to a skilled workforce and talent base, and creating important innovations and inventions that are commercialized by Silicon Valley-based firms (Adams, 2005). This view has led to a theory of sorts that postulates that world-class research universities are the engines of growth in high-tech regions and that fostering knowledge-based economies might not be feasible if a region does not have such a university. Another often mentioned prerequisite of high-tech growth is the presence of large amounts of venture capital, and Silicon Valley has been credited with the rise of the modern venture capital industry (Banatao and Fong, 2000; Hellmann, 2000; Kenney and Florida, 2000).

Most efforts to imitate Silicon Valley have failed, and an analysis of these attempts discredits the aforementioned myths. For example, consider the activities of Frederic Terman, Stanford's provost and dean of engineering (himself an entrepreneurial individual who led Stanford's efforts to nurture Silicon Valley's high-tech economy). By the mid-1960s, he had travelled to other regions in the US and abroad in an effort to replicate the Silicon Valley model. Terman believed that Silicon Valley could be copied if the right kind of university was in place. He tried to set up higher education institutions that resembled Stanford in places as far-flung as northern New Jersey; Dallas, Texas; and South Korea. His attempts failed because he overemphasized the role of the research university and did not fully appreciate the importance of the local environment. He ignored the fact that even in Silicon Valley, industry and the university grew up together and developed a symbiotic relationship over time. He also failed to see that the right kind of environment – one that fosters networks and cooperation – would be necessary to leverage the presence of higher education institutions (Leslie, 2001; Leslie and Kargon, 1996).

Silicon Valley's growth in the 1980s and 1990s mobilized policymakers and business leaders in the US and across the world to strive to transform their regions into the 'next Silicon Valley' (Miller and Cote, 1985; Rogers and Larsen, 1984). Most often these attempts failed because they did not acknowledge the complex nature of the evolution of a high-tech region. Rather, they tried to follow the simple recipe outlined earlier.

While many accounts of the history of Silicon Valley start with a focus on the role of Stanford's Terman in the formation of companies like Hewlett-Packard (Saxenian, 1994b), they ignore the region's long-standing history in technology and innovation. Sturgeon (2000), for example, traces Silicon Valley's success to the emergence of the radio industry and the formation of the Federal Telegraph Corporation (FTC) in Palo Alto in 1909. FTC was an important incubator for other pioneering firms such as one of the companies that developed and manufactured vacuum tubes,

Litton Industries. Sturgeon's account shows that the history of Silicon Valley cannot be reduced to the roles played by Stanford University and Hewlett-Packard.

Further evidence of the importance of firms in high-tech industry development can be seen in the history of Fairchild Semiconductors. This company was established in Palo Alto in 1957 by a group of eight scientists who had left Shockley Semiconductor Laboratory (Lecuyer, 2000). Fairchild spawned over two dozen semiconductor-related start-ups, including Intel, Advanced Micro Devices (AMD), and LSI Logic (Berlin, 2001). Fairchild's research laboratory, which was set up separately from its manufacturing operation, turned out to be 'the source of much of the technology used by firms that eventually spun out' (Gibbons, 2000: 216). Firms and their research laboratories may have played a more important role than universities in developing the semiconductor industry, one of Silicon Valley's signature industries.

Conventional wisdom also ignores the fact that the region's high-tech economy is quite heterogeneous. The network of small and medium-sized high-tech firms that cooperate and compete with each other represents only one aspect of the industrial structure. Often overlooked is the role of large firms in the industrial ecosystem. Large firms, such as Intel, often dominate networks in Silicon Valley (Gray et al., 1999). These large firms can exert power over local economies and determine the ways in which regions develop (Christopherson and Clark, 2007). Large corporations, especially those operating in capital-intensive industries, can also retain barriers to entry for small firms. Yet large firms can positively impact regional economies: their resource base allows for greater investments in talent and innovation, and they can serve as incubators for start-up firms (Mayer, 2005a, 2005b). They can take on the lead role in facilitating the emergence of a regional economy and they therefore can act as the region's lead firms.

Saxenian's account of Silicon Valley also overlooks the heterogeneity of high-tech industry sectors (Gray et al., 1999; McCann and Arita, 2006). Her account primarily focuses on flexibly specialized semi-conductor design firms, such as Cypress Semiconductors or Cirrus Logic and overlooks the large vertically integrated semiconductor manu-facturers, including Intel, Texas Instruments, and Toshiba (Arita and McCann, 2007).[1] Semiconductor firms like Intel have expanded outside of Silicon Valley (Gray et al., 1999). Interestingly, these firms not only relocated production from Silicon Valley into lower-cost regions (as the product cycle theory would predict) but also shifted important R&D activities to other locations, thus giving rise to alternative high-tech locations.

Relevant to the emergence of second tier high-tech regions like Boise and Portland is the fact that Silicon Valley firms started to expand outside of California in the 1950s and 1960s. Initially firms like Hewlett-Packard and Fairchild Semiconductor set up sales offices or manufacturing plants to take advantage of emerging markets and lower labour costs. Hewlett-Packard, for example, opened sales offices and manufacturing facilities in Switzerland and Germany in 1959 (Packard, 1995). Fairchild Semiconductor built manufacturing plants in Portland, Maine, in 1962 because wages 'were only half of those in the Bay area' (Lecuyer, 2005: 204) and because the workforce was anti-union. Fairchild also ventured into Asia, establishing a subsidiary in Hong Kong in 1963 and one in South Korea in 1965 (Lecuyer, 2005). Expansions outside of Silicon Valley continued into the 1970s: Hewlett-Packard opened a branch facility in Boise, Idaho, in 1973, and Intel established its first branch manufacturing plant in a suburb of Portland, Oregon, in 1976 (Mayer, 2009a). The push to expand outside of Silicon Valley coincided with the tremendous growth of a commercial market for high-tech products and the need to lower production costs. Expansions outside the Valley were accompanied by a shift from Fordist mass production to a model characterized by flexible specialization, production networks, and the integration of R&D into the manufacturing process (Piore and Sabel, 1984; A. Scott, 2008). This shift, in turn, influenced branch facilities, which evolved from focusing solely on production (and taking advantage of low costs) to engaging in innovation.

Firm relocation and branching outside of Silicon Valley has not received much attention because the dominant focus of the literature has been on the inner workings of Silicon Valley. Second tier regions like Portland and Boise, however, have benefited from firms like Intel and Hewlett-Packard setting up branches. Firms have been relocating and branching out of Silicon Valley since the 1950s. Zhang (2003), for example, shows that during the decade of the 1990s more firms and employees moved out of Silicon Valley and California than moved in. At Intel in 2008 there were more than 15 500 employees at branch locations in Oregon, more than twice the number at the firm's Santa Clara headquarters (Intel, 2008).

In sum, the case of Silicon Valley shows that the commonly held myths about the region's emergence and growth as a high-tech centre do not fully reflect the various facets of its growth. First, the overemphasis on the role of the university as an engine of economic growth led scholars to underemphasize the importance of large firms. Large firms in Silicon Valley have played an instrumental role in attracting and developing talent, creating innovations, and incubating spin-offs. Second, the implications of firm relocation and branching out have not received enough attention. Silicon Valley is not an island of innovative activity cut off from other regional economies. Rather, like many other regions, it functions like a node in a global network of regional economies (Amin and Thrift, 1992). If we want to fully grasp the implications of high-tech regional development in the US, it is important to understand Silicon Valley and other regions – particularly second tier high-tech regions – as connected nodes in a global economic web.

THREE MODELS OF HIGH-TECHNOLOGY DEVELOPMENT

There are a variety of models of high-tech growth, and there is a lively debate in the academic literature about the role of the university in catalysing and maintaining a region's high-tech economy. This debate can be structured by considering three models (Mayer, 2007). The first is the classic Silicon Valley model characterized by successful high-tech development where a world-class research university is present. Other regions that represent this model are North Carolina's Research Triangle Park and Boston's Route 128 in the US, and Cambridge in the United Kingdom. The second model describes regions that host significant research institutions such as a large university or federally funded research laboratories, but have failed to leverage this infrastructure for high-tech economic development, such as Baltimore or Cleveland. The third model, including the case studies in this book, describes regions that lack a world-class university or research institution but nonetheless have successfully developed a high-tech industrial base.

The most popular perspective is associated with the first model. Saxenian (1994b) describes how MIT's and Stanford's close partnerships with high-tech industries benefited regional economic growth in Boston and Silicon Valley. Luger and Goldstein (1990) point to the prominent role North Carolina's universities played in the planning and development of Research Triangle Park, which was deliberately located in close proximity to Duke University, the University of North Carolina, and North Carolina State University. The so-called Cambridge Phenomenon describes the ways in which a high-tech industry agglomerated around the University of Cambridge in the UK and how the majority of companies there can directly or indirectly (as children of university-related spin-offs) trace their genealogy to the university (Segal, 1985; Wicksteed, 2000a, 2000b). The theory of the university as an economic engine has also been applied to second tier high-tech regions. In Austin, Texas, the University of Texas has played an important role in promoting home-grown companies (some of them as university spin-offs) and in attracting large technology firms from outside (Smilor et al., 1989). One study addresses the need for a university and even notes that 'if such a research university is not in place, and has not attained an acceptable level of overall excellence, then a technology centre is not likely to develop very rapidly' (Smilor, Dietrich, and Gibson, 1993: 204).

The model of the university as an economic engine and the cases cited above have contributed to a new understanding of the role of the university in regional economic development. A new paradigm of the 'entrepreneurial university' (Etzkowitz, 2001) has emerged whereby higher education institutions, aiming to increase their economic and societal contributions, go beyond traditional functions like teaching and research to engage in activities more typically associated with private corporations. Programmes related to technology transfer, licensing, spin-off activities, and the like play a more prominent role in this entrepreneurial model.

The second model describes regions that have failed to develop a high-tech economy despite the presence of a university. Studies of such regions challenge the theory of the university as an economic engine and suggest that the presence of a university or a research infrastructure is not sufficient for growing a high-tech economy. A region also needs to develop an economic infrastructure and a supportive local environment capable of translating knowledge spillovers into commercialization and job creation. The two cases described below represent this model.

Feldman (1994) presents a case study of the Baltimore, Maryland, region, which hosts one of the most prominent medical research universities in the US, Johns Hopkins University. She finds that the region was not able to develop an innovation infrastructure around the university. Baltimore lacked a critical mass of technology-intensive firms that could commercialize university research; it also lacked large firms that focused on R&D and could absorb the university's spillovers. Nor did the region have specialized producer service firms and an entrepreneurial culture that would have encouraged researchers to start new companies. Consequently the local economy did not capture the benefits available as a result of its proximity to the university. A biotech cluster emerged not too far from Baltimore and Johns Hopkins University, along the Route 270 corridor in the Washington, DC, metropolitan region. The push for this development came from federal government downsizing (Feldman, 2001; Feldman and Francis, 2003), which resulted in increased start-up activity. According to Feldman and Francis, 'the majority of entrepreneurs came from private laboratories or companies (65 per cent) in the combined time period, 1973–1985' (2003: 783). With a critical mass of entrepreneurial start-up companies, the region then developed a vibrant innovation milieu that traced its roots not to universities but to the transformation of the public and private sectors. Rather than being proactive, policymakers and higher education representatives responded to the budding biotech economy and established university-based programmes to support it. Local universities have built incubators, and the state is a leading investor in efforts to link universities with industry.

Cleveland, Ohio, is another instructive case demonstrating that the mere presence of research organizations is not sufficient. Forgarty and Sinha (1999) examined patent citations and presented evidence for failed university engagement in the Cleveland region. Faced with severe industrial decline, regional leaders decided to invest in aspects of the research infrastructure such as science and technology centres, technology transfer, and commercialization programmes. These investments, however, did not induce major economic development and restructuring. Instead, the researchers found that important technological breakthroughs that had been developed in Cleveland's laboratories quickly diffused to other regions, namely Silicon Valley and Boston. Cleveland simply did not have the supportive local environment and entrepreneurial infrastructure necessary to absorb the knowledge spillovers.

The third model describes cases of successful high-tech development that occur without the presence or engagement of a world-class university. These cases present evidence that challenges the theory of the university as necessary for high-tech growth. The regions compensated for the lack of a university by hosting firms, private research laboratories, or military facilities that acted as catalysts for high-tech growth. Two examples are instructive here: Colorado Springs, Colorado, and Seattle, Washington.

In the case of Colorado Springs, the region had no research university; it also lacked a skilled labour force. Instead, military facilities built the basis of regional economic development and high-tech growth. Labour was attracted from other states by the rapidly expanding military facilities (Markusen et al., 1991). Local leaders pushed to improve the higher education system and 'forced the state' to set up a university so that 'university involvement has followed the creation of the complex, not the other way around' (p. 241). Seattle represents a case where the university did not provide the impetus for the growth and evolution of a certain sub-sector of the high-tech economy. The software and information technology industry emerged there primarily because of the presence of Microsoft Corporation (Gray et al., 1996; Gray et al., 1999).[2]

The three models of high-tech development illustrate that universities contribute to a regional high-tech economy in a variety of ways but are neither a sufficient nor a necessary component of high-tech success.[3] The evidence also seems to point to the importance of the firms themselves in creating successful high-tech regions.

THE RISE OF SECOND TIER HIGH-TECH REGIONS

Silicon Valley's prominence in the literature about regional high-tech development may have overshadowed insights emerging from other regions, particularly regions typically considered second tier. The literature regarding successful high-tech development in second tier regions is small but insightful and relies primarily on case studies of particular regions. In the following examples from the US and Europe, I highlight some general patterns that are emerging from the case studies. Before I describe these cases, I will focus on a set of larger economic trends that have shaped the emergence of these second tier regions.

In the US larger economic trends have been partially responsible for the emergence of second tier high-tech regions, particularly in the South and West. One of the most important trends was the shift of economic and political power from the traditional industrial cities in the Northeast and Midwest – commonly called the manufacturing belt (later the rustbelt) – to emerging, fast-growing metropolitan areas in the South and West whose economies have specialized in high-tech manufacturing (Abbott, 1981). These regions, often referred to as the Sunbelt, started to prosper during and after the Second World War, as new military facilities opened and federal defence investments spurred new industries such as aerospace and electronics (Markusen, et al., 1991). Referring to the period between 1963 and 1998, Ceh and Gatrell note that 'surprisingly, some of the peripherally located "software" states, such as Arizona, Idaho, South Dakota, and Utah, did now show notable R&D growth' (2006: 540). Other researchers found that during the 1980s the fastest growing metropolitan regions, such as Phoenix, Arizona; Dallas, Texas; and San Diego, California experienced high growth and specialization in only one or two industry sectors, indicating that these emerging second tier regions were highly specialized (Pollard and Storper, 1996). These Sunbelt regions continued this pattern into the 1990s (Gittell and Sohl, 2005).

The shift of economic activity from the Northeast and Midwest to the South and West was augmented in the 1960s and 1970s by a shift of economic activity out of successful high-tech centres such as Silicon Valley as those firms expanded. At the time, Silicon Valley already faced enormous diseconomies of agglomeration such as high land cost and lack of talent due to competitive labour markets. Many firms responded by setting up branch plants in smaller metropolitan areas that were still accessible by a two-hour flight. Glasmeier notes that 'this forced exodus resulted in the creation of a number of dependent technical centres outside the core regions of high-tech development' (1988: 290). Some of the branch facilities, however, not only focused on manufacturing but also started to incorporate higher-level activities such as design, engineering, prototyping, and testing. These spatial shifts led to the emergence of second tier high-tech regions that evolved into important locations for innovation and product development.

Several case studies of locations that became second tier high-tech regions provide useful insights. For example, Austin, Texas, attracted numerous high-tech manufacturing branch plants in addition to foster-ing home-grown technology firms (Oden, 1997). During the 1960s the region attracted IBM and Texas Instruments with traditional location factors such as low cost of land, availability of talent, relatively low wages, good infrastructure, and convenient access to emerging growth markets in the South and West. During the 1970s the semiconductor industry there began to expand after Illinois-based Motorola and several Silicon Valley-based firms such as AMD opened manufacturing branches there. Over time, these branch facilities transformed into sites that integrated cutting edge R&D into production processes, a shift that started to take place in response to competitive pressures from Japanese companies. In addition, local boosters attracted several industry research groups such as Microelectronics and Computer Technology Corporation (MCC) and SEMATECH. Specialized business and producer services emerged, local networks and linkages developed, and local universities – especially the University of Texas – started to engage with industry.

Another region that successfully transformed a branch plant economy into an industrial district is the adjacent cities of Denver and Boulder, Colorado (Lyons, 1995; Neck et al., 2004). In the late 1950s and early 1960s advanced high-tech manufacturing facilities for IBM, Martin Marietta, and Ball Brothers Aerospace initiated successful economic development, albeit with limited local inter-firm linkages. Studies of this region indicate that access to universities or government research labora-tories was not important in the location decisions of those firms (Lyons, 1995). The Denver/Boulder high-tech economy grew primarily because of entrepreneurship. A few dominant large firms played the role of incuba-tors for start-up companies (Neck, et al., 2004). About 32 per cent of the firms examined for one study (Lyons, 1995) were founded by entrepre-neurs who used to work for other local firms. At least four generations of spin-offs emerged from these lead firms, indicating that the region success-fully developed endogenous entrepreneurial dynamics.

The extent to which lead firms contributed to local entrepreneurship was influenced by a series of critical events that shaped the organizational structure and strategy of those firms: layoffs, corporate growth and decline, initial public offerings, and bankruptcies increased local start-up activities. Spin-offs not only diversified the economy but also created important agglomeration economies such as a skilled and specialized labour pool. The influence of the few lead firms extended into the business environment as local leaders forced the state to establish a university presence. During the 1960s, for example, Hewlett-Packard demanded the establishment of a branch of the University of Colorado in Denver (A. Markusen, et al., 1991). These two case studies indicate that local economies that start out as branch plant locations can indeed evolve into more embedded and innovation-based second tier high-tech regions. Key to such a successful transition are the organizational strategies of lead firms, their impact on local entrepreneurship, and the ways in which the local economy develops.

Several case studies of locations that have *not* been able to develop entrepreneurial or networked second tier high-tech regions can be found across the US.[4] Colorado Springs, Colorado, for example, also benefited from the shift of economic activity into the Sunbelt. During the 1940s and 1950s the region successfully recruited military installations such as the Air Force Academy. Local boosters started to recruit electronics branch plants in the 1970s, sports organizations in the 1980s, and religious non-profit organizations in the 1990s. During each round of recruitment local assets built in previous rounds were used to attract firms and organizations. This 'recruit and parlay' strategy (Gray and Markusen, 1999: 312) led to the creation of economic assets that were harnessed by subsequent rounds of recruitment: military assets created a reliable workforce, which was leveraged by the electronics branch plants. These in turn recruited engineers from across the nation. The region's quality of life and low costs helped firms to attract qualified labour easily. The electronics industry, however, never developed strong local ties. Only the religious organizations sector formed strong local linkages and resembles a flexibly specialized industrial district.

Richardson, Texas, a suburban city in the Dallas-Fort Worth metropolitan region, experienced similar development (Lyons, 2000). In 2000 the region was home to about 600 high-tech firms and about 70000 workers, most of whom were employed by lead firms such as Texas Instruments, Alcatel, Ericsson, and MCI. The city's high-tech roots go back to the 1950s when both Texas Instruments and Collins Radio (later Rockwell International) located facilities there. These two firms created a large pool of highly skilled labour, particularly engineers. As the firms went through significant corporate changes such as downsizing, employees left and started their own businesses. Over time a local venture capital industry emerged that supported local entrepreneurship. Other firms started to move to the region to take advantage of the emerging agglomeration economies. Even though local entrepreneurship and new firms diversified the economy, the firms never formed strong inter-firm relationships. Rather, they tended to develop more links to markets and suppliers in the rest of the US, primarily because they wanted to tap the knowledge capacities of other industrial districts. Only a small group of the most innovative firms have developed higher levels of trust and cooperation locally.

There are also regions that have failed to leverage the presence of home-grown high-tech firms or branch plants. Glasmeier (1988) examined the influence of lead high-tech firms in three regions in the US (Phoenix, Arizona; Melbourne, Florida; and Austin, Texas). Each region failed to leverage the presence of lead firms such as Motorola, Harris Corporation, and Rolm Corporation. She concludes that firm structure and strategy influence a region's development trajectory. The firms, for example, did not encourage linkages with the local economy (either supplier linkages or other relationships). The nature of the labour pool was also an important determinant. Firms that employ mostly production workers may fail to stimulate local entrepreneurship, as those workers are very different from the types who may become the next entrepreneur. A firm's business model, product, and market; its corporate culture towards human resources and entrepreneurship; its 'non-compete' regulations for former employees; and the type of R&D the company conducts – all influence the extent to which a firm can encourage or inhibit the creation of start-ups and local business opportunities. A firm that mass produces a product that is based on price rather than features, employs a higher share of production workers than so-called manager-engineers, and has a culture that discourages experimentation and entrepreneurship will not contribute to the local economy. The nature of this type of firm and its relationships to entrepreneurship will be discussed in more detail later in this chapter.

The biotechnology industry in the US experienced slightly different regional development patterns. The industry emerged in the 1970s when scientists in San Francisco discovered a new method to use recombinant DNA to develop pharmaceutical products. These scientists co-founded one of the first biotech firms, Genentech (Genetic Engineering Technology, Inc.). Traditionally the biotech industry has shown strong clustering along the West and East Coasts. Cortright and Mayer (2002) have shown that only nine regions in the US can be considered biotech leaders, as they show disproportionately high concentrations of commercialization and entrepreneurship. The biotech industry, which consists predominantly of small research and capital-intensive firms, differs from its counterpart, the pharmaceutical industry, which is characterized by large multinational corporations. Research-intensive biotech firms most often cluster around universities, because often so-called 'star scientists' (the most productive in discoveries related to genetic sequencing) are typically employed by universities and they tend to be engaged in founding the ventures (Zucker and Darby, 1996).

Despite the strong agglomeration tendencies in the industry, a few areas have emerged as second tier biotech regions. One of these, Kansas City, Missouri, is detailed in this book. Indianapolis, Indiana, represents another interesting case of a second tier biotech region. Walcott (1998, 2001) examined the role of Eli Lilly and Company (Lilly), a global pharmaceutical company headquartered in Indianapolis where the firm employs about 12 000 workers, in economic development. Walcott refers to Lilly as a 'technological oligarch' (2001: 513). Being far away from biotech centres in the Mid-Atlantic region and the West Coast, Lilly compensates by leveraging benefits from the agglomeration of other firms in the medical device and health sectors. In-house research laboratories and extensive research collaborations with universities and start-ups across the world ensure a continued supply of new commercialization opportunities. Lilly also taps into other regions such as Research Triangle Park in North Carolina; San Diego, California, and Shanghai in eastern China through firm acquisitions and branch facilities. In addition, Lilly's civic engagement and local influence ensure its success in recruiting and retaining a highly qualified but mobile labour force of scientists and engineers. Both Lilly and Indianapolis' universities benefit from joint appointments, where Lilly's researchers can teach at academic institutions and interact with their university colleagues.

The studies of second tier high-tech and biotech regions reviewed here illustrate some important insights into the ways in which agglomerations of knowledge-based economic activity emerge. Common to the studies is the role of large, dominant, innovative, and often market-leading firms. These firms shape the regional environment through spin-offs (by functioning as incubators and becoming parents of new ventures); they attract and develop labour; they exert political power and shape the region's business environment; they provide business opportunities for other firms; they can implant their resources in a region; and – through market relationships – they link to other regions. In all these activities, the organizational structure, and the corporate strategies of these firms play a significant role, and we need to pay attention to these firm-specific aspects. Moreover, corporate changes and evolution can affect the local economy. For example, negative corporate events such as acquisitions, lay-offs, and restructuring can have positive impacts on the local economy. Second tier regions may not immediately develop strong inter-firm relationships, but they can do so over time, indicating that clusters also go through evolutionary processes. While local connections do not seem to be critical, second tier regions benefit from external links. As we have seen in the review of the role of universities in regional high-tech development, higher education institutions are neither necessary nor sufficient for the formation of high-tech clusters. However, they can function as important support institutions that help anchor lead firms and start-ups. They are probably more important in later stages of a region's development. In addition, the various case studies describe a set of general characteristics of second tier regions: They seem to possess a set of generic location factors (such as low land costs, a fairly skilled labour force, and a moderate climate) that foster specific high-tech sectors. The next section develops a coherent theory of cluster evolution in second tier regions.

CLUSTER EVOLUTION

How do regions emerge as high-tech locations if they do not have the ingredients that are conventionally considered prerequisites, such as a world-class research university, large amounts of venture capital, or high levels of start-up activity? How can we theorize the process by which regions like Austin, Denver/Boulder, and Colorado Springs evolved as locations for high-tech activity? In this section, I focus on the emergence of clusters of economic activity and describe the ways in which high-tech regions evolve, highlighting the unique aspects of a second tier region.

Cluster evolution is an understudied area; only recently have scholars started to focus on the dynamics of regional economies (Braunerhjelm and Feldmann, 2006; Brenner, 2004; Fornahl et al., 2010). The majority of studies about industry clusters do not provide satisfying explanations for why certain locations develop agglomeration economies in the first place. Porter (2000a), for example, explains how industry clusters work, but he does not theorize how clusters form, merge, decline, or rejuvenate. He merely notes that 'new business ideas will tend to bubble up within clusters because of the concentration of firms, ideas, skills, technology, and needs there. Once an idea is perceived, the barriers to entry and growth are lower at cluster locations' (Porter, 2000b: 269). Typically, however, while second tier regions may have generic location advantages, they lack the specific factors Porter mentions. Thus, cluster theory is imprecise, especially regarding the dynamic aspects of cluster formation and growth (Lorenzen, 2005; Martin and Sunley, 2003). Furthermore, cluster theory does not pay particular attention to the ways in which industries and firms are organized and the implications this may have for regions (Iammarino and McCann, 2006). In addition, theories of clusters, industrial districts, regional innovation milieux, and so on do not distinguish among different types of regions, such as pioneer high-tech regions versus second tier high-tech regions. In order to understand the process of building agglomeration economies, we have to examine the ways in which various agents such as firms, entrepreneurs, and policymakers shape the regional context, particularly for second tier regions.

There are two competing explanations of how clusters grow and evolve. On one hand, scholars like Michael Porter (2000a, 2000b) argue that clusters grow because of agglomeration economies. From their perspective clusters simply 'bubble up' because of physical proximity to factors that benefit firm development. This perspective assumes that agglomeration economies provide cost advantages that reside outside the firm and thus yield efficiencies stemming from labour market pooling and physical proximity to other firms such as suppliers and customers. Agglomeration economies provide positive externalities in the form of knowledge spillovers. These spillovers benefit local industry and contribute to path-dependent development processes (Arthur, 1987, 1996). This perspective implies that a certain level of economic activity must be present for a cluster to emerge. Second tier regions might not meet this prerequisite.

The agglomeration perspective does not account for cases in which a highly innovative cluster has emerged in the absence of a favourable environment that encourages spillover effects – a situation much more common to second tier high-tech regions. For these cases, a more fitting explanation is that clusters grow through spin-off processes and that regions will develop agglomeration economies over time and as a result of entrepreneurship. In such a situation second tier regions develop or emerge into spin-off regions. Existing firms are the source of entrepreneurship and they act as incubators. Spin-off processes are often triggered by corporate changes such as mergers and acquisitions, and corporate downsizing. The spin-off process is important for the cluster and leads to the densification of the entrepreneurial environment (Benneworth, 2004). Spin-off processes can also lead to diversification of the regional economy. These processes are often path-dependent because they reflect local processes and dynamics (Martin and Sunley, 2006) and because the actors involved in spin-offs – such as parent firms and entrepreneurs – shape institutions, rules, and routines in the region. Particularly in locations that do not benefit from urban density or close proximity to economic centres, spin-off processes from one or two corporate anchors or lead firms can have large effects on cluster formation and the diversification of the local economy. These spin-off processes can create clusters if the right types of anchor institutions (large, R&D-oriented, innovative firms) are present and provide the sources for entrepreneurial action (Klepper, 2001b). Often entrepreneurs engage in building the local cluster because they become financial investors in new enterprises or they engage in networking and mentoring activities (Feldman et al., 2005). These processes have not been sufficiently theorized and tested. We will discuss them below and through-out the case studies presented in this book.

The debate about cluster formation highlights the need to examine the processes that give rise to the emergence of second tier high-tech regions. Only a few studies have focused on the dynamic nature of the emergence of industry clusters. These studies agree on four important key assump-tions. First, clusters can be triggered by a chance occurrence that does not have a spatial logic. Boschma and Lambooy argue that 'the location of new firms or innovations may be quite random, determined by arbitrary factors like the home town of the entrepreneur. It is then by accident that new firms or innovations emerge and expand in regions where the local selection environment happens to be right, that is where they fit into the particular regional environment' (1999: 414). The growth of an industry can be such a trigger; for example, the rise of the commercial electron-ics industry after the Second World War led to the expansion of Silicon Valley. Second, entrepreneurship drives cluster growth. The importance of the 'entrepreneurial spark' (Feldmann and Braunerhjelm, 2006: 3) accentuates the role of spin-off processes in cluster formation. Third, while chance plays an important role in initiating a cluster, and entrepreneurship leads to cluster growth, institutions and social structures ensure that the effects of the chance event and spin-off processes do not dissipate. A cluster does not grow and evolve if the initial trigger and the chance event are not followed by processes that embed the economic activity. Entrepreneurship and firm building are particularly important. Firm building refers to the role of corporations in building a skilled labour pool, providing backward and forward connections inside and outside the region, developing mana-gerial talent, and building capabilities (Bresnahan, et al., 2001). Fourth, clusters evolve through four distinct phases of development, described below: emergence, growth, maturation and specialization, and stagnation and decline (Feldmann and Braunerhjelm, 2006; Menzel and Fornahl, 2007; ter Wal and Boschma, 2007).

Cluster Emergence

The first phase of cluster evolution is referred to as cluster emergence. In this phase, a region's economy does not display the classic characteristics of a functioning industry cluster such as strong and dynamic inter-firm relationships, an entrepreneurial environment, or a set of specific location factors that support the cluster's growth. During this phase, only a few firms are present in the region. These firms might not cooperate with each other and they are often small. Menzel and Fornahl (2007) argue that the types of firms that settle in a region determine its development path and future technology orientation. Specific location factors such as the presence of venture capital, a well-developed higher education infrastructure, and a supportive business climate are less important during this phase. This in turn allows second tier regions to capture the growth dynamics of emerging clusters. However, some argue that generic factors such as a stable labour supply and workers with basic skills and knowledge are so important that if a region lacks them, a cluster might not emerge (Storper and Walker, 1989; ter Wal and Boschma, 2007).

Economic developers and scholars may not identify an emerging cluster as such because the region does not yet exhibit trends of spatial concentration (Menzel and Fornahl, 2007). If clustering happens, the processes by which it occurs are unstable and unpredictable (ter Wal and Boschma, 2007). Thus many different locations – such as large cities, second tier regions, peripheral regions, and old industrial areas – may be candidates for emerging clusters. Second tier regions that enter this phase can either develop flourishing clusters or fail to do so. Successful regional economies enter the next phase and grow clusters through entrepreneurship and the development of clustering processes. The 'entrepreneurial spark' (Feldmann and Braunerhjelm, 2006: 3) needs to be combined with a process of 'de-locking' (Martin and Sunley, 2006: 423) the region's industrial potential.

Second tier high-tech regions may represent a unique model of cluster emergence. High-tech industry sectors are considered to be highly innovative and entrepreneurial. Many scholars argue that this industry depends on knowledge spillovers and that geographic proximity plays an important role in generating innovation activity (Audretsch and Feldmann, 1996). It is less clear, however, what kind of initial factors need to be present in a location to spur the clustering of high-tech firms. Boschma and van der Knaap argue that new high-tech industries can cluster anywhere and that many types of locations thus have the potential to host emerging high-tech clusters, especially during the initial stages of growth. They note that 'new high-tech industries reflect a high rate of discontinuity because they place new demands on their local production environment' (1999: 73). They further argue that such industries have the creative ability to shape the local environment in ways that suit them. They can therefore transform the local environment into one that provides specific support factors. Thus, second tier regions can become viable locations for high-tech industries because firms and entrepreneurs can play a proactive role in shaping the local environment. Boschma and van der Knaap also note that 'a local favourable environment is more often a result *of*, rather than a condition *for*' (1999: 76) the rise of high-tech industries. In the case of second tier high-tech regions, small chance events, such as the relocation of a firm into the region, can become initiating factors in their emergence.

Cluster Growth

An emerging cluster will grow and specialize if it can create a critical mass of companies that interact with each other and can incubate new start-up firms. The numbers of firms and employees increase because existing firms become successful and expand their operations in a region (firm building) and/or new firms start in the region (entrepreneurship). The location may also become attractive to other firms which may begin to relocate there (ter Wal and Boschma, 2007). The growing density of firms creates more opportunities for networking and interactions (Menzel and Fornahl, 2007). The region then begins to develop positive externalities such as a specialized labour pool, specialized suppliers, and supportive institutions. This in turn creates regional competitive advantages, and the region begins to show clustering trends that scholars and practitioners of economic development start to detect. During this phase, some firms may go out of business while others survive. This shakeout process limits the diversity of firms in the cluster and increases specialization. If a shakeout is not harvested in positive ways, for example through spin-offs, then the cluster may stagnate or even decline. Shakeouts, however, can contribute to increased entrepreneurial dynamics because adverse events such as mergers and acquisitions or corporate lay-offs motivate entrepreneurs to start their own ventures (Klepper and Thompson, 2005).

Firm building and entrepreneurship processes are important mechanisms for growing second tier high-tech regions. A special set of firms is necessary to take the cluster from emerging to growing. They are typically large; as lead firms they tend to dominate their markets and at times they may also dominate the cluster and its evolution; they are innovative; and they go through a process of organizational evolution. These firms also function as incubators for start-up firms and as 'surrogate universities' (Mayer, 2005b). In addition, their employees become entrepreneurs and start new firms.

Previous cluster studies have not paid enough attention to the role of firms as agents of change. A firm-based perspective takes into account the ways in which firms are organized and how they influence a region's evolution. Firms have the ability to foster the growth of an industry cluster because they may engage in backward and forward linkages and can create business opportunities for start-up firms. Second tier high-tech regions especially benefit from the ability of firms to implant resources (Longhi, 1999). These large firms essentially orchestrate economic activity in a region (Lazerson and Lorenzoni, 1999). They attract and develop talent and form specialized labour pools. These labour pools are the source of nascent entrepreneurs who drive the cluster's growth. It is important to pay attention to the nature of these firms because they can also function as intermediaries that connect the region with the global economy.

Cluster Maturation and Specialization

Second tier high-tech regions become mature and specialized once they are stable and able to maintain a level of employment and industry specialization that is above the national average. Changes in the size and composition of the cluster during this phase are typically cyclical, and the cluster may endure even if it experiences periods of significant restructuring and decline (Menzel and Fornahl, 2007). The region solidifies its competitive advantage (Feldman and Braunerhjelm, 2006) as the environment continues to specialize and provide specific inputs such as education, workforce development, and capital. Through physical proximity and interactions, firms begin to shape their strategies in relation to each other, developing stable inter-firm relationships. Inter-firm networks facilitate learning which in turn leads firms to upgrade their activities and to adjust their firm strategies based on their experiences with their competitors or other firms in their industry. These networks may also benefit entrepreneurial ventures, as the new firms may be able to act as suppliers and business partners to older firms. During the maturation phase, the region's business environment becomes more specialized. Large firms, in particular, may begin to exert power over the regional economy to shape the labour supply, higher education infrastructure, and other factors – especially those related to public policy – that are necessary to improve their operations (Christopherson and Clark, 2007).

Maturing and specializing clusters in second tier high-tech regions can take advantage of extra-local networks. This improves their performance which in turn influences the cluster's performance. Ter Wal and Boschma found that 'clusters that are characterized by strong local knowledge dynamics and a high degree of integration in global networks outperform other clusters' (2007: 12). Similar to the growth phase, firm building plays an important role in maturation and specialization. Certain types of corporations – particularly those that are leaders in their markets – can function as 'extrovert firms' (Tappi, 2005: 293) that funnel new knowledge and innovations to the region through their non-local networks and linkages to the global economy. Second tier regions in particular will benefit from the presence of extrovert firms, because they can implant resources and thereby stimulate cluster growth, maturation, and specialization.

During the maturation and specialization phase, existing firms continue to spawn start-up companies, especially in response to critical events in their own organizations. Entrepreneurial dynamics are, however, augmented by subsequent generations of spin-offs. Second-, third-, and fourth-generation spin-offs benefit from the improved entrepreneurial milieu formed by the pioneering entrepreneurs who became involved as mentors and financiers at the regional level (Feldman and Francis, 2003).

During this phase second tier regions may be able to develop a higher-than-average innovation capacity. While clustering by itself does not promote innovative activity in a region, the presence of highly innovative firms that operate in the same sector seems to foster the growth of other innovative firms and advance the cluster's innovativeness (Beaudry and Breschi, 2003). According to Beaudry and Breschi 'positive agglomeration externalities are likely to flow only from innovative firms' (Beaudry and Breschi, 2003: 339). Thus, second tier regions need to foster innovative firms if they are to develop specialized clusters.

Cluster Stagnation and Decline

Second tier high-tech regions may stagnate and eventually decline if their clusters fail to rejuvenate. In this phase, employment decreases and the number of firm deaths exceeds the number of births. Simply put, the cluster loses its ability to regenerate (Menzel and Fornahl, 2007). Cluster stagnation and decline are due to a combination of firm failures and firm exits. Both firm building and entrepreneurial processes end, so they no longer contribute to the cluster. Stagnating and declining clusters may experience lock-in effects (Grabher, 1993) whereby the region's socioeconomic structure becomes too narrowly focused and fails to embrace new ideas and innovations. Second tier high-tech regions may be more vulnerable to cluster stagnation and decline than their pioneering counterparts because they may be more specialized in certain industry sectors and thus more vulnerable to lock-in effects.

FIRM BUILDING AND ENTREPRENEURSHIP

The previous sections described the various ways in which high-tech regions can evolve. Each phase of cluster evolution describes processes of firm building and entrepreneurship. During the emergence of a cluster, second tier regions benefit from a few key firms that take root in the region. Firm building processes such as hiring and developing personnel, growing the business in the region, and developing market connections are key. These firms can function as incubators for start-ups or they can attract customers, suppliers, and competitors. This, in turn, leads to the growth of the cluster. Specialization and maturation of the cluster takes place when more firms in similar industry sectors are present in the region. Thus, firm building and entrepreneurship are important mechanisms by which second tier high-tech regions evolve. The discussions clarified the importance of two dynamics: firm building and entrepreneurship. High-tech regions – either pioneering or second tier – have to form successful firms (so-called lead firms), which in turn provide the fertile ground for new ventures. The concepts of firm building and entrepreneurship can help us understand how second tier high-tech regions form and evolve.

The Role of Firms in Cluster Evolution

Critics have questioned the model of university-led growth in high-tech regions and research has shown that the mere presence of universities is not sufficient to spur it (for example, Leslie, 2001; O'Mara, 2005). Another necessary precondition seems to be the presence of an environment that is able to absorb spillover effects from university activities (Fogarty and Sinha, 1999). More important, however, and often overlooked is the role of the firms themselves in cluster emergence. In particular, large firms that are characterized by a dynamic and innovative internal environment, and strong linkages inside as well as outside the region, seem to play a very important role in cluster formation and development. The way firms are organized, how they evolve, and how they integrate with the local economy determines the ways in which regional economies evolve. Regions may host a cluster of technology-oriented firms, but the way in which these firms are structured may or may not lead to cluster evolution.

Much of the literature on regional economic development has ignored the fact that firms differ in their capabilities (Taylor and Oinas, 2006). For example, ideas about industry clusters and industrial districts have overemphasized the role of small and medium-sized firms and neglected the role of large firms (Florida and Kenney, 1990b; Gray et al., 1999; Harrison, 1994). The literature on industrial districts argues that districts form because of a unique industrial organization based on flexibly specialized production networks common to smaller firms. This production structure, however, is not incompatible with large firms. In fact, Martinelli and Schoenberger (1991) argue that large firms can also adopt flexible specialization models and adjust to new industrial paradigms.

In short, firms are heterogeneous and can influence a region in different ways (Giuliani, 2005; Lazerson and Lorenzoni, 1999; ter Wal and Boschma, 2007). Glasmeier (1988), for example, noted the importance of studying firm-level dynamics and their influence on the regional economy, high-lighting several influencing factors, such as product type (mass produced or customized), corporate policies (especially towards human resource management and labour policies), product markets (internal to the region but also external), and organizational evolution (such as mergers and acquisitions). For example, if a firm is heavily focused on mass production of standardized products that do not require much research and devel-opment, discourages employees from forming their own firms, and does not develop intra-regional supplier networks, then the firm has limited influence on clustering in the region. In all three cases that she studied, Glasmaier found that the large firms did not engage locally; as a result, the respective regions did not develop into vibrant high-tech economies.

Bresnahan et al. echo Glasmeier's concerns and suggest that 'factors like firm-building capabilities, managerial skills, a substantial supply of skilled labor and connections to markets were crucial for the take off' (2001: 835) of high-tech regions such as Silicon Valley, Northern Virginia, and Cambridge, UK. They further highlight the critical role large firms can play in the development of a region's skill base, noting that:

> in the Silicon Valley story, one should not neglect the potential training pro-vided by established firms like Hewlett-Packard or Intel. Large firms often nurture technical competencies. . . . Similarly, many offer managerial train-ing and possibly even managerial connections. Moreover, this technical and managerial training can encourage spin-offs. (2001: 846)

In addition to building a skill base, large firms often provide backward and forward linkages that small firms may not be able to provide. These large firms may help familiarize their employees with global production networks and influence a region through intra-organizational change processes. Herrigel (2000, 2004) notes that large firms drive change in regional economies because firms that operate in industries such as automobile or electronics production have been reorganizing their local production relationships (to suppliers, for example). These large firms can either 'deregionalize' by breaking off all their ties to local suppliers (or not developing many in the first place) or 're-regionalize' by redefining their supplier relationships to be more locally oriented (Herrigel, 2004). The former can lead to regional industrial decline and the latter may lead to the creation of an industrial district (Harrison, 1992). Glasmeier (1988) notes that some large firms may not develop deep local relationships; as a result a region may not benefit from the presence of these firms.

Certain large firms – particularly lead firms – can serve as so-called 'focal points' around which a cluster develops (Menzel and Fornahl, 2007). They can function as intermediaries that connect the region to a global economy (Simmie, 1998). If they do so, they can act as knowledge gatekeepers (Caniels and Romijn, 2003). Large firms can also play the role of incubators for start-ups (Menzel, 2005), which may emerge because of corporate changes such as mergers, acquisitions, or lay-offs. They are also often considered anchor organizations (Agrawal and Cockburn, 2003; Feldman, 2003; Lucas et al., 2009).

In second tier regions, large firms can play a very important role. They can build networks and technologies and can 'implant' resources in the region (Longhi, 1999). Some have argued that large firms can create industrial districts because they organize production systems, orchestrate economic activity, initiate transfer of ideas and knowledge from outside, provide a foundation for the creation of small firms, spawn an industrial culture, and outsource and subcontract (Lazerson and Lorenzoni, 1999). Through these functions, a few large firms (or often a single company) can contribute to cluster emergence and growth.

Entrepreneurship in Cluster Evolution

One important mechanism of cluster evolution is entrepreneurship. It is new firm formation, rather than the presence of agglomeration economies, that fosters the emergence of clusters (Klepper, 2001b) and contributes to a region's economic growth and diversification. Research often identifies the general characteristics of a region that hinder or support entrepreneurship (Taylor, 2006). Most of these studies note the importance of venture capital, a skilled labour force, proximity to universities, and the availability of support services (Bruno and Tyebjee, 1982). These studies and policy approaches, which merely focus on a list of ingredients, are limited in that they do not consider how a region's preconditions foster or hinder the development of entrepreneurs. Why are some regions more entrepreneurial than others? It is important to analyse the sources of entrepreneurship in a regional economy if we want to understand how an industry cluster is created. Here, insight emerges from examining the backgrounds of entrepreneurial firm founders, their motivations, their technical and managerial skills, and their relationship to their parent firms (their previous employers) and other firms in a regional economy.

If we examine the regional conditions that yield new firms, we need to focus on two perspectives. The first relates to the individual entrepreneur and his or her background, motivations, and skills. This is generally referred to as the supply side (Thornton, 1999). The second perspective considers the demand side of entrepreneurship and focuses on a region's opportunity structure. On the demand side, resources, market relationships, organizational models, and regional embeddedness may influence entrepreneurs (Thornton, 1999).

The parent firm or incubator of the start-up is critical in determining the type of venture and its success. Most technology ventures are started by entrepreneurs who have gained experience at existing firms (Gompers et al., 2003; Mitton, 1990; Zhang, 2003). In some industries, such as biosciences, universities have played a more prominent role as incubators for start-up companies (Schachtel et al., 2004), but generally it is existing companies that act as 'incubator organizations' for start-up firms (Cooper, 1971). Cooper notes that the incubator organization

> hires and often brings the potential founder into an area; it trains him [or her] and helps him [or her] to develop technical, market, and managerial skills and knowledge; it provides the organizational framework which may allow the potential founder to work closely with men [or women] of varied skills who might join him [or her] in an entrepreneurial team. In addition, the established organization, through the satisfactions and frustrations it provides, helps to influence the motivation of the prospective entrepreneur. (p. 11)

Therefore it is important to consider the nature of the incubator organization and the ways in which this firm evolves, changes, and relates to start-up companies.

Linking Firm Building and Entrepreneurship

If we want to analyse the emergence of second tier high-tech regions through the perspective of firm building and entrepreneurship, we need to pay attention to the role of the firm in economic geography. The literature contains only a few studies of the theory of the firm (Maskell, 2001; Taylor and Oinas, 2006); an even deeper theoretical gap exists for the role of the firm in entrepreneurship (Taylor, 2006). Currently, scholars do not completely understand what types of firms encourage or inhibit the emergence of high-tech clusters and the role of the firm as an incubator of start-ups. Yet, as explained above, entrepreneurs play a critical role in the emergence and growth of clusters, and it is important to understand where they come from and how their previous experiences shape cluster evolution. To develop a general understanding, I will draw on an emerging literature on the theory of the firm in economic geography. I will connect this literature with another emerging field, the ecology of entrepreneurship.

Taylor (2006) and Maskell (2001) review a set of three theories of the firm that are relevant to entrepreneurship and regional development. The first theory is the resource-based theory, which Penrose developed in the late 1950s (Penrose, 1959). This theory focuses on the internal conditions, structures, and resources of the firm and embraces the notion of firm heterogeneity. Firms are different, especially in their resource endowment. Firms can have excess resources that are not used internally but may be exploited by employees who would like to start new firms. Here this theory connects with the knowledge spillover theory of entrepreneurship (Audretsch and Lehmann, 2005). One strand of the resource-based theory sees people – employees – as the essential knowledge resource of the firm (Kogut and Zander, 2003). The second theory is the behavioural theory, which was developed by Cyert and March (cited in Taylor and Oinas, 2006) in the early 1960s. This theory focuses on the firm's decision-making process and the roles of conflict, search, and learning. The firm's decision-making involves different parties (stockholders, employees, suppliers, and customers). Start-up activity may be influenced by a firm's actions (that is, the ways in which a firm interacts with start-ups and provides them with business opportunities, and how corporate decisions influence employees who might want to start a business, and so on). The third theory is the evolutionary theory, which was developed by Nelson and Winter in the early 1980s (Nelson and Winter, 1982). Like Penrose's view, this theory sees firms as having competencies and resources. The ways in which they implement these resources, however, changes depending on their environment. The theory focuses on three important elements of firm behaviour and context: routines, searches, and the selection environment. The three theories add to our understanding of the firm, but they fall short when it comes to explaining the spatial implications of the ways in which the firm searches, arranges and develops its resources, its decision-making process, and its evolution. Moreover, the theories do not explain the degree to which existing firms spawn new companies, how spin-off firms evolve in relation to their parents, or what the spatial implications of these entrepreneurial events are. Taylor (2006) also laments the failure of the theories to incorporate entrepreneurship. They do, however, develop a good perspective of the firm building process.

These theories of the firm allow us to understand the key characteristics of corporations. Considering the firm-entrepreneur nexus, we need to outline a theory of entrepreneurship and connect it with ideas of firm building as they emerge from the theory of the firm. Here organizational ecology theories provide a useful perspective, and we can focus on one of those theories, the ecology of entrepreneurship (Carroll and Khessina, 2005). The field of organizational ecology studies the various populations of organizations and focuses on how they change over time. The field highlights the need to understand background conditions and how they determine organizational founding. Unfortunately, scholars of entrepreneurship have largely ignored this field (Carroll and Khessina, 2005), as have economic geographers. The ways in which firms are organized, how they are structured, their products, their business and innovation models, and the kind of culture they develop all shape regional development, particularly regional entrepreneurship (Glasmeier, 1988). We therefore need to investigate how these firm-building characteristics influence start-up activity and how firm heterogeneity influences entrepreneurship, which has a direct impact on the spatial context and the emergence of second tier high-tech regions.

Firm-building characteristics at established firms in a region influence entrepreneurship. Cooper (1971) notes that

> any established firm is a potential incubator organization, employing and influencing potential entrepreneurs who may 'spin-off' to establish their own firms. Regional entrepreneurship is closely related to the established firms or incubator organizations located in that same region. New firms are typically founded by entrepreneurs who are already employed in organizations in the same geographic area. (p. 18)

Thus we need to pay attention to the internal dynamics of the incubator organization and how they influence entrepreneurship.

The following firm-building characteristics are important, and we can hypothesize their influence on start-ups (see also Table 2.1):

- Corporate changes
- Linkages
- Connections to markets
- Product types
- Nature of production process
- Innovation
- Corporate policies and culture
- Capital assets
- Labour

Corporate changes. The behavioural theory of the firm assumes that the firm goes through a decision-making process that involves various partners. These decisions lead to corporate changes that, in turn, facilitate entrepreneurship because they create critical moments at which established firms experience an increased rate of spin-off activity (Klepper, 2001a; Mitton, 1990; Neck, et al., 2004). Corporate changes can be positive or negative. The growth of a firm constitutes a positive change, while lay-offs or restructuring may constitute a negative change. Positive corporate change also influences entrepreneurship in more indirect ways. More successful firms will attract more capable employees, who in turn will be better entrepreneurs (Klepper, 2001b). Growing firms can learn and improve their routines, and better routines lead to better performing firms, which in turn can lead to better performing start-ups (Klepper, 2001a). Cooper (1971) notes that if the incubator firm is in a rapidly growing industry, it offers opportunities for small firms with good ideas. Growth may also encourage entrepreneurship because of its symbolic value; for example, it may indicate an increasing demand for the sector's products or services (Romanelli and Schoonhoven, 2001). Negative corporate changes also facilitate entrepreneurship because they can act as push factors, meaning that employees may leave if changes at their firm affect them negatively (Feldman, et al., 2005). Corporations undergoing crises show higher rates of spin-off (Cooper, 1985). Crises such as mergers and acquisitions, a change in corporate leadership, and slow growth also facilitate entrepreneurship by affecting employees (Brittain and Freeman, 1986). Slow growth, for example, blocks career mobility and may encourage the entrepreneurially minded employee to leave. New corporate executives often bring new ideas that may not be popular with key employees. Mergers and acquisitions may lead to restructuring, including lay-offs which can directly affect those interested in entrepreneurship. Together these corporate changes facilitate disagreement among employees, which can also be a motivating entrepreneurial factor (Klepper and Thompson, 2005). Frustration can be a powerful entrepreneurial force and can motivate employees to leave their parent firm (Benneworth, 2004; Bhide, 2000; Cooper, 1971).

Linkages and connections to markets. Corporate linkages and connections to markets also impact how, and the extent to which, firms influence entrepreneurship in a region. If firms engage in supplier or subcontractor relationships with other firms within the region, then these linkages can be important business opportunities for start-ups (Glasmeier, 1988). Especially large and dominant firms produce backward and forward linkages (Bresnahan, et al., 2001). Spin-offs may start out with contracts with their parent firms or with customers of that firm; thus they do not have to go out and create new markets (Glasmeier, 1988). New firms can also become subcontractors that the lead firms in a region can draw on (Tappi, 2005). In addition, the relationship of an incubator firm to its market is important. Firms that are leaders in their markets show a higher spin-off rate (Klepper, 2001b) and may provide entrepreneurs with important contacts and connections to potential partners, subcontractors, and suppliers. These firms can channel important knowledge and industry-specific information to the region and to the potential start-ups (Tappi, 2005). Spin-offs most often exploit niches and markets that are similar to those of their parents (Bhide, 2000; Cooper, 1971; Klepper and Sleeper, 2005).

Product types. The nature of an incubator organization's products and business lines also influences start-up activity. Firms with products that show more variation have more start-ups. The spin-off rates are higher in industries that are in the early stage of the product life cycle (Klepper, 1996). This may indicate the level of experimentation within a firm and the degree to which the firm produces new ideas and knowledge that can then be exploited by entrepreneurs. Spin-offs are also more likely if a firm's products are based on attributes rather than price, and less likely for firms that specialize in standardized products and focus heavily on production and execution (Glasmeier, 1988). Firms with more varied products also show more start-up activity because they have a richer learning environment than firms that are focused on a single product (Klepper, 2001a). Yet, if the firm's focus is too scattered and its energies are channelled in too many directions, innovations may not commercialize in-house because corporate leadership might miss them (Chesbrough, 2002; Mayer, 2005a).

Nature of production process. Closely related to the types of products a firm produces is the nature of the production process. As mentioned earlier, high-tech regions are often described as flexibly specialized industrial districts. In such regions, firms gain a competitive advantage by subcontracting with other firms and specializing in niche areas within a larger production process. Flexibly specialized firms may have more start-ups because they may offer more business opportunities for entrepreneurs. In contrast, firms characterized by vertical integration and/or mass production may show limited start-up rates because they have fewer connections to the local economy (Glasmeier, 1988; Saxenian, 1994b).

Innovation. Innovation is another key determinant of spin-off activity. Generally, more innovative firms have more spin-offs (Klepper, 2001a). But the nature of the innovation process could influence entrepreneurship in different ways. Firms that focus mainly on product innovation may invest more in ideas and knowledge, not all of which may be exploited in-house. In contrast, firms focused on process innovation may not display such great variation in products and may focus more on improving the production process. Start-ups may exploit innovations when the incubator firm does not recognize the opportunity (Chesbrough, 2002; Christensen, 1997).

Corporate policies and culture. Corporate policies and the firm's culture can also influence spin-off activity. Firms that foster an environment in which employees can develop their skills, particularly managerial and sector-specific skills, may have more and better spin-offs than those that do not have such a focus. Similarly, firms that encourage entrepreneurial behaviour – either internally (called intrapreneurship) or externally through financial support for entrepreneurial ideas – may have more spin-offs. Firms also need to develop highly skilled labour and have in place human resources policies that give employees a chance to hone not only their technical skills but also their managerial skills. In the high-tech sector, for example, the 'engineer manager' combines these two critically important skills (Breshnahan and Gambardella, 2004; Bresnahan, et al., 2001). Firms that allow their former employees who turned to entrepreneurship to return if a spin-off fails may also have more spin-offs than other firms. The knowledge spillover theory of entrepreneurship predicts that entrepreneurial activity will be higher in the context of high knowledge investments (Audretsch and Lehmann, 2005). Thus, if the incubator firm is focused on innovation, it invests in ideas and knowledge and fosters the talent of its employees. The organizational structure of a firm can also influence entrepreneurship. If the incubator organization is organized as a series of small businesses, then it can contribute to more spin-offs (Cooper, 1971) because smaller firms provide more useful lessons to employees about how to manage a start-up. Also, start-ups are social products (Staber, 2005) and they tend to emulate their parents. Thus the incubator organization leaves an important imprint on the new firm (Aldrich and Martinez, 2001; West and Simard, 2006).

Capital assets. The extent to which the firm's ideas and knowledge are embedded in physical or human capital influences the degree to which it can function as an incubator organization. Firms with richer, broader, and more transferable assets tend to spawn more spin-offs than those with fixed assets (Klepper, 2001a). Klepper (2001a) further argues that the easier it is to access a firm's know-how, the lower the barriers are for start-ups to commercialize ideas and knowledge. Firm know-how that is embodied in physical assets is harder to access. Thus the kind of assets a firm develops determines the rate of spin-off activity.

Labour. The knowledge-based theory of the firm emphasizes the importance of human capital; that is, the employees of a firm who are also potential entrepreneurs. Firms with superior labour spawn more spin-offs (Klepper, 2001a) and firms that are good at recruiting ambitious and capable people will function as fertile incubators (Cooper, 1971).

Entrepreneurs tend to enter industries in which they have some kind of experience (Cooper, 1985; Sorenson and Audia, 2000). The incubator firm has to have the right mix of labour and develop technical as well as managerial talent. High-level employees tend to become the founders of start-ups and the leading firms in an industry tend to have superior managerial employees and will therefore produce more and better spin-offs (Klepper, 2008). In addition, such employees tend to develop a broad background and contacts that may help with starting a company (Cooper, 1971). If a firm hosts only technical workers, it will have fewer spin-offs and therefore will not function as an incubator in the region (Glasmeier, 1988).

Some of the key characteristics detailed above critically influence the nature of spin-off activity and they are summarized well by Cooper:

> A firm with the following characteristics probably would be a very good incubator. It would be in a rapidly growing industry which offered opportunities for the well-managed small firm with good ideas; it would be a small firm or would be organized as a series of 'small businesses'; it would be good at recruiting ambitious, capable people; and it would periodically be afflicted with internal crises sufficient to frustrate many of its professional employees and lead them to believe that opportunities were being missed and that '*even I could manage the business better*'. This, incidentally, is a fairly good definition of many of the firms which have been established in the Palo Alto area in the past ten years. (1971: 25)

Table 2.1 summarizes the connections between firm-building characteristics and entrepreneurship that form the foundation of this research.

CONCLUSIONS

For a second tier high-tech cluster to emerge, a region needs to engage in firm building and then initiate entrepreneurship. Bresnahan and Gambardella note that successful high-tech regions created 'old economy' inputs such as 'organizational and firm building activities, investment in general and industry-specific human capital, larger companies and related economies of scale at the level of the firms, and lengthy periods of investment in capability before their exploitation at a firm, regional or national level' (2004: 333). These inputs contributed to cluster take-off. The case studies presented in this book will examine these processes. Firm building is a dynamic process because corporate strategies change in response to market opportunities, demand, and competition (Berger, 2005). The regions examined in this book were influenced by these changes. The lead firms in these regions have undergone major restructuring processes in response to changes in national and global markets. Even though these

Table 2.1 Connecting firm-building characteristics with entrepreneurship

Theory of firm	Firm building		Entrepreneurship
Behavioural theory	**Corporate changes**		**Corporate changes, especially crises, facilitate entrepreneurship; they represent critical moments in a region's entrepreneurial history (Mitton, 1990; Neck, et al., 2004).**
	Positive: corporate growth		Growing firms have more spin-offs:
			– attract more capable employees who in turn are potential founders (Klepper, 2001a)
			– modify and change existing routines; better routines lead to more spin-offs (Klepper, 2001a)
			– are in growing industries, which offer opportunities for start-ups (Cooper, 1971)
			– growth indicates demand for products or services, which encourages entrepreneurs (Romanelli and Schoonhoven, 2001)
	Negative: corporate crisis		Firms undergoing corporate crises have a higher rate of spin-offs (Cooper, 1985):
			– negative events can pull employees into entrepreneurship (Feldman, et al., 2005)
			– mergers and acquisitions, new corporate leadership, slow growth facilitate entrepreneurship (Brittain and Freeman, 1986)
			– disagreement with employer leads to entrepreneurship (Klepper and Thompson, 2005)
			– frustration with employer leads to entrepreneurship (Cooper, 1971; ; Bhide, 2000 Benneworth, 2004)
Contractual theory	**Linkages**		**The ability to link with existing firms in a region represents important business opportunities for start-up firms; parent firms also provide important market connections to other regions.**
	Backward/supplier		– Firms, especially large and dominant firms, can produce backward linkages (Bresnahan, et al., 2001)
			– Spin-offs tend to contract with parent firm or with customers and thus do not have to create new markets (Glasmeier, 1988)
			– New firms can become subcontractors (Tappi, 2005)

43

Table 2.1 (continued)

Theory of firm	Firm building	Entrepreneurship
	Forward/markets	– Firms, especially large and dominant firms, produce forward linkages (Bresnahan, et al., 2001) – Links with external markets are important because of knowledge flows (Tappi, 2005)
	Connections to markets	**The parent firm's position and connection to markets is an important factor in a start-up's success. Thus the degree to which the parent firm is connected to firms in other regions is critical.**
	Position within industry	– Firms that are leaders in a market have a greater spin-off rate (Klepper, 2001b) – Spin-offs often exploit a similar niche or market as their parents (Cooper, 1971; Bhide, 2000; Klepper and Sleeper, 2005)
	Connection to outside markets	– A parent firm's ties to other regions is important (Tappi, 2005)
Evolutionary theory: assets and routines	**Product types**	**Firms with more varied products have more spin-offs.**
	Customized	– Spin-off rates are higher when industry is in early state of product life cycle (Klepper, 1996)
	Standardized	– Spin-offs are more likely when a firm's market is based on product attributes rather than price (Glasmeier, 1988) – Spin-offs are less likely from firms that specialize in standardized products (Glasmeier, 1988)
	Varied	– The broader the product line of a firm, the greater the number of spin-offs because all the firms have a richer learning environment (Klepper, 2001a) – If product lines are too varied and not connected to core business, then innovations are not commercialized in-house, which in turn can lead to more spin-offs (Chesbrough, 2002; Mayer, 2005a)

Nature of production process	**Firms engaged in flexible production techniques have more spin-offs, which tend to be local because of the need to engage in face-to-face contact.**
Flexible specialization	– Firms engaged in flexible specialization have more spin-offs than those that do not (Saxenian, 1994b)
Mass production	– Vertically integrated firms have fewer spin-offs because they have fewer connections to the local economy (Glasmeier, 1988; Saxenian, 1994b)
Innovation	**More innovative firms have more spin-offs.**
Process innovation	– Firms focused on process innovation may not display such great variation in products and show a greater focus on improving the production process
Product innovation	– Firms that focus mainly on product innovation may invest more in ideas and knowledge, which in turn may not all be exploited in-house.
Radical innovation/ competence destroying	– Spin-offs will exploit innovation their parents do not pursue because the innovation may threaten the parent's business model/success (Chesbrough, 2002; Christensen, 1997)
Corporate policies and culture	**Firms that develop entrepreneurial skills and encourage entrepreneurial behaviour among employees have more spin-offs; firms that are decentralized and organized into small business units have more spin-offs; spin-offs are social products shaped by their parent and their regional environment.**
Human resources	– Human resources policies influence the rate of entrepreneurship – A firm's employees are the potential entrepreneurs and they need to have the ability to develop not only technical but also managerial skills (Breshnahan and Gambardella, 2004; Bresnahan, et al., 2001)
Entrepreneurship	– Success of spin-off can be determined by parent encouragement and how parent views those who leave to start a firm (Glasmeier, 1988) – Corporate policies towards entrepreneurship is important, that is whether firm allows internal entrepreneurship (intrapreneurship), how it supports potential entrepreneurs, and so on (Glasmeier, 1988)

Table 2.1 (continued)

Theory of firm	Firm building	Entrepreneurship
	Innovation/ technology	– Knowledge spillover theory predicts entrepreneurial activity to be higher in the context of high knowledge investments (Audretsch and Lehmann, 2005) – Firms that are involved with R&D have more spin-offs than those that focus on execution/production (Glasmeier, 1988) – If parent does not commercialize innovation, spin-off will (Klepper, 2001a) – Spin-offs may become R&D partners (Chesbrough, 2003a)
	Organization structure	– Firms organized into small businesses will have more spin-offs (Cooper, 1971) – Smaller firms provide more useful lessons to employees who start firms (Klepper, 2001a) – Spin-offs are social products (Staber, 2005) and they tend to emulate their parents (Aldrich and Martinez, 2001) – Parents imprint their culture on spin-offs (West and Simard, 2006)
Resource-based/ knowledge-based theory	**Capital assets**	**Firms with richer, broader and transferrable assets spawn more spin-offs.**
	Human assets	– The richer a firm's know-how associated with a product variant, the lower the organizational skills required to start a spin-off and the more spin-offs produce a related product (Klepper, 2001a) – If a firm's knowledge is embodied in human capital, it is more accessible to employees and thus easier to use in a spin-off (Klepper, 2001a) – Investments in a firm's R&D and marketing know-how generate knowledge that can be exploited by spin-offs (Klepper and Sleeper, 2005)
	Physical assets	– If a firm's know-how is embodied in physical assets, there are fewer spin-offs (Klepper and Sleeper, 2005)

46

Labour	**Firms with superior labour spawn more spin-offs; firms that are good at recruiting ambitious, capable people also have more spin-offs.**
Industry expertise	– Spin-off founders tend to enter industries in which they have experience (Sorenson and Audia, 2000)
Technical	– Spin-offs are founded by well-educated and experienced employees of firms with similar technologies and markets (Cooper, 1985)
	– Highly skilled labour is especially important for the growth of high-tech clusters (Bresnahan, et al., 2001)
	– A large pool of only technical/production workers leads to fewer spin-offs (Glasmeier, 1988)
	– Engineering and scientific talent is important for spin-offs and their innovation (Lyons, 1995)
Managerial	– High-level employees tend to be founders of spin-offs, and top firms tend to have superior employees; such a spin-off will be better able to compete in industry (Klepper, 2008)
	– Professional employees develop broad background and contacts that help with start-up (Cooper, 1971)
Engineer-manager	– The combination of skills in engineering and in management can be deployed in start-up (Breshnahan and Gambardella, 2004)

Source: Author's analysis of literature cited in table.

events were experienced as crises at the regional level, they influenced the regions in positive ways because the lead firms functioned as incubators of an abundance of start-ups. Firm-building activities lead to entrepreneurship, and it is this process that leads to the evolution of high-tech regions.

As the literature review suggests, there may be a sequence of events in a cluster's evolution that begins with spin-off processes and ends with the mobilization of the region's economic actors. Entrepreneurial firm formation as a response to corporate changes can sow the seeds for the development of a high-tech cluster and the emergence of spin-offs can lead to the growth of the clusters. The clusters mature and specialize as these spin-offs add to the region's specialization. Lead firms determine each region's initial specialization, and their spin-offs occupy niches and exploit opportunities within the same or adjacent sectors. In each region, the processes of firm building and entrepreneurship mobilize local actors and institutions such as economic development agencies, higher education institutions, venture capitalists, and trade associations. As a result a networked regional economy may emerge.

Overall the cluster life cycle model suggests that the initial impetus for cluster take-off comes from firm building, which is followed by entrepreneurial firm formation. The cluster matures and specializes as actors and institutions adjust and respond to the growth of the industry. Unlike the traditional Silicon Valley perspective, which emphasizes the role of the university as an engine of growth, second tier high-tech regions emerge in the absence of a strong university. In this study I hypothesize that high-tech firms can function as surrogate universities within a region. Using this framework, I assume that in second tier regions that lack world-class research universities, leading high-tech firms contribute to the development of the high-tech economy by attracting and developing talent, serving as incubators for start-ups, fostering innovation, and conducting research and development. Firms that function as surrogate universities foster entrepreneurship and the creation of successful clusters by exercising the unique firm-building characteristics presented in Table 2.1.

NOTES

1. In contrast to the software industry (and other high-tech sub-sectors such as semiconductor or computer manufacturing), Seattle's biotech industry is more closely aligned with local research organizations. The University of Washington has played an important role in creating the region's biotechnology industry, primarily through university-based spin-offs. For example, it was the parent of one of the region's pioneering biotechnology firm, ZymoGenetics. Founded in 1964, the Fred Hutchinson Cancer Research Center is an industry leader and encourages the commercialization of its research. Several of the

region's earliest and largest biotechnology companies, including Genetic Systems Corp and Immunex Corporation, were started by researchers from 'the Hutch' (Cortright and Mayer, 2002). As the case of Seattle illustrates, universities may play different roles depending on the type of industry they are engaged with.

2. The literature seems to indicate that their role and influence depends on the industry sector and that there are different levels or 'tiers of engagement' of universities with their regional economies (Boucher et al., 2003). James Gibbons, former Dean of Stanford University's School of Engineering, states that 'for the silicon semiconductor industry, Gordon Moore, a co-founder of both Fairchild Semiconductor and Intel, believes that Stanford's principal contribution to Silicon Valley is in replenishing the intellectual pool every year with outstanding graduates at both the masters and PhD levels' (Gibbons, 2000: 201). Gibbons claims that Stanford University contributed substantially to the creation of very successful start-up companies in the field of computing and information networking. Companies such as Silicon Graphics, Sun Microsystems and Cisco Systems make up an important part of the Silicon Valley economy. Biotechnology (Zucker et al., 1998) or networking and computing may rely more closely on the commercialization of academic knowledge than other high-tech sectors. Industries that are characterized by incremental innovation and depend more on a talented workforce than on cutting edge basic research (such as the semiconductor industry) may engage universities in very different ways.

3. A handful of European cases highlight the ways in which some key elements of the emergence of second tier high-tech regions might be relevant across national contexts. Longhi (1999) examines the emergence of the French high-tech centre Sophia-Antipolis, near Nice. Benneworth (2004) examined a declining branch plant location in North East England where the electronics firm Joyce-Loebl had spun off about 40 new firms that now employ more than 1000 workers. A case where a nation benefited from the presence of large, dominant firms is Ireland (Barry, 2006; O'Malley and O'Gorman, 2001). In the field of biotechnology, Austria presents some interesting insights into how regions may be able to develop industry capacities. Trippl and Toedtling (2007) examine three biotech clusters in Austria where endogenous spin-off processes led to the formation of firms emerging from academic institutions.

3. Identifying emerging high-tech regions

'No longer do Silicon Valley and Route 128 have the monopoly on innovation; there are other alternatives, and many cases equally satisfactory.'

Herbig and Golden (1993: 29)

High-tech industries have a special allure among policymakers and economic development practitioners. The industries are typically associated with rapid employment growth and a high capacity for innovation. High-tech firms are viewed as having potential to spin-off new firms, leading to renewed entrepreneurial dynamics in a region. Many policymakers consider high-technology to be a more or less 'clean' industry without polluting smokestacks. Since the 1970s, high-tech industry has become a desirable target of urban and regional development efforts. In this chapter, I discuss the nature of high-tech industry sectors and their industrial organization. In addition, I explain three key drivers of high-tech growth: talent, innovation, and entrepreneurship. Defining the industry and its key drivers is important if we want to gain a nuanced understanding of how cities and regions benefit from the growth of high technology.

I also present a typology of high-tech regions. While many analysts have ranked cities based on the size of their high-tech economy, I employ a substantively different approach. This approach focuses on the degree to which different metropolitan areas share similar industrial, innovation, human capital, and entrepreneurship dynamics. Simply ranking metropolitan areas by the number of high-tech jobs favours regions with a large high-tech economy such as Silicon Valley or Boston. It also favours regions that are merely large, and places where urbanization economies may lead to large high-tech economies.[1] In contrast to size rankings, the methodology presented here organizes metropolitan regions according to the degree to which they share certain growth dynamics. This allows us to focus on emerging second tier high-tech regions that have not traditionally been in the spotlight.

ROOTS OF HIGH TECHNOLOGY

The roots of high-tech industries go back to the invention of the radio telegraph by Guglielmo Marconi in Italy in the late nineteenth century and his advances in radio in the early twentieth century. Innovations in wireless transmission triggered a slew of inventions such as the vacuum tube (invented in 1906 by American physicist Lee De Forest) that were critical to the development of electronic technology, including television, telephones, computers, and measurement instruments. High-tech industries in the US began to flourish, especially in the 1950s when military support for research in physics, electrical engineering, and mathematics increased dramatically (Ceruzzi, 2000). In addition to investing in research, the US built a competitive advantage through various institutional innovations; for example, entrepreneurship was fuelled by the rise of the venture capital industry during the 1940s (Kenney and Florida, 2000). The commercialization of research and technology transfer was made possible by important policy changes in the 1980s (most notably the passage of the Stevenson-Wydler Technology Innovation Act and the Bayh-Dole University and Small Business Patent Act, which allowed the transfer of publicly funded intellectual property to industry). The combination of investments in university research, the build-up of an appropriate finance infrastructure, and the development of a robust commercialization infrastructure facilitated the rapid growth of high-technology industries in the US and the rise of high-tech regions like Silicon Valley and Boston's Route 128.

The invention of the radio ushered in a completely new era in electronics research and commercialization. The development of the vacuum tube in 1904 enabled the amplification of radio waves and the transmission of sound over long distances. This was vividly demonstrated when the Titanic sank in 1912, and its distress call was received in New York. During the 1920s radio was commercialized and small radio stations sprang up across the US. As a result the production of radio equipment surged. One of the centres of the radio industry was the San Francisco Bay area where the FTC, based in Palo Alto, was started in 1909 to produce radio transmission technology (Sturgeon, 2000). The FTC led to numerous spin-off companies including Magnavox (loudspeakers), Fisher Research Laboratories (metal detectors), and Litton Industries (vacuum tube manufacturing). These early developments formed the basis of modern Silicon Valley.

DEFINING HIGH TECHNOLOGY

The high-tech industry is composed of many sub-sectors, which have unique organizational structures and geographic location patterns. This section discusses a range of high-tech sub-sectors in the areas of instruments and computers, semiconductors, and life sciences and biotechnology. These sub-sectors are all part of the broader high-tech industry definition, yet they differ significantly in their geographic location patterns, industry structures, innovation and business models.

Instruments and Computers

The early radio and electronics pioneers needed reliable test and measurement equipment. Lee notes that the main technical limitation of radio engineers was their 'inability to make more precise electrical measurements. The complex circuitry of all but the most elementary radio required special equipment to diagnose wiring problems, measure resistance, and test both components and entire circuits' (1986: 7). Several electronics firms at the time tried to fill this void by developing more precise test and measurement instruments. Hewlett-Packard (HP), founded in Palo Alto in 1938, was one of these firms. HP's first product was the audio oscillator, which 'represented the first practical, low-cost method of generating high-quality audio frequencies needed in communications, geophysics, medicine, and defense work' (Packard, 1995: 41). Tektronix, founded in Portland, Oregon, in 1946, commercialized the first oscilloscope that incorporated the triggered sweep circuit, an innovation that allowed users to pick up and display high-speed electronic events without delays or interruptions. These new firms began to incorporate innovations that allowed them to become market leaders in their respective segments.

Demand for test and measurement instruments soared as another industry – computers – began to emerge. The first computers were developed during the Second World War to calculate artillery firing tables for the US Army (Ceruzzi, 2000). In 1951 the Eckert-Mauchly Computer Corporation of Philadelphia introduced the first commercial computer, the UNIVAC. This computer stored information on magnetic tapes rather than cumbersome punch cards. This advance allowed businesses to search for stored information much more efficiently than was possible using labour-intensive punch cards. These mainframe computers also included compilers capable of batch processing, a type of computer programming that ushered in the commercial software industry. Mainframes, however, were large machines that were typically operated by specialists in separate rooms. The next stage of computer evolution was the minicomputer, developed in the 1960s and commercialized by Digital Equipment Corporation (DEC) in Boston. The minicomputer's advantage over the mainframe was its ability to be reprogrammed for different applications. At this time, the industry's geographic centre was the East Coast, particularly the area around Boston's Route 128. Saxenian (1994b) notes that the Boston area was home to more than 35 new computer firms during the 1960s and 1970s.

The computer industry next began to take advantage of the invention of the integrated circuit (see below for a more detailed discussion of the semiconductor industry). Integrated circuits replaced transistors in the central processing units of computers. This allowed the combination of multiple operations on a single circuit. Integrated circuits also facilitated the development of personal devices such as calculators. In the 1970s, for example, HP introduced the first inexpensive pocket calculator to use these circuits. Pocket calculators, in turn, unleashed tremendous creative potential which led to the development of the microcomputer in the 1970s. Computer enthusiasts at MIT and Stanford developed a hacker culture that helped modify devices. A supporting social infrastructure that included informal gatherings like the Homebrew Computer Club, which met in the Menlo Park area of Silicon Valley, allowed knowledge exchange and innovation. In 1974, the electronics firm MITS in Alberquerque, New Mexico, developed the Altair 8800 microcomputer, ushering in the use of the personal computer. It was a 'capable, inexpensive computer designed around the Intel 8080 microprocessor' (Ceruzzi, 2000: 226). The Altair 8800 consisted of a $400 kit, which buyers could assemble, add to, and modify.

The geographic location patterns of the minicomputer and personal computer industries differed in important ways. While the minicomputer industry was centred around Boston on the East Coast, the personal computer industry began to flourish on the West Coast. Ultimately the high-tech industry on the West Coast developed more successfully than its Eastern counterpart. Saxenian (1994) attributes the success of Silicon Valley to the corporate culture of a network of flexibly specialized firms that used collaborative practices, horizontal communications, risk taking, and entrepreneurship. The semiconductor industry that emerged in Silicon Valley played an important role in this success.

Semiconductors

The semiconductor is a key component of many electronic devices such as computers, telephones, digital cameras, televisions, and radios. As a result, firms producing semiconductors are important cornerstones of the US high-tech economy. The semiconductor sub-sector is characterized by short product life cycles, large investments in R&D, and continuous upgrading of the manufacturing infrastructure. Firms in this sector fiercely compete on a multitude of dimensions, including price, innovation, product differentiation, and speed of market introduction. The industry is geographically concentrated in Silicon Valley but in recent decades has shifted away from here to areas in predominantly non-coastal Western states such as Oregon, Idaho, Arizona, and New Mexico (Arita and McCann, 2007).

The semiconductor industry began in 1947 when Bell Laboratories in New Jersey invented the transistor. During the 1950s the industry was located primarily on the East Coast because of the traditional concentration of vacuum tube manufacturers there (Ketelhöhn, 2006). This geographic pattern changed in 1955 when William Shockley, who had worked on transistor research at Bell Labs in New Jersey, founded Shockley Semiconductor Laboratory in Mountain View, California. Differences in opinion over the direction the company should take led to the exodus of eight Shockley employees who founded Fairchild Semiconductor in 1957. This group included Robert Noyce and Gordon Moore who would later found Intel (Berlin, 2005). This flurry of start-up activity solidified Silicon Valley's leadership in the industry, with new firms heavily engaged in new technology development. In 1959, John Kilby at Texas Instruments in Dallas, Texas, and Robert Noyce at Fairchild Semiconductor in Silicon Valley patented their invention of the integrated circuit (IC). This was a major improvement to the semiconductor because the IC integrated a large number of tiny electronic circuits on a microchip.

From the 1960s to the early 1980s employment in the semiconductor sub-sector rose from 54 000 to 178 000, an increase of 229 per cent (Ketelhöhn, 2006). US semiconductor firms dominated because they were able to commercialize cutting-edge inventions. Angel (1994) also credits large-scale US investments in science and engineering that began during the Second World War. These investments fuelled basic research and the training of scientists and engineers. As a result firms like Shockley and Fairchild took leadership roles. In addition, the US – and in particular Silicon Valley – provided entrepreneurial start-up firms such as Fairchild and Intel with many other benefits, such as the ability to draw on venture and angel capital, a high degree of labour mobility, proximity to specialized suppliers and leading academic institutions, contracting opportunities with the local military industry, and a more or less open flow of knowledge and information (Angel, 1994; Ketelhöhn, 2006).

During the 1980s, however, the US semiconductor industry lost its market leadership to Japan. Angel notes that 'the US share of worldwide open-market semiconductor sales fell from 58 per cent to 37 per cent;

during the same period, Japanese firms increased their market share from 26 per cent to 49 per cent' (1994: 65). Deficiencies in the production process were mainly responsible for the decline of the US industry. While US firms were stellar inventors and able to commercialize their innovations, they had a hard time increasing production yields and they suffered from poor manufacturing quality and fluctuating capacities. Japanese semiconductor manufacturers were able to outperform their US counterparts, especially in the price-sensitive commodity markets such as memory chips (DRAMs).

The debt crisis of the 1980s, however, led to major restructuring in the US semiconductor industry. US producers initially shifted to different types of semiconductors and also sought political solutions such as trade agreements. More importantly, however, were the industry's efforts to restructure its innovation and manufacturing processes. The industry's poor manufacturing performance stemmed from US semiconductor firms' bifurcated manufacturing system, in which innovation and R&D were separate from the production process (Angel, 1994). The restructuring efforts during the 1980s led to significant changes. First and foremost was a closer integration of innovation and manufacturing. Angel (1994) describes several of these efforts in detail. US firms began to create teams within their organizations that combined key personnel from research, development, manufacturing, and marketing. Firms increasingly sought partnerships with external partners, such as equipment and materials suppliers, because they saw the value in co-developing technology. Another improvement was the adoption of concurrent product development, which allowed firms to overlap the development of new products. One of the most important organizational innovations was the adoption of continuous innovation. In the traditional model, innovation was separated in-house from manufacturing; after a new idea was developed it was transitioned into the prototyping and later into the production process. This model introduced errors into the process because different engineers and scientists were involved at different stages. To address these problems US semiconductor firms introduced a new form of manufacturing that had important spatial implications, especially for second tier high-tech regions like Portland, Oregon. In the new model, firms (like Intel, for example) no longer separated innovation from manufacturing. Rather, they integrated the two in what they called 'process development facilities'. These facilities served as the 'primary centres of semiconductor technology development for the company, integrating process and equipment development, product development, productization, and yield enhancement' (Angel, 1994: 111).

The semiconductor industry's efforts to link innovation more tightly with production influenced the growth of second tier high-tech regions in important ways. The industry had begun to disperse production activities by the 1960s, and a unique spatial division of labour emerged. Angel (1994) notes that three types of locations characterized this phase of development: centres of innovation such as Silicon Valley, routinized high-volume fabrication facilities located in low-wage sites outside major metropolitan areas in the US, and labour-intensive assembly operations in low-cost locations offshore. This spatial organization, however, was based on the bifurcated process described above. Organizational innovations, such as Intel's process development facilities, changed the nature of the branch location. These locations – like Portland, Oregon, where Intel had initially relocated routine mass production facilities because of low labour costs, availability of labour, and other production factors such as abundant water and cheap electricity – transitioned into emerging second tier high-tech regions. The tighter integration of innovation with production meant that branch locations also played an important role in shaping product innovation and manufacturing process development. As a result, the labour force changed from one focused on manufacturing (primarily technicians) to one with multidimensional teams (technicians, engineers, and scientists). In addition, the proliferation of strategic partnerships and alliances, especially with equipment and materials suppliers, led to the co-location of these firms in the regions.

Life Sciences and Biotechnology

The life sciences and biotechnology industries in general are special cases of high-tech development. In contrast to other high-tech sub-sectors such as computers and semiconductors, life sciences industries rely more heavily on a scientific knowledge base and include a broad range of subdivisions such as pharmaceuticals, medical devices, agriculture, environmental sciences, and so on. Life sciences can be defined as using 'biological techniques and supporting technologies with a goal to improve human and animal health, address threats to the environment, improve crop production, contain emerging and existing diseases, and improve currently used manufacturing technologies' (Kochut and Humphreys, 2007: 1). As an industry, life sciences include companies that deal with biotechnology, pharmaceuticals, food processing, environmental remediation, and medical devices, among others.

The most prominent subdivisions of life sciences are pharmaceuticals and biotechnology. These subdivisions differ in important ways (Cortright and Mayer, 2002). The pharmaceutical industry's main focus is drug manufacturing. Pharmaceutical firms are typically large and fairly mature. They tend to have large-scale operations that combine in-house corporate functions such as manufacturing and marketing. The industry is led by multinational firms such as Pfizer, Eli Lilly, Merck, Bristol-Myers-Squibb, Bayer, and Novartis. These companies develop strategic alliances and research agreements with much smaller biotechnology firms. In contrast, biotechnology firms undertake cutting-edge research and apply new biological knowledge and techniques in molecular, cellular, and genetic processes. Biotechnology firms tend to be smaller and younger than their pharmaceutical partners. They are capital intensive because they focus heavily on R&D. The biotechnology industry as a whole has not been profitable, sparking criticism by observers who note that the industry is challenged by high levels of risk, uncertainty, great complexity, and the challenge of integrating diverse areas of scientific knowledge (Pisano, 2006). Both pharmaceuticals and biotechnology face long time horizons: the development and approval of a drug typically takes between five and 12 years.

The US has been a leader in the development of the modern bio-technology industry (Cooke, 2001). Several factors contributed to this leadership (Bagchi-Sen et al., 2004). Federal research funding allowed the infusion of capital and the buildup of a strong scientific research base, on which the industry relies. Strong intellectual property rights protection incentivizes the commercialization of scientific knowledge. In addition, policies regarding university-industry collaboration and entrepreneurship encourage knowledge transfer. Lastly, the growth of a venture capital industry allowed capital-intensive biotechnology firms to invest in their operations. Industry observers estimate that in the US there are about 1500 biotechnology companies that employ about 195000 people (Ernst and Young, 2008). About 389 of them are public companies. Some observers, however, note that biotechnology's share of total US manufacturing employment is rather small (Cortright and Mayer, 2002).The US biotechnology and pharmaceutical industries have unique location patterns. One study found that there are only nine metropolitan areas where the biotechnology industry has a substantive presence (Cortright and Mayer, 2002). 'These nine areas account for three-fourths of the nation's largest biotechnology firms and for three-fourths of the biotech firms formed in the past decade' (Cortright and Mayer, 2002: 3). These areas have strong research capacities, but more importantly they are leaders in the commercialization of biotechnology innovations. For example, as a group the nine areas accounted for 75 per cent of the new venture capital in biotechnology between 1995 and 2001. They captured 74 per cent of the research contracts with pharmaceutical firms between 1996 and 2001 and they hosted 56 per cent of the new biotech firms that were formed during the 1990s. Cortright and Mayer (2002) find that even though every metropolitan area in the US gained biotechnology research capacity, only the nine biotech leaders were able to commercialize this capacity successfully.

These nine regions differ in important ways. New York and Philadelphia are traditional centres for the pharmaceutical industry, and their biotechnology firms built on this base of knowledge. Boston and San Francisco were able to build on their first mover advantage: the first biotechnology firms started in these areas in the 1970s. In recent years, other regions have challenged these pioneering biotechnology and pharmaceutical centres. Raleigh-Durham, North Carolina; Seattle, Washington; and San Diego, California have seen rapid growth in commercial biotechnology activity. Other regions with significant biotechnology activity are the Washington, DC-Baltimore, Maryland area and the Los Angeles region. The presence of research-intensive universities and hospitals in these biotech regions plays an important role because the biotechnology industry relies heavily on scientific knowledge. In fact, the presence of so-called 'star scientists' has determined the location of biotechnology firms (Zucker and Darby, 1996; Zucker et al., 1998). Another important location determinant is the availability of venture capital (Powell et al., 2002).

Economic geographers and industry scholars focus mainly on leading biotechnology centres while overlooking other regions that may have emerged as second tier biotech or life sciences regions. Meanwhile there is strong evidence that life sciences industry activity is not confined to the most prominent regions. For example, Feldman (2003) analyses the geographic location pattern of biotechnology firms and finds that while the industry is highly concentrated in a few places, it has also become more distributed. Some of the more dispersed locations specialize in biotechnology sub-fields such as R&D in animal products (Des Moines, Iowa), in veterinary products (Kansas City, Missouri), and in medical devices (Minneapolis-St Paul, Minnesota). She attributes the growth of these specialized centres to the presence of large established firms that play the role of anchor institutions. Another dynamic that leads to geographic dispersal is the industry's trend towards subcontracting, outsourcing, and the development of complex inter-firm alliances. For example, Gray (2006) shows how biotechnology and pharmaceutical firms employ numerous strategies to benefit from other regions' R&D or manufacturing capacities. Genentech, the oldest biotech firm in the US, conducts R&D at its headquarters in San Francisco while cooperating with Eli Lilly, a large pharmaceutical manufacturer in Indianapolis, for clinical trials, manufacturing, and marketing. Pharmaceutical firms tend to outsource research and manufacturing to other organizations that are referred to as contract research organizations (CROs) or contract manufacturing organizations (CMOs) (Armstrong-Hough, 2006). Two of the US centres for contract research in biotechnology are the Research Triangle Park region in North Carolina (Lowe, 2007) and the Kansas City region in Kansas-Missouri (Mayer, 2006). In addition to focusing on dispersed cooperation strategies of biotech and pharmaceutical firms, scholars have begun to focus on the global nature of the biotechnology value chain (Birch, 2008; Zeller, 2010).

WHAT DRIVES HIGH-TECH REGIONAL DEVELOPMENT?

The discussion of the development of the high-tech industry shows that the industry is diverse, not only in technology and products but also in terms of location patterns. While certain regions in the US clearly stand out as high-tech centres, others have emerged as alternative sites. Corporate relocations and the development of home-grown technology firms often sparked the development of these emerging high-tech regions. As the semiconductor industry illustrates, corporate restructuring facilitated the emergence of these regions because places like Portland, Oregon, evolved from being merely cheap manufacturing sites to being regions with significant innovation advantages.

What drives high-tech regional development? What factors keep high-tech firms rooted in a place? Why do high-tech firms cluster in certain locations? In recent years scholars of economic geography have started to answer these questions. They have analysed the location behaviour of high-tech firms and examined why certain regions – particularly pioneering high-tech regions such as Silicon Valley – are home to an agglomeration of firms that locate in close proximity to each other. These analyses have identified three crucial drivers: talent, innovation, and entrepreneurship. Each has important implications for the spatial arrangement of the high-tech industry, and I will discuss them all briefly.

High-tech firms depend heavily on the creation of new knowledge, technology, and products and they typically invest heavily in R&D. Specialized talent is key for creating innovation. Research has shown that industries like high technology tend to cluster because of the importance of new knowledge and the spillovers created through investments in skilled labour and R&D (Audretsch and Feldmann, 1996). Innovation is therefore a highly localized phenomenon and the spillovers that occur through labour mobility, co-location of competitors or suppliers, and so on contribute to the spatial agglomeration of high-tech industries. Marshall (1920) observed that firms located in agglomerations or specialized industrial districts benefit from three externalities: the formation of a skilled labour pool, the presence of specialized suppliers and intangible knowledge spillovers. Entrepreneurship is another important factor in the creation of high-tech regions. Entrepreneurs typically do not leave the region where they start their ventures. One reason is that existing social networks and other benefits that emerge from being in a familiar place allow entrepreneurs to start their firms without high transaction costs. Thus, entrepreneurship is also a highly localized phenomenon. To analyse the geographic pattern of high-tech industries, we used these three key drivers.

A TYPOLOGY OF HIGH-TECH REGIONS

This study identifies different types of high-tech regions. We examine the ways in which smaller metropolitan areas emerge as high-tech locations from a broad variety of data on the aforementioned drivers of high-tech development.[2] To examine the ways in which US metropolitan statistical areas (MSAs) differ in their high-tech development, we employ a principal component and model-based cluster analysis (see Appendix). This type of analysis clusters observations into groups that share similar features and then investigates the ways in which the groups differ. In developing the typology, we use a wide range of data that reflect the economic perform-ance of each MSA and its associated degrees of industrial specialization, as well as input-based characteristics, such as employment concentration, quality of the labour force, and R&D funding. The data can be grouped broadly into four categories: economic performance, innovation, talent, and entrepreneurship.

We identified 359 regions that fit into the following types: high-tech centres (36); emerging high-tech regions, called challengers (68); emerging high-tech regions, called hidden gems (71); old economy regions in transi-tion (85); and regions with no significant high-tech activity (99).[3] Figure 3.1 shows the different types of regions, highlighting those with a location quotient above 1.10 in 2005.[4]

There are two main rationales for this approach. First, metropolitan areas are clustered into groups that share similar features and second, by examining the way in which these clusters vary, we obtain additional insights into the different economic dynamics that influence each region. For example, high-tech challenger regions are generally more innovative and entrepreneurial than the metropolitan average. However, they differ from high-tech centres in other measures such as their growth dynamics. Similarly, high-tech hidden gem regions as a group show improving meas-ures of high-tech specialization and growth in industry R&D funding.

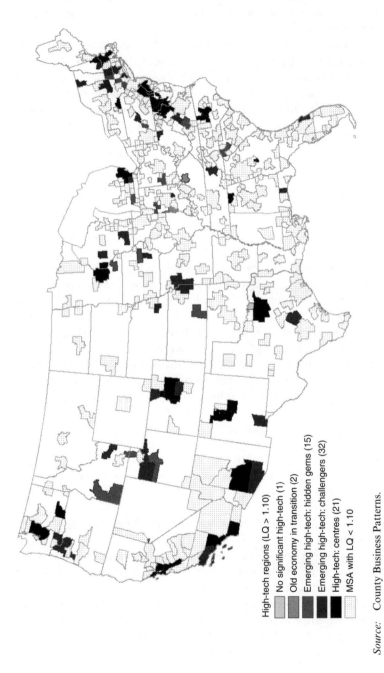

High-tech regions (LQ > 1.10)

☐ No significant high-tech (1)

▨ Old economy in transition (2)

▨ Emerging high-tech: hidden gems (15)

▨ Emerging high-tech: challengers (32)

■ High-tech: centres (21)

☐ MSA with LQ < 1.10

Source: County Business Patterns.

Figure 3.1 High-tech regions with location quotients larger than 1.1 by type, MSAs, 2005

The method lets us identify metropolitan areas that are similar to each other as measured by the variables that reflect talent, innovation, and entrepreneurship.

Unlike simply ranking MSAs by a small set of variables (such as the number of high-tech firms, number of high-tech jobs, or location quotients), this method allows us to use the additional information contained in our much broader set of variables by reducing the dimensionality of the data via the principal component analysis. We can form model-based clusters which, in contrast to other clustering or ranking techniques, are not based on arbitrary cut-off points. Since we are most interested in identifying emerging high-tech regions, we are able to look beyond the largest high-tech centres and examine other regions in more depth. The analysis yields the following major findings, which will be discussed in detail below:

- The majority of high-tech firms and jobs still concentrate in a few dominant metropolitan areas. The four leading ones are Washington, DC, Boston, Los Angeles, and San Jose.
- Smaller metropolitan areas are emerging as high-tech regions of two types: high-tech challengers and hidden gems. Entrepreneurial and innovative, these regions attract talent. They typically leverage the presence of anchor institutions such as a university or a corporation.
- Emerging high-tech centres, in particular the smaller hidden gems, display a higher degree of specialization than other regions. Specifically, they tend to specialize in manufacturing and service-intensive high-tech industries. While the high-tech industry has above-average productivity that is independent of geographic location, the absolute level of productivity is highest in regions that are not considered high-tech centres, suggesting diminishing marginal productivity associated with high-tech specialization.
- More than half of the nation's metropolitan areas are struggling to restructure their economies or have no significant high-tech industry activity.

Our analysis shows that between 1998 and 2005, high-tech employment in the US increased by 10.8 per cent, from 4 881 075 to 5 408 231 jobs. During the same period, the number of high-tech firms increased by 166 per cent from 231 182 to 568 129. The numbers seem surprising, especially when we consider that the dot.com bubble grew and finally burst in 2001. Despite these periodic ups and downs, the high-tech economy in the US seems to be alive and well. As many analysts have shown, high-tech jobs are geographically concentrated (Chapple, et al., 2004; Cortright and Mayer, 2001). Regions such as Silicon Valley and Boston capture the majority of industry activities and dominate because they are highly innovative and entrepreneurial. Most studies have focused on these dominant centres, and the findings presented here corroborate their conclusions. However, as I will show, these high-tech centres are challenged by other, often smaller, metropolitan areas that are emerging as viable high-tech locations.

High-tech Centres

The majority of high-tech firms and jobs concentrate in a few metropolitan areas. Washington, DC, Los Angeles, Boston, and San Jose are the nation's dominant high-tech centres and together capture almost two-thirds of US high-tech jobs (63.6 per cent or 3 430 981 jobs). Average high-tech employment in these centres is 95 305 jobs – about six times higher than the overall MSA average. The analysis shows that of 36 metropolitan areas that can be characterized as high-tech centres (see Table 3.1), 21 are highly specialized and show location quotients between 1.15 (Minneapolis) and 4.6 (San Jose). On average, these high-tech centres have a location quotient of 1.57 (see Table 3.2), indicating that their high-tech industries constitute more than one and a half times as large a share of the local economy as the national economy. In contrast, the average high-tech location quotient for all MSAs in the US is only about half as large (0.78).

High-tech centres like Boston and San Jose (which is representative of Silicon Valley) are highly innovative and entrepreneurial. As a group, high-tech centres account for almost half (48.8 per cent) of all university R&D funding and more than a third (37.8 per cent) of all industry R&D funding. Of all patents, 43.6 per cent are issued to inventors in high-tech centres.

Besides capturing the majority of innovation activities, high-tech centres host 43 of the 90 universities classified as research-intensive. Boston, for example, hosts five, and Los Angeles is home to four. High-tech centres also capture a significantly high share of the nation's population with bachelor's degrees (20.8 per cent) and share of employment in so-called 'Creative Class' (Florida, 2002b) occupations (28.5 per cent).

High-tech centres like Los Angeles, San Jose, and Boston show very high levels of entrepreneurial activity. The rate of high-tech firm births in these regions is more than five times higher than the MSA average. Venture capital investments are highly concentrated in these regions as well: on average, high-tech centres had three times more venture capital deals from 2000–5 than the other types of region. During this period, San Jose captured 86 venture capital deals per 1000 people, Boston received 35, Los Angeles 18, and Washington, DC 11.

Table 3.1 compares the top ten MSAs in high-tech centres with the top ten MSAs in regions of the other types. All top ten MSAs in high-tech

Table 3.1   Top ten MSAs in each type of high-tech region, ranked by high-tech employment in 2005

MSAs by type of high-tech region	High-tech employment (2005)	High-tech employment LQ (2005)	% Change in high-tech employment (1998–2005)	% Change in high-tech establishments (1998–2005)	Specialization
High-tech centres					
Washington-Arlington-Alexandria, DC-VA-MD-WV	306 271	2.64	23%	141%	IT
Los Angeles-Long Beach-Santa Ana, CA	302 194	1.17	–17%	81%	Diversified
Boston-Cambridge-Quincy, MA-NH	218 392	1.96	–9%	70%	Diversified
San Jose-Sunnyvale-Santa Clara, CA	197 253	4.64	–25%	45%	Diversified
Dallas-Fort Worth-Arlington, TX	196 248	1.61	16%	142%	Diversified
San Francisco-Oakland-Fremont, CA	178 160	1.89	14%	73%	IT
Seattle-Tacoma-Bellevue, WA	162 713	2.31	71%	99%	Diversified
Philadelphia-Camden-Wilmington, PA-NJ-DE-MD	155 891	1.25	9%	146%	Diversified
Detroit-Warren-Livonia, MI	116 309	1.31	32%	112%	Services
San Diego-Carlsbad-San Marcos, CA	107 306	1.87	22%	134%	Diversified
Emerging high-tech regions – challengers					
Austin-Round Rock, TX	68 455	2.40	8%	113%	Diversified
Portland-Vancouver-Beaverton, OR-WA	58 646	1.35	–9%	121%	Manufacturing
Kansas City, MO-KS	49 918	1.14	–2%	159%	IT
Hartford-West Hartford-East Hartford, CT	38 516	1.42	69%	86%	Manufacturing
Tucson, AZ	33 651	2.18	50%	125%	Manufacturing
Salt Lake City, UT	32 989	1.32	5%	143%	Diversified
Bridgeport-Stamford-Norwalk, CT	31 682	1.45	27%	89%	Manufacturing

Oxnard-Thousand Oaks-Ventura, CA	26 872	2.03	63%	112%	Diversified
Palm Bay-Melbourne-Titusville, FL	26 136	2.97	14%	115%	Manufacturing
Springfield, MA	22 161	1.77	333%	112%	IT
Emerging high-tech regions – hidden gems					
Wichita, KS	37 317	2.98	436%	209%	Manufacturing
Dayton, OH	27 725	1.60	21%	95%	IT
Poughkeepsie-Newburgh-Middletown, NY	21 691	2.16	75%	97%	Manufacturing
Boise City-Nampa, ID	18 969	1.76	-15%	219%	Manufacturing
Greenville, SC	15 422	1.16	-14%	146%	Services
Provo-Orem, UT	12 738	1.81	7%	146%	IT
Cedar Rapids, IA	10 654	1.90	-55%	141%	Manufacturing
Kalamazoo-Portage, MI	10 327	1.67	49%	157%	Services
Lynchburg, VA	5 626	1.24	-26%	154%	Diversified
Rochester, MN	5 256	1.18	-51%	126%	Manufacturing
Old economy regions in transition					
Virginia Beach-Norfolk-Newport News, VA-NC	31 569	1.04	22%	154%	Services
Milwaukee-Waukesha-West Allis, WI	30 582	0.79	4%	127%	Diversified
Richmond, VA	16 565	0.66	3%	146%	Diversified
Buffalo-Niagara Falls, NY	16 256	0.70	2%	142%	Diversified
Jacksonville, FL	16 113	0.64	19%	175%	IT
Tulsa, OK	13 695	0.77	-1%	178%	Diversified
Birmingham-Hoover, AL	13 491	0.59	6%	138%	Diversified
New Orleans-Metairie-Kenner, LA	13 149	0.52	-18%	141%	Services
Omaha-Council Bluffs, NE-IA	13 076	0.69	-40%	137%	IT
Syracuse, NY	12 083	0.95	-8%	135%	Diversified

Table 3.1 (continued)

MSAs by type of high-tech region	High-tech employment (2005)	High-tech employment LQ (2005)	% Change in high-tech employment (1998–2005)	% Change in high-tech establishments (1998–2005)	Specialization
Regions with no significant high-tech activity					
Sarasota-Bradenton-Venice, FL	6165	0.57	–11%	195%	Diversified
Mobile, AL	5709	0.74	25%	136%	Diversified
Spokane, WA	5427	0.63	–40%	144%	Diversified
Bakersfield, CA	5393	0.64	21%	230%	Services
El Paso, TX	4731	0.49	13%	204%	Diversified
Cape Coral-Fort Myers, FL	4609	0.52	43%	181%	Diversified
York-Hanover, PA	3856	0.49	–11%	163%	Services
Scranton--Wilkes-Barre, PA	3687	0.33	–54%	180%	Diversified
Reading, PA	3537	0.49	–41%	148%	Services
Vallejo-Fairfield, CA	3438	0.66	45%	181%	Biotech

Source: County Business Patterns.

centres have a high-tech employment base of at least 100 000 people and a location quotient of at least 1.1. From 1998–2005, high-tech employment in high-tech centres grew by 9.7 per cent, and the number of high-tech establishments during this period increased by 138 per cent. Most regions saw positive job growth, except for San Jose, where high-tech jobs declined by 25 per cent from 1998–2005, and Los Angeles, which saw a 17 per cent decline.

While high-tech centres captured the most innovative and entrepreneurial activities, their growth in jobs and establishments lags that of other regions. Compared to emerging high-tech regions, which are classified as high-tech challengers and hidden gems, high-tech centres have seen smaller changes in measures of concentration and specialization. The high-tech location quotient in these centres changed by 14.9 per cent while on average it changed by 45.6 per cent for all MSAs.

Emerging High-tech Regions: Challengers and Hidden Gems

The most striking finding of this analysis is that a number of smaller MSAs are emerging as high-tech regions. We classified 68 of these emerging regions as high-tech challengers and 71 as high-tech hidden gems. The high-tech challenger regions added more high-tech jobs and establishments from 1998–2005 than the high-tech centres, their more prominent counterparts. Both types of regions also outperformed high-tech centres in industry R&D funding and firm births during the period 2000–5. Even though these emerging high-tech regions are smaller in terms of the absolute number of high-tech jobs and high-tech establishments, they have been able to develop innovative, entrepreneurial high-tech economies.

High-tech challenger regions

Of the 68 high-tech challenger regions, 32 have a high-tech location quotient larger than 1.1, and they average 1.23, indicating that they are highly specialized in high-tech industries. Some regions, such as Corvallis, Oregon, and Idaho Falls, Idaho, have location quotients comparable to those of high-tech centres. They are typically regions with strong universities (Oregon State University in Corvallis) or research facilities (Idaho National Laboratory in Idaho Falls). In addition, high-tech challenger regions have become more specialized in high-tech, as indicated by the percentage change of their location quotient (see Table 3.2). In Burlington, Vermont, for example, it increased from 2.09 in 1998 to 2.57 in 2005, and in Austin, Texas from 2.36 in 1998 to 2.40 in 2005.

On average, high-tech challenger regions have a much smaller high-tech employment base than high-tech centres, ranging from 552 jobs (Merced,

Table 3.2   Comparison of characteristics by type of high-tech region

Characteristics	All MSAs	High-tech centres	High-tech challenger regions	High-tech hidden gem regions	Old economy regions in transition	Regions with no significant high-tech
Number of cases	360[1]	36	68	71	85	99
Economic performance						
Average high-tech (HT) employment (2005)	15025	95305	14711	5397	5003	1555
Total change in HT employment (1998–2005)	10.8%	9.7%	37.9%	14.1%	6.0%	–5.6%
Total change in HT establishments (1998–2005)	166.4%	137.6%	138.6%	167.3%	99.5%	79.3%
Average annual GDP growth (2000–5)	3.03%	3.73%	3.76%	3.05%	1.93%	3.23%
MSA GDP per capita ($ nominal 2005)	36199	46005	40432	34150	37422	30147
High-tech location quotient (2005)	0.78	1.57	1.23	0.81	0.56	0.37
Cumulative change in LQ (1998–2005)	45.6%	14.9%	100.1%	33.2%	51.3%	23.4%
Innovation						
Share of R&D employment (2005)	11.8%	43.0%	21.6%	10.7%	4.1%	1.1%
Total industry R&D funding ($M, 2000–5)	458467	314052	80798	31871	24850	6896
Total university R&D expenditures ($M, 1997–2000)	115081	56125	39667	6376	12702	211
Total patents (per 1000 people, 1990–99)	110	476	70	89	69	53
Total SBIR grants (per 1000 people, 2000–5)	6	13	8	11	1	1

Talent					
Share of residents age 25+ with bachelor degree (2005)	16.8%	20.8%	21.1%	16.6%	15.3%	13.7%
Employment share of 'creative class' occupations (2005)	22.5%	28.5%	25.6%	22.2%	21.9%	19.0%
Total number of research-intensive universities (2008)	90	43	31	3	13	0
Entrepreneurship					
Average annual number of HT firm births (1997–2000)	29	166	25	11	14	7
% Self-employed residents (2005)	12.5%	12.2%	13.9%	12.9%	12.8%	11.1%
Cumulative number of firm births (2000–5)	10412	55606	9445	4096	5558	3339
Cumulative number of firm deaths (2000–5)	9457	49845	8647	3694	5243	3079
Total venture capital deals (per 1000 people, 2000–5)	4	12	5	3	2	2

Notes: 1. We analysed 360 MSAs in terms of their high-tech economic activity. We combined, however, the MSAs for Durham, NC and Raleigh, NC into one region and labelled this region 'Research Triangle Park'. As a result, we come up with 359 regions that are classified into the five different types. See also notes in Appendix.

Source: Author's analysis of data from County Business Patterns, US Census, Small Business Administration, National Science Foundation, and US Patent and Trademark Office.

69

California) to 68 455 (Austin, Texas). Within this group, only Austin and Portland have more than 50 000 high-tech jobs (see Table 3.1). Except for Kansas City and Portland, the top ten regions in this group have seen substantial job gains from 1998–2005. Portland lost 9.5 per cent of its high-tech jobs (due to its concentration in high-tech manufacturing-related sectors), but increased the number of high-tech establishments. High-tech challenger regions have outperformed high-tech centres in job and establishment growth. As a group they increased high-tech jobs by 37.9 per cent and high-tech establishments by 138.6 per cent. In addition, the average annual gross domestic product (GDP) growth rate in high-tech challenger regions was 3.76 per cent from 2000–05, the highest of all regions examined in this study (see Table 3.2).

High-tech challenger regions are above average for all US MSAs in measures of innovation, entrepreneurship, and talent (although they are still below high-tech centres on most of these measures). They stand out because they have the highest educational attainment and the highest percentage of self-employed individuals (13.9 per cent) of all MSAs. Measures of research and knowledge creation show that these regions have been able to develop an innovative high-tech economy. Their share of R&D employment is about twice the metropolitan average. Industry and university R&D funding from 2000–05 were also above average. The only measure in which high-tech challenger regions do not perform as well is the number of patents issued. These regions rank below average in terms of patents per capita, but the measure may be biased by the dominance of high-tech centres (see Table 3.2).

Half of the high-tech challenger regions host at least one university that is classified as having very high research intensity. Albany, New York, is home to two such institutions, Rensselaer Polytechnic Institute and SUNY at Albany. Of the top ten largest high-tech challenger regions, only Austin (University of Texas), Hartford (University of Connecticut), Tucson (University of Arizona), Salt Lake City (University of Utah), and Springfield (University of Massachusetts at Amherst) are home to a research-intensive university. Regions like Portland or Kansas City represent areas that have been able to root high-tech economies without the presence of a world-class research university. High-tech regions without universities capture higher levels of industry R&D funding than their college-town counterparts. As I will show in greater detail in subsequent chapters, high-tech challenger regions like Portland and Kansas City have leveraged corporate assets and are developing unique university-industry partnerships with existing universities and colleges.

High-tech challenger regions perform well when it comes to attracting and retaining talented people. Their educational attainment is the highest among all regions: 21.1 per cent of the population aged 25 years and older has a bachelor's degree, compared with 20.8 per cent in high-tech centres and 16.8 per cent on average in all metropolitan areas. High-tech challenger regions are also in a good position to attract and retain talented individuals because they generally have high quality of life.

In terms of entrepreneurship, high-tech challenger regions perform at or below the metropolitan average. An average of 25 new high-tech firms started in each region during the period 1997–2000 (see Table 3.2, Entrepreneurship). There is no clear pattern as to which regions are most entrepreneurial in terms of high-tech start-up growth, and it is interesting to note that those regions generally known for having entrepreneurial high-tech economies, such as Austin, were no more entrepreneurial than metropolitan areas in the Midwest and some that are considered old economy regions. For example, from 1997–2000 Austin counted an annual average of 86 high-tech firm births, while Cincinnati had 87 and Cleveland had 88. On average, however, high-tech challenger regions have not been able to match the high-tech firm births of the high-tech centres, which at an annual average of 166 is almost six times higher than the metropolitan average of 29 (see Table 3.2, Entrepreneurship). Firm births in general are slightly lower than the MSA average, while firm deaths are also slightly lower. While the high-tech centres dominate in terms of venture capital investments, high-tech challenger regions perform above the MSA average. As a group these regions captured an average of five venture capital deals per 1000 people from 2000–5. The measures of entrepreneurship indicate that high-tech challenger regions may have developed entrepreneur-friendly milieus and support systems.

High-tech hidden gem regions
Among emerging high-tech regions, 71 MSAs can be classified as high-tech hidden gems. They represent metropolitan areas that are not as well known for their high-tech economies. They are often dominated by a few large firms and have a less competitive industry structure. These regions show positive high-tech employment and establishment growth, and they are slowly becoming more specialized in high-tech industries. Fifteen regions in this group have high-tech location quotients that are larger than 1.1. These regions, however, lag behind the high-tech challenger regions in measures of innovation, talent, and entrepreneurship.

Among the high-tech hidden gem regions are Wichita, Kansas; Dayton, Ohio; Poughkeepsie, New York; and Boise, Idaho (see Table 3.1 for a list of the top ten). Wichita, for example, is often referred to as 'the Air Capital of the World', and the region is home to major aircraft manufacturing companies such as Boeing, Cessna Aircraft, and Bombardier Aerospace.

Dayton represents a classic manufacturing town in the Midwest where the automobile industry is still prominent. Poughkeepsie is home to IBM, which established manufacturing facilities there in the 1940s and today employs more than 11 000 people. Boise, which will be discussed in detail in a later chapter, leveraged the presence of a home-grown semiconductor firm and a branch of Silicon Valley-based Hewlett-Packard.

The high-tech employment base in hidden gem regions is on average rather small (5397), not exceeding 40 000 (for example, 37 317 jobs in Wichita). Overall these regions have seen substantial growth in the number of high-tech jobs (14.1 per cent) and high-tech establishments (167 per cent). However, this job growth is sharply divided. From 1998–2005, half the top ten regions recorded significant increases (for example, in Wichita high-tech jobs quadrupled), while the other half experienced cuts (for example, Cedar Rapids, Iowa, and Rochester, Minnesota, experienced declines of 55.2 per cent and 51.4 per cent, respectively). All high-tech hidden gem regions have had substantial growth in the number of high-tech establishments, but the majority do not have high levels of high-tech specialization. The average high-tech location quotient for this group is 0.81, and only 15 of the 71 hidden gem regions have a location quotient larger than 1.1. GDP in these regions has grown at a rate similar to the overall MSA average.

Even though hidden gem regions have had a larger percentage increase in industry R&D funding and in the number of new firms than high-tech centres, they are average or below-average in measures of innovation, talent, and entrepreneurship. Their share of R&D employment is slightly below the overall MSA average. They capture only a third of the average amount of university R&D funding. This is not surprising as only three hidden gem regions host a research-intensive university (University of Rochester in Rochester, New York; Purdue University in Lafayette, Indiana; and Virginia Tech in Blacksburg, Virginia). Even though hidden gem regions had a larger percentage change in industry R&D funding from 2000–5, the average level is very low, about 40 per cent of the overall MSA average. Surprisingly, however, in that same period these regions captured more federal Small Business Innovation Research (SBIR) grants than high-tech challenger regions (11 versus 8) and almost as many as high-tech centres (13).

Hidden gem regions show below-average performance in attracting and retaining talent. Only 16.6 per cent of the population aged 25 years and older has a bachelor's degree, and only about 22.2 per cent of jobs count as creative class occupations. Combined with the general lack of research-intensive universities, hidden gem regions show significant weakness in developing an adequate workforce.

While the level of self-employment in hidden gem regions is higher than the overall MSA average and higher than in high-tech centres, these entrepreneurial dynamics do not seem to translate into more high-tech start-ups. Hidden gem regions on average only saw 11 annual new high-tech firms from 1997–2000. The cumulative numbers of firm births and deaths – generally considered a measure of entrepreneurial churning – were also significantly lower than the MSA average.[5] In addition, with only three venture capital deals per 1000 people from 2000–5, hidden gem regions seem to have difficulties in developing an entrepreneurial high-tech economy.

Regions with Minimal High-tech Activity

More than half the nation's metropolitan areas have minimal high-tech activity. This may run counter to the assumptions of economic developers in these areas who are trying to attract high-tech firms. Of the MSAs we analysed, 184 are in two types of regions, old economy regions in transition and regions with no significant high-tech activity. Both types have very low levels of high-tech employment and few high-tech establishments, and both are below average in measures of talent, innovation, and entrepreneurship. Each type of region is discussed in more detail below.

Old economy regions in transition. We identified 85 regions as old economy regions in transition. From 1998–2005, these regions have added only a modest, below-average total percentage of high-tech jobs (6.0 per cent) and establishments (99 per cent) and they have become more specialized in high-tech industry sectors. Furthermore, their average annual GDP growth rate has also been significantly below the overall MSA average, indicating that their economies might be struggling to restructure. Examples of this type of region are Virginia Beach, Virginia; Milwaukee, Wisconsin; Richmond, Virginia; and Buffalo, New York. The economic base in these regions is focused on old-economy sectors such as shipbuilding (Virginia Beach) and traditional manufacturing sectors such as automobiles or steel (Milwaukee, Richmond, and Buffalo). Old economy regions in transition show low levels of innovation and entrepreneurship. In 2005, their share of R&D employment was 4.1 per cent (see Table 3.2). Total industry R&D funding from 2000–5 amounted to about $24.8 million, which was less than one-tenth of that in high-tech centres. As a group, they host about 13 research-intensive universities, but their levels of educational attainment and share of creative class occupations were just below average. In addition, measures of entrepreneurship such as number of firm births, percentage of self-employed residents, and venture capital deals per 1000 people were each at or significantly below its respective overall MSA average.

Regions with no significant high-tech activity.   There are 99 regions with no significant high-tech activity. Only one MSA in this group has a high-tech location quotient above 1.0 (Sherman-Denison, Texas, with 1.1). These regions have on average 1555 high-tech jobs, and from 1998–2005 these jobs diminished by a non-trivial amount (–5.6 per cent). In addition, their average high-tech location quotient is only 0.37, the lowest of all region types.

These regions do not have significant levels of innovation and entre-preneurship activity. Their average share of R&D employment is a mere 1.1 per cent. Industry and university R&D funding are both very low, and these regions capture few SBIR grants. The educational attainment level (13.7 per cent) is also below overall MSA average, and the employ-ment share of creative class occupations is only 19 per cent. Furthermore these regions do not grow an entrepreneurial economy, and they have very low levels of high-tech entrepreneurship. Regions with no significant high-tech activity are not necessarily stagnating, as their average annual GDP growth rate (3.23 per cent) shows evidence of economic expansion, but their economies might be growing for reasons other than high-tech development.

ANALYSIS OF HIGH-TECH SPECIALIZATION AND PRODUCTIVITY

Specialization

The analysis of the data for these five types of regions shows that emerging high-tech regions, in particular the smaller hidden gem regions, display a higher degree of high-tech specialization than other regions. Specifically, emerging high-tech regions tend to specialize in manufacturing and service-intensive high-tech industries (see Table 3.3). Indeed, 40 per cent of the hidden gem regions specialize in high-tech manufacturing, and 27 per cent of this group have a service-based or an R&D focus. Similarly, almost a third of the challenger regions specialize in manufacturing, and a quarter concentrate strategically in service-based high-tech. By contrast, almost two thirds of the high-tech centres have no specific industrial specializa-tion. This strong difference in specialization between emerging high-tech regions and other regions is also reflected in Table 3.1, which shows that only three of the top ten high-tech centres are specialized, whereas the

Table 3.3   *High-tech specializations for regions with MSAs with*
          LQ >1.10, 2005

Type of high-tech region[1]	Biotech- nology	Manufac- turing	IT	Services & R&D	Diversi- fied
High-tech centres (21)	0%	10%	10%	19%	62%
High-tech challenger regions (32)	3%	31%	13%	25%	28%
High-tech hidden gem regions (15)	7%	40%	13%	27%	13%
Old economy regions in transition (2)	0%	50%	0%	0%	50%
Regions with no signif. high- tech (1)	0%	100%	0%	0%	0%

Notes: 1. The number of MSAs per type of high-tech region is given in parentheses.

Source: County Business Patterns.

vast majority of the two sets of top ten emerging high-tech regions show a specific concentration in one of the four high-tech industry types.

Productivity

While the high-tech industry has above-average productivity that is independent of its geographic location, the absolute level of productivity is highest in regions that are not considered high-tech centres, suggesting that diminishing marginal productivity is associated with high-tech specialization (see Table 3.4). This relationship implies that the importance of high-tech industries to a region's productivity is greatest in regions that are not high-tech centres. Focusing on high-tech economic development pays off more in emerging high-tech regions, old economy regions in transition, and regions with no significant high-tech activity than it does in regions that are already high-tech centres. High-tech industries' national share of output is almost three times its national share of employment, and at the national level the GDP per high-tech job is close to 4.5 times that of an average job. This indicates that high-tech industries are critically important to the prosperity of the nation's metropolitan economies.

As Table 3.4 indicates, the contribution of high-tech industries to productivity is highest in regions that do not have a large and diversified high-tech base. In high-tech challenger regions the high-tech output share is 13 per cent, while the high-tech employment share of the overall economy is 6

Table 3.4   High-tech productivity by type of region, 2005

Productivity measure	All MSAs	High-tech centers	High-tech challenger regions	High-tech hidden gem regions	Old economy regions in transition	Regions with no significant high-tech
High-tech output share	11%	16%	13%	10%	9%	12%
High-tech employment share	4%	8%	6%	4%	2%	3%
Labour productivity	2.9	2.0	2.1	2.6	4.9	4.4
MSA GDP per capita ($, nominal)	36199	46005	40432	34150	30147	37422
MSA GDP per job ($, nominal)	96337	115497	103849	90845	87751	94757
MSA GDP per HT job ($, nominal)	431403	301762	322823	426960	470696	502715

Source: Author's analysis.

per cent. Similarly their GDP per high-tech job is three times higher than the GDP per job in the overall economy. Hidden gem regions have a high-tech output share of 10 per cent and a high-tech employment share of 4 per cent.

Old economy regions in transition and regions with no significant high-tech show even higher measures of high-tech productivity. Old economy regions have a high-tech output share of 9 per cent and a high-tech employment share of 2 per cent, both significantly below the overall MSA average. Their GDP per high-tech job is five times higher than the GDP per job in the overall economy. A similar pattern emerges for regions that have no significant high-tech activity. The marginal contribution of one additional high-tech job is much smaller in high-tech centres than in emerging high-tech regions. One additional high-tech job contributes the most in old economy regions that are restructuring or have no significant high-tech activity.

CASE STUDIES OF EMERGING HIGH-TECH REGIONS

As this analysis shows, emerging high-tech regions are different from the well-known high-tech centres such as Silicon Valley, Boston, Washington,

DC, or Seattle. Unlike these prominent areas, emerging regions are less known as high-tech locations. The following chapters present case studies of three emerging high-tech regions. Two are challenger regions (Portland and Kansas City) and one is a hidden gem region (Boise). Both Portland and Boise are located in the western US and are within a two-hour flight from Silicon Valley. Each region is highly specialized. The Portland region, often nicknamed 'the Silicon Forest', is home to a cluster of high-tech manufacturing firms that specialize in measurement instruments, computers, and semiconductors. Boise's high-tech economy specializes in semiconductors and computer peripherals such as printers. Kansas City represents a different type of emerging high-tech region, as its economy specializes in life sciences, particularly contract research manufacturing, biotechnology, and animal health sciences. In entrepreneurship, innovation, and research, all three regions rank below their prominent counterparts, Silicon Valley and Boston, and all three have a significantly smaller high-tech economy. In 2005, Portland's high-tech employment stood at 58 646, Kansas City's was 49 918, and Boise's was 18 969. The following case studies will add insights into the evolution of these high-tech regions and they will provide explanations of how emerging high-tech regions develop, what role firms and universities play and how policymakers respond to these developments.

NOTES

1. Urbanization economies describe external effects or advantages that arise from the location in an urban area (such as availability of labour, access to markets and consumers, infrastructure). Advantages to the firm occur because of spatial agglomeration in general. In contrast, localization economies describe advantages that occur as a result of spatial concentration of firms in the same industry (Feser, 1998).
2. We use a variety of variables that measure a region's capacity in talent, innovation and entrepreneurship (for a detailed discussion of the methodology, see Appendix): Employment in high-tech, change in employment in high-tech, growth rates in employment in high-tech, high-tech establishments, business density, GDP from high-tech, percentage creative and bohemian employment in the MSA, percentage of population with a bachelor's degree, percentage self-employed, cumulative R&D funding, number of patents, firm births and deaths, and small business innovation research grants.
3. We analysed 360 MSAs and combined the Metropolitan Statistical Areas of Raleigh-Cary, North Carolina, and Durham-Chapel Hill, North Carolina, into one area called 'Research Triangle Park'. This reflects the typical view of this area as one functionally integrated high-tech region. As a result a total of 359 regions were analysed and categorized for this research.
4. The high-tech location quotient, a measure of the extent to which a metropolitan area is specialized in high-tech industries, is the ratio of the percentage of a metropolitan area's employment that is in high-tech industries to the percentage of nationwide employment in those industries. A location quotient above 1.00 indicates some degree of high-tech

specialization, and the higher the location quotient the greater the metropolitan area's high-tech specialization.

5. Entrepreneurial churning describes the rate of entry and exit of new firms into the economy.

4.   Portland: two anchor firms seed the Silicon Forest

'In the long run, a region that can develop businesses in the new technologies ensures its economic future. A regional economy can be compared to a forest. The large, mature trees stand out by their importance. But the source of future growth lies among the seedlings and young saplings.'

Miller and Cote (1985: 123)

BEGINNINGS OF THE SILICON FOREST

For much of the year, Portland is a rainy place, which some people find uncomfortable. Yet the rain is responsible for a lush vegetation of tall trees and verdant undergrowth. It is not surprising that Portland's high-tech economy has been nicknamed 'the Silicon Forest'. Although tracking its origin is rather difficult, this epithet has been used since at least the late 1970s (Francis, 1995). The roots of the Silicon Forest, however, go back even further to the 1930s and 1940s when a handful of electronics firms and a radio research facility located in the area. Today, the Silicon Forest is a very specialized high-tech economy. The region is home to major high-tech firms that include Intel, Tektronix, Hewlett-Packard, and Xerox. To extend the metaphor, Intel and Tektronix represent the large, mature trees that anchor the forest. Over time, spin-off companies and new firms moving to the region have become the seedlings and young saplings noted in the quote above. Portland's anchor firms were responsible for seeding the Silicon Forest because they have functioned as incubators of a variety of start-up companies. The region has managed to develop an ecosystem that supports entrepreneurship and innovation. In this chapter I trace the evolution of the Silicon Forest and highlight the ways in which Tektronix and Intel shaped high-tech growth. In tracing their role, I examine the link between firm building and entrepreneurship and explain how a region can overcome its initial location disadvantages.

The Portland region was never home to a world-class research university like Stanford or MIT. Oregon's more prominent universities are located in the smaller towns of Eugene and Corvallis, which are between 50 and 100 miles south of the Beaverton area, the geographic heart of the

Silicon Forest. Portland hosts several small liberal arts colleges (such as Reed and Lewis and Clark Colleges) and one public university (Portland State University) which by now is the largest university in the state. But none of these higher education institutions can be considered the main drivers of high-tech growth. Portland also trails other regions in terms of venture capital investments. From 1998–2008, Portland area start-up firms received on average of $242 million in venture capital; during the same period, firms in Denver – a similarly sized region – received on average of $1.02 billion. In 2008, Portland merely ranked twentieth in terms of venture capital investments (PricewaterhouseCoopers, 2009). Yet by other measures, the Silicon Forest can be considered highly entre-preneurial and innovative. Considering the rate of patenting activity, for example, Portland is more inventive than Boston (260 versus 223 patents per 1000 people). How, then, could this region develop a vibrant high-tech industry, overcoming the disadvantages stemming from the lack of a world-class research university and low investments of risk capital?

High-tech development in Oregon's largest city seems unusual. The state is better known for its resource-based sectors such as timber and agriculture. Portland offers great advantages for these industries because of its deep-water shipping, interlocking rail and highway systems, and water connections to the Pacific Ocean and the Columbia-Snake River system. The most important goods shipped are grains, woodchips, lumber, and logs (Abbott, 1983). Increasingly, however, Portland has become an important exporter of other merchandise, including silicon chips, comput-ers, footwear, and sports clothing. This shift indicates a major transfor-mation of the state from a resource-based economy to a knowledge-based economy.

Indeed, early developments of Portland's high-tech industry were closely related to Oregon's resource base. During the early 1930s the US Forest Service established a radio laboratory in Portland. The so-called Forest Service Radio Laboratory (FSRL) – located in Portland from 1933 until 1951 – pioneered the development and use of low-power, lightweight, shortwave wireless radio sets (Gray, 1982). This innovation provided a way for forest rangers and firefighters to communicate in the rugged, forested terrains of the Pacific Northwest. Wireless radio was much more reliable than carrier pigeons (used during the 1919 Oregon fire season) or telephone networks, which required the expensive installation of lines throughout the forests.

Even though the FSRL was small (it never employed more than eight engineers), it was an important institution for the development of local radio technology. It offered radio schools to train forest workers on the new equipment and was the nucleus of the local chapter of the Institute of Radio Engineers (IRE), providing local radio enthusiasts such as Tektronix co-founder Howard Vollum a place to exchange ideas with peers. Several of the lab's employees – such as Logan Belleville, who became Tektronix's second engineer, and Douglas Strain, co-founder of Electro Scientific Industries, another local high-tech firm – would become part of the budding high-tech economy in Portland. The FSRL also contracted with local firms who worked closely with it to produce radio equipment. In this way, the FSRL laid the groundwork for Portland's emerging high-tech economy.

Portland's high-tech economy is quite small when compared to Silicon Valley or Boston (see also Chapter 3). In 2005, 5614 high-tech firms employed 58 646 people. Silicon Forest firms specialize in semiconductor manufacturing, computers, measurement instruments, and software development. Part of a well-functioning semiconductor industry cluster, they produce silicon wafers, supply semiconductor manufacturing equipment, and develop electronic design automation. Related and supporting industries include engineering firms that specialize in clean room construction, chemical suppliers, and professional service firms. Other industrial specializations include display technologies, printers, software development, and test and measurement instruments. The Portland region has become a desirable place for high-tech activities and innovative entrepreneurs. In 2004, Linus Torvalds, the founder of Linux, relocated to Portland from Silicon Valley, further validating the region's strength in high tech (Rogoway, 2005).

Portland's emergence as a high-tech region builds on the presence of two anchor firms: Tektronix and Intel. Both high-tech firms have shaped the Silicon Forest in important, albeit different, ways. Tektronix is a leading manufacturer of test and measurement instruments, mainly oscilloscopes. Established in 1946, Tektronix located in Portland because two of its founders were natives who had returned to the region after their service during the Second World War. Over the years, Tektronix set industry standards with its products and became the world's leading manufacturer of oscilloscopes. Tektronix fulfilled the role of a 'surrogate university' because it attracted and developed talent, conducted research and development, and commercialized innovation. It also played the role of an incubator for a myriad of spin-off firms that helped to diversify the Silicon Forest. In later years, however, Tektronix ceased to function as a wellspring of entrepreneurial activity. In 2007, its local ownership came to an end when it was acquired by Washington, DC-based Danaher Corporation. Today Tektronix employs about 4500 workers worldwide, fewer than 2800 of them in the Portland region.

The other anchor firm of the Silicon Forest is Intel. Intel opened its first branch manufacturing facility in Portland in 1976 and has expanded it since then into a state-of-the-art manufacturing process development facility for semiconductor production. Consequently, most of Intel's innovations are 'Made in Oregon' (a marketing slogan developed in the 1970s to promote the state's products). During the 1990s, for example, the majority of Intel's patents were assigned to Oregon-based inventors. In contrast to Tektronix, Intel shaped the evolution of the Silicon Forest by attracting suppliers, subcontractors, and competitors. It functioned to a lesser extent as an incubator of start-ups. Intel's evolution in the Silicon Forest illustrates the changes taking place in the semiconductor industry (Angel, 1994). As I show in this chapter, the firms differ in important ways, and these differences shape the ways in which firm building influences regional entrepreneurship.

This chapter traces the growth of Portland's Silicon Forest. The region's high-tech economy grew because Tektronix and Intel built critical corporate assets. These corporate assets rather than public policy or government-led economic development created high-tech growth. Public policy in Oregon is generally reactive to the growth of the high-tech industry. The main policy efforts have been geared towards strengthening the state's higher education system and connecting industry assets with the research capacity of the area's universities. In the following I review the history of Tektronix and Intel and I pay particular attention to their role in shaping the region's talent, innovation and entrepreneurship dynamics. I then highlight the results of a survey of high-tech firms and finish with a discussion of policy efforts in the region.

A SHORT HISTORY OF TEKTRONIX

In the 1930s, the FSRL put the Portland region on the map for innovations in radio development. Besides the lab, however, only a few other electronics firms emerged in the Silicon Forest early on. Among them were Radio Specialties, a supplier of radio equipment to FSRL, and Pacific Scientific OECO, which was founded in 1946 and since then has been based in Milwaukie, Oregon. Yet the most important seedling of the Silicon Forest was Tektronix, a company that grew into the world's leading manufacturer of oscilloscopes.

After the Second World War ended, the nation's high-tech industry was still in its infancy. The emerging high-tech centres were California's Silicon Valley and the Boston area along Route 128. Due to the presence of high-profile research organizations and companies that served as military contractors, after the war these regions continued to receive federal funding aimed at supporting electronics research and its commercial applications (Leslie, 1993, 2000). Portland remained in the shadow of these regions and was largely unrecognized by many electronics insiders until the success of Tektronix in the late 1940s and early 1950s. Tektronix was started in 1946 to develop and manufacture test and measurement instruments. As the Second World War ended, a budding commercial electronics industry began to flourish, creating a ready market for instruments with which engineers could measure and display electrical wave forms and currents. At the time the inability to make precise measurements limited the work of electrical engineers interested in complex circuitry design, so there was a ready market for these instruments. Tektronix's success was not hampered by its isolated location in the Pacific Northwest. Rather, it leveraged a growing national and international market that needed sophisticated electronics instruments and it drew on the technical expertise of its founders. That Portland was the home of Tektronix happened purely by chance, as a result of the founders' desire to stay in their home town (Lee, 1986).

Tektronix became Portland's most important high-tech firm. Corporate expansion from the 1950s through to the early 1980s led to a peak in employment of 24 028 worldwide, with about 15 000 employees in the area. Following that, Tektronix went through significant corporate changes, lay-offs, and business divestitures. Tektronix profoundly influenced the growth of the Portland region's high-tech industry because its success attracted many talented high-tech workers, and the innovations created at Tektronix seeded the growth of various spin-off firms. These spin-off activities were facilitated by a unique corporate culture and the effects of corporate restructuring. The history of the company is summarized in Table 4.1.

Early Years: 1946 to 1970

Tektronix was founded in the mid-1940s in Portland, Oregon, by a team of engineers who had gained critical expertise during their military service. This team was not only skilled in electronics, but also had insights into the needs of emerging markets. And above all, they had a desire to build a small business in their home region, the Pacific Northwest. In 1946, Jack Murdock and Howard Vollum, together with Miles Tippery and Glenn McDowell, formed Tekrad, the company that would become Tektronix (Lee, 1986). They set up their firm in the basement of Murdock's house on SE Foster Road in Portland. One year later they moved to a new location on SE Seventh and Hawthorne where they also operated Hawthorne Electronics, a radio retail and service business that subsidized their entrepreneurial venture in its early years.

Table 4.1   History of Tektronix in the Silicon Forest, 1946–2007

Period	Activities
1946	Tektronix founded
1949–70	Start of vertical integration (transformers, cathode ray tubes, integrated circuits)
	Development of unique 'Tek Culture'
	Commercial success with oscilloscope and corporate growth
	Limited competition
1969–71	Downturn
1972	Formation of Tek Labs
1971–83	Diversification into many new product areas
	Creation of business units (including information display, communications, laboratory instruments, service instruments, and test and measurement instruments)
	Increased tension over decentralization or centralization of engineering
1981–3	Resignation of key personnel
1984	Tektronix Development Company (TDC)
1983–91	Period of restructuring
1991–2007	New CEO introduces new sales and productivity targets
	Major restructuring
	Tek Labs dissolved and R&D integrated into business units
	Refocus on oscilloscope
2007	Danaher Corporation acquires Tektronix

Source: Author's analysis.

Howard Vollum had graduated with a physics degree from Reed College in Portland in 1936. While in college he had built his own oscilloscope, which already included the features of the instruments that he would later commercialize with Tektronix. After college Vollum briefly worked for local radio firms (including Radio Specialties and Sears Roebuck) and ran his own radio repair shop before he was drafted into the army and joined the Signal Corps. He was assigned to the Corps' Electronics Training Group and posted with the British radio laboratory and then with Evans Signal Lab in Belmar, New Jersey, where he had a chance to meet Bill Hewlett, one of the future co-founders of Hewlett-Packard. In these positions Vollum gained critical expertise in the development of radar and was also exposed to the growing demand for sophisticated instruments.

Jack Murdock opened his own business in Portland, Murdock Radio and Appliance, instead of going to college. During the war, Murdock stayed in the Pacific Northwest and served in the Coast Guard, where he maintained and repaired radio equipment. During this service, Murdock met Miles Tippery who would join them as Tektronix's first service engineer. Accountant Glenn McDowell became Tektronix's first secretary-treasurer.

Working with wartime surplus parts, Vollum and his colleagues developed their first commercially successful oscilloscope, the 511, which went into production in 1947. The oscilloscope has since then become a critical tool for the electronics industry because it enables engineers to view and measure electronic signals. The 511 was an instant success: it was small and portable, enclosed in a well designed metal case, and above all made more accurate measurements because of its novel triggered sweep circuit. With this new circuit, along with a calibrated amplifier and time base, the oscilloscope was able to pick up and display high-speed electronic pulses. Previously, such devices were very slow and did not meet the demands of advanced research in emerging industries because they could only measure repetitive electronic signals. By incorporating an innovative solution, Tektronix was able to offer an improved instrument to a growing community of engineers eager to develop new commercial electronic products.

Throughout the next three decades Tektronix set industry standards for test and measurement instruments. Net sales rose from $1.2 million in 1950 to more than $31 million in 1959 (Lee, 1986). As a result, Tektronix became one of the most important employers in the Portland metropolitan area, with employment growing from 16 in 1947 to 8991 in 1971 (Lee, 1986). This growth was ironic, because the founders initially wanted to build a small business with an informal atmosphere and only a handful of employees who would know each other well. None of them envisioned much of a demand for their products. But the reality was very different. Throughout the 1950s, Tektronix became known as the world's leading manufacturer of oscilloscopes and was recognized by high-tech companies such as Hewlett-Packard, government laboratories, and research organizations as a serious competitor and capable supplier of high-quality products. Its oscilloscopes were in high demand because they could be applied to many different projects. Thus Tektronix had a broad spectrum of customers ranging from commercial electronics firms to government laboratories.

The founders were dedicated to high quality. The engineers working at Tektronix were the most sophisticated and critical users of the oscilloscope, thereby pushing the envelope of research and development. Only three years after Tektronix was started, the founders introduced a plan to share profits with employees. This not only ensured higher productivity and a smaller backlog of orders, but increased employee identification and loyalty. Another organizational innovation aimed at increasing product quality was Tektronix's policy of not making a profit on orders of replacement parts. In addition, trained technicians, known as field engineers, worked as sales representatives, assisting the emerging electronics industry with their knowledge. This network of technical assistance ensured Tektronix an increasing market share and enhanced the value customers placed on Tektronix products.

The most important organizational innovation Tektronix used to ensure quality was vertical integration, controlling all the inputs used for making the oscilloscope – wires, circuitry, and metal case enclosures – as well as sales and marketing. At the time, Tektronix was not the only technology firm with a strong belief in vertical integration: IBM and Digital Equipment Corporation (DEC) 'became highly integrated vertically and not only assembled equipment, but [DEC] also manufactured many of its own inputs, from semiconductors to equipment cases, and handled its own sales' (Langlois, 1992: 7). Vertical integration was not just rooted in Tektronix's commitment to high-quality products, but also the result of the firm's remote location. 'We were isolated up here', a former vice president noted, describing Portland's business climate in the company's early days (Walker interview, 2001). The practice began when Tektronix decided to manufacture its own transformers in 1949. After bad transformers supplied by outside sources compromised the 511, Vollum decided to wind and assemble them in-house. This decision set the stage for deepening the practice of vertical integration.

One telling example is the company's venture into the production of cathode ray tubes (CRTs), one of the most critical components of the oscilloscope as it helps to display the electrical waveforms. Tektronix had been purchasing the tubes from RCA and DuMont Laboratories, companies that also produced oscilloscopes and were, therefore, competitors. This situation created a variety of problems. First, Tektronix was not in the position to ask either company to manufacture more advanced CRTs for fear of giving away its plans for future instruments. Second, Tektronix discovered that DuMont had shipped them substandard tubes, after employees in early 1950 compared a shipment of flawless replacement tubes to the initial shipment of flawed tubes. In response to these issues, Tektronix decided to manufacture its own tubes and the company shipped the first products containing these tubes in 1954. Tektronix's production grew into an increasingly large component of the company (Lee, 1986).

Vertical integration accelerated the growth of Tektronix, while increased competition (mainly from Hewlett-Packard) by the mid-1950s and 1960s pushed the company to accelerate product innovation. Consequently, by the early 1970s, Tektronix had evolved from a company merely focused on one product, the oscilloscope, to an organization with a diverse product portfolio. Engineers worked on a wide range of products, including graphic display terminals, computer-aided workstations, and printers.

The Tektronix co-founders wanted to create a place with a relaxed atmosphere where everyone knew everyone. The firm developed a unique corporate culture, which was known as 'Tek Culture'. It resembled the well-known 'HP Way' of Hewlett-Packard (Packard, 1995), one of Tektronix's competitors. At Tektronix everyone was on a first name basis, an honour system was used instead of tracking workers' times, and there were no special privileges for the owners. Participatory management techniques involved everyone. In addition, the firm established an engineering culture by hiring top talent and investing in research and development. Lee (1986) notes that the Tek Culture encouraged a climate that allowed experimental thinking and the free exchange of ideas. This atmosphere was more akin to other firms on the West Coast than the older electronics firms on the East Coast that were characterized by hierarchical organization (Saxenian, 1994b). In the early decades it helped Tektronix to stay a step ahead of its competitors.

During the 1960s, as competition from other electronics firms increased, Tektronix started to diversify by building teams that were focused on the development of new technologies and products. One team worked on computer graphics terminals, and by 1970 a new group formed which was known as the Information Display Products Group. The mastermind behind display products was Norm Winningstad. He would later leave Tektronix to pursue an MBA degree at Portland State University and to found Floating Point Systems (FPS). FPS was one of the most successful spin-offs from Tektronix because it resulted in an additional eight spin-offs.

Tektronix pursued display technologies because it had developed a new type of oscilloscope, in response to a threatening new 1964 oscilloscope from HP. In 1969, Tektronix issued the first 7000 Series oscilloscopes. Lee argues that this new instrument series was a true 'breakthrough technology' (Lee, 1986: 266) because it had a digital readout, greater plug-in capabilities, and automatic triggering of the signals. The 7000 Series also used special integrated circuits that were designed and manufactured in-house. At the start of the 1970s, Tektronix had managed to grow a diverse range of engineering capabilities, which in later years influenced the development of new products and technologies that were commercialized by Tektronix spin-offs.

Corporate Restructuring: 1971 to 2007

As outlined above, the 1960s had ushered in the process of diversification at Tektronix. By 1971, the company offered more than 110 products and various new technology development efforts were underway. At the same time, however, Tektronix experienced its first real downturn. In 1971, sales fell by more than 11.6 per cent and the firm had to lay off more than 350 manufacturing employees (Lee, 1986). The crisis was aggravated by the death of Jack Murdock in an airplane accident that same year. To get out of this crisis, Tektronix chose to invest more heavily in R&D. In 1972, the company formed an in-house R&D organization known as Tek Labs to conduct innovative research and to propel Tektronix into new business areas by commercializing promising research. But Tek Labs faced serious challenges in accomplishing these goals. As was the case with Xerox PARC (Chesbrough, 2002) and other high-tech labs, Tek Labs was separate from the product divisions. The result was a failure to commercialize research. It was a dilemma that many corporate R&D laboratories faced at the time, when functional specialization and increased separation of R&D from product development and production made it increasingly difficult to transfer knowledge into the manufacturing process.

Functional specialization characterized Tek Labs, with its research groups set up to focus on specific areas. Two main groups, applied research and component research, housed nine sub-groups: systems and cybernetics research, computer research, display research, data acquisition, signal processing, semiconductor design, semiconductors, cathode ray tubes, and hybrid circuits. Within those groups, breakthrough research was conducted. One project, for example, involved work on a new software programming language invented at Xerox PARC, called Smalltalk, that had the promise of being the first programming language to use a visual interface. In the early 1980s, Tektronix was one of only four high-tech companies licensed to work with Smalltalk. Another Tek Labs group began work on a new type of semiconductor, gallium arsenide, as an alternative to silicon. This technology would later build the foundation for TriQuint Semiconductors, a Tektronix spin-off. Researchers in the labs also laid the foundations for colour projectors (later commercialized by former Tek Labs employees in the Silicon Forest start-up Planar Systems) and colour printers (which formed the basis for Tektronix's printer division, later sold to Xerox).

With no world-class research university nearby, Tek Labs made strong connections to the nation's top academic institutions. Senior-level researchers were hired from academia, and the majority of the lab managers had advanced degrees from well-known US universities such as Purdue, Rensselaer Polytechnic Institute, and MIT. A former employee of the labs recalled that many hires – especially in the computer science field – had been faculty members at universities before they joined Tektronix

(London interview, 2001). These recruits helped shape Tek Labs' culture, which resembled a university more than a company. However, this academic culture did not encourage the transfer of knowledge from the labs into other units of the firm.

By the mid-1980s, rival US and Japanese firms had chiselled away Tektronix's competitive edge. In 1986 Howard Vollum, the company's most visionary founder, died, leaving Tektronix struggling to regain its market share. Under new leadership, Tektronix began to reorganize. While worldwide employment peaked in the early 1980s, Tektronix significantly reduced its local employment, using lay-offs and incentives such as voluntary retirement and compensation packages. From 1985–1995, Tektronix shed more than half of its workforce, about 16 025 jobs. Personnel reductions were not the only restructuring policy. After years of product diversification, by the mid-1990s Tektronix management decided to meet market challenges and increase operating efficiency by refocusing on its core product, the oscilloscope, and divesting business units that were not profitable or did not have the potential of being market leaders (Colby, 1992, 1993).[1] In 1995 Tek Labs was eliminated (Hurt interview, 2011). Additionally, sales of excess buildings and other real estate during the 1990s trimmed the company's organization and costs.

A much leaner and more focused company, Tektronix was sold in 2007 to Washington, DC-based Danaher Corporation for $2.85 billion and now operates as a wholly-owned subsidiary located in the Portland suburb of Beaverton. Since the acquisition, Danaher has cut Tektronix's worldwide workforce by about 10 per cent, and local employment stood at about 2113 in December 2007 (Portland Business Journal, 2008). The firm is still among the top ten high-tech firms in the area, but by 2008 it had fallen to ninth place (Portland Business Journal, 2008).

TEKTRONIX'S ROLE AS A SURROGATE UNIVERSITY

For the high-tech industries in the Silicon Forest, Tektronix has played the role of a surrogate university. In the absence of a major research university, Tektronix itself attracted talent, fostered innovation, and enabled entrepreneurship to flourish. The sections below detail the ways in which Tektronix fulfilled this role. The company placed great emphasis on technological excellence, which involved large investments in talent and innovation. Tektronix also contributed to entrepreneurship in the region, starting in the early to mid-1980s, becoming a wellspring of spin-offs.

Talent

Many talented and highly motivated people came from all across the US to work at Tektronix. These employees valued Tektronix's informal and egalitarian culture. Tektronix also placed great emphasis on promoting professional development and education, making sure that their skills and capabilities developed while at the company. In the 1950s it established the Tektronix education programme whose offerings rivalled those at local community colleges and universities. The programme filled a critical gap because the Portland region did not have a strong research university similar to Silicon Valley's Stanford University or Boston's MIT.

Especially in the first decades (1950s to early 1970s), Tektronix built a critical mass of high-tech talent in the Portland metropolitan area. This labour pool was then available to the growing high-tech economy that emerged around the firm. Things began to change in the Silicon Forest in the 1950s and 1960s when Portland's high-tech industry gained more visibility and was recognized in state government reports and newsletters. A 1962 Pacific Power & Light Company report identified five high-tech firms in the Portland metropolitan area in 1950 'employing about 300 persons and with sales of about $4 000 000' (Portland Chamber of Commerce, 1950). Twelve years later, the report indicated that 22 such companies were operating in the Portland region, 'with more than 5000 employees and sales estimated to be in excess of $60 000 000' (Soher, 1962). During the 1970s, employment in high-tech grew from 17 378 employees in 1976 to 29 836 in 1979. During the same period, Tektronix's worldwide employment grew from 12 907 to 21 291. Even with the growth in the industry in Portland, there was not a rich enough agglomeration of high-tech firms for Tektronix to benefit from, so it had to attract and develop its own labour pool.

Tektronix's national reputation for being a leading high-tech company attracted people from all over the world. One former Tektronix employee later remembered that 'Tektronix had a reputation for hiring and creating really, really good people. Engineers, business people, all kinds' (Taylor interview, 2001). Another engineer emphasized that Tektronix served as a magnet for talented people, noting, 'We attracted some of the very best and brightest people from around the world in the early days because they wanted to be at the centre of technology development' (Hallen interview, 2001).

Senior-level positions were generally filled through an internal job-posting system. The effect of this policy, one human resources person recalled, was that most of the jobs that were open to outside candidates were entry-level positions which tended to be filled by recent college graduates who were motivated and brought in new ideas from their studies (Kunkel interview, 2001). The drawback, however, was that managers at Tektronix were often engineers who had climbed up the ranks, but who may not have had good marketing or finance skills. Leading up to the 1970s, managers were often ignorant of new products that deviated too much from the oscilloscope. Such disregard by management would later become a push factor for some employees to leave Tektronix and pursue an entrepreneurial venture. Yet, for entry-level employees, Tektronix was a 'great finishing school'. Engineers were able to rotate into management positions and be exposed to the business side through learning-by-doing. This process was enhanced by the company's vertical integration. Because of these opportunities, Tektronix employees who later left the company to start their own businesses took with them not just technical skills, but also critical business and management skills.

Many Tektronix employees, of course, had come from colleges or companies outside Oregon. Once they got to know the region and appreciate its quality of life, they tended to stay in the state, even when they were laid off or accepted voluntary retirement in the 1970s–1990s. During that period, in particular, other high-tech firms leveraged Tektronix's lay-offs for their own growth. The founder of one Tektronix spin-off company recalled that the regional labour market was populated with many former Tektronix employees. He noted that 'there are Tektronix people all over the place around the Silicon Forest' (Taylor interview, 2001).

Tektronix made an important contribution to the Silicon Forest labour market when it assumed an influential role as a provider of education. Former Tektronix president Bill Walker later remembered that one of the reasons Tektronix built an extensive in-house education and training programme was the lack of local higher education opportunities (Walker interview, 2001). That is why in the late 1950s, the company took the first steps in this direction and started the Tektronix Education Program (TEP), which was conceived as a separate department and followed in the tradition of establishing multiple units within the vertically integrated company (Lee, 1986).

Between 1965 and 1972, an average of 6000 Tektronix employees participated in TEP each year. 'During profitable times,' one Tektronix human resources manager recalled, 'the in-house Tek Education and Training Program offerings grew and rivaled most local community colleges' (Kunkel interview, 2001). By the end of the 1960s, the programme offered more than 180 classes, with a catalogue that contained more courses and was thicker than the catalogue of any local community college. In 1974, Tektronix's employee newsletter, *Tekweek*, compared TEP offerings to those at nearby colleges:

> The Tek student body totals 2200 (give or take a few), almost equal to the combined enrollment of Reed College and Pacific University. . . . And here's the clincher: Tek classes are held four days a week in 42 rooms or work areas, plus available space in four cafeterias. Classrooms are scattered throughout 17 buildings including Sunset and Westgate. Jim Sayer (E&T manager) said the 99 classes constitute the greatest number of job-related courses of instruction ever offered at Tek. (Tekweek, 1974)

Making continuing education available to all workers was at the core of Tektronix's human resources policy. TEP classes were offered in electricity and electronics, physical sciences, materials and processes, computer technology, and professional development, with technical classes added as demand and need emerged. Course instructors were required to have advanced degrees, and most of them were recruited from the Tektronix workforce. As TEP expanded, it also included classes such as piano and organ lessons, winemaking, and cross-country skiing.

Tuition reimbursement programmes were put in place for employees pursuing degree programmes at area schools. An on-campus MBA programme was offered through the University of Portland, and in 1973 Tektronix made an agreement with Oregon State University in Corvallis to offer electrical engineering master's programme classes on the corporate campus in Beaverton. In these degree programmes, most classes were offered in the evening and used Tektronix employees as teachers.

By making training and degree programmes available to all of its employees during the early days of the region's high-tech growth, Tektronix played an important role in the development of the Silicon Forest. It was able to play that role because it held a leadership position in the oscilloscope market for a long enough time that it could invest additional resources in professional development programmes. TEP and other company programmes helped keep Tektronix employees at the cutting edge and they helped create a specialized regional labour pool.

In addition to holding its own classes, Tektronix actively promoted and lobbied for more engineering education opportunities at Portland-area schools. By the early 1970s, these efforts bore fruit as educational institutions started to expand to meet the demand for high-tech workers. The Oregon Graduate Institute, which had been established in 1963, granted its first degrees in 1973, and Portland Community College's Rock Creek campus opened in Beaverton three years later. Consequently, Tektronix decreased its in-house educational offerings, especially general education development courses.

Innovation

Tektronix's commercial success and market leadership allowed the firm to invest heavily in R&D. Tek Labs was established in 1972 to conduct research in areas as diverse as integrated circuits, solid-state devices, cathode ray tubes, and software programming. Numerous PhD-level researchers were allowed to freely experiment and contribute to the knowledge base of the emerging electronics industry. As noted earlier, several technologies developed at Tek Labs built the foundation for numerous spin-off firms that still operate in the Silicon Forest.

Another important component of Tektronix's success was the company's open, informal, and egalitarian culture, which was pivotal in promoting the transfer of knowledge among the company's groups and divisions. In that sense, Tektronix was like other West Coast high-tech companies such as Hewlett-Packard, where employees saw the benefits of sharing knowledge and helping each other out (Lecuyer, 2003; Packard, 1995; Saxenian, 1994b). A retired Tektronix engineer recalled that

> there were ongoing informal seminars that occurred on a regular basis. Sometimes someone would have special knowledge and there would be two or three people that would be very interested in that topic, so they asked that person to make a presentation. Or sometimes it would just be one on one or so, but that was as important as the formal classes that were taught. (Hallen interview, 2001)

Tektronix's culture of teamwork and cooperation extended into research projects. R&D work was done in teams, and engineers did not hesitate to exchange memos and ask for help from colleagues in other divisions. Employees recall that they were able to go to anybody in the company and ask for information. Sometimes colleagues from other groups would informally help solve research problems, as one engineer remembered:

> I had a friend . . . who was a process development engineer, and he would come around and talk to me, and I told him what I was doing, so we would just exchange ideas and he just sort of independently went off and developed the basis of a new semiconductor process that enabled us to do this project that I was working on with no formal proposal or anything. (Hallen interview, 2001)

This informal sharing of knowledge, however, did not overcome the structural problems associated with having a diversified and vertically integrated multi-unit firm. While Tektronix's corporate culture encouraged personal contact among employees, Tek Labs operated separately from the other units – a structure that inhibited technology transfer to other functions such as manufacturing.

The company's emphasis on research and development and its focus on staying on the leading edge of technology resembled in many ways the traditional culture of a university. In fact, many current and former Tektronix employees who were interviewed for this research referred to their employer as 'the University of Tektronix'. Until the 1980s, the company's commercial success and market leadership made it possible for Tektronix to support innovation through R&D. It became easy to obtain funding for research activities. Tektronix historian Marshall Lee notes that

> the company had become profitable enough to fund a variety of experimental research projects. There was never a question of resources and funds, virtually every interesting idea was encouraged. . . . High profits spurred a liberal policy with respect to project funding, and that was all the encouragement that most engineers needed to push new projects. (Lee, 1986: 220)

Informal procedures to decide what kinds of projects were to be funded encouraged the pursuit of new ideas. A former Tektronix engineer recalled that a conversation with company executives over a cup of coffee was often sufficient to gain their approval for a new project. The result of this liberal policy toward funding research was the development of a diverse range of research competencies. Early on, oscilloscope innovations encompassed pioneering work on cathode ray tubes, which later led to the development of a line of display technologies such as the T4002 Graphics Computer Terminals. Over time, electronic circuitry became more complex, and by the early 1980s Tektronix was deeply involved in semiconductor R&D. The desire to capture the display of electronic currents on paper in addition to the oscilloscope screen led to research and development efforts in printing. To further this research, Tek Labs operated like other high-tech firms, such as Xerox's Palo Alto Research Center (Xerox PARC), which had also institutionalized innovation within separate R&D laboratories (Ceruzzi, 2000; Florida and Kenney, 1990a; Smith and Alexander, 1988).

Industrial research laboratories in large corporate enterprises have a long history. At the end of the eighteenth century, firms in the German chemical industry were among the first in the world to institutionalize innovation and knowledge creation within corporate R&D laboratories (Freeman and Soete, 1999). America's pioneer industrial research laboratories, such as Edison, General Electric, Bell, DuPont, and Eastman Kodak, emerged in the late nineteenth and early twentieth centuries (Noble, 1977). It was in these research laboratories that the fundamentals of electronics innovation were laid during the late 1940s. In 1948, for example, two engineers at Bell Laboratories – one of them a University of Oregon graduate – invented the transistor under the leadership of William Shockley. In 1955, Shockley started Shockley Semiconductor

Laboratory in Palo Alto. Just a year later, Robert Noyce, co-founder of Intel, joined Shockley in California (Wolfe, 1983). These laboratories had several things in common: they were set up separately from other corporate units (namely, manufacturing and marketing), their research activities were usually separated by distinct scientific fields, and the culture of work resembled that of academic institutions (Florida and Kenney, 1990a). Tek Labs had all of these characteristics.

During the 1980s, Tek Labs was the most important research institution in the Portland metropolitan area. A former Tek Labs researcher boasted:

> I always tell people that we had the best computer science department in the State of Oregon . . . if you only count those of us that had already been in academia. We had the best computer science department south of Seattle, north of Palo Alto or Berkeley, and west of Madison, Wisconsin. (London interview, 2001)

In fact, Tek Labs incorporated many characteristics of an academic environment. Work there was less time pressured and structured than in Tektronix's product units. Researchers were able to travel to and take part in academic conferences, and management allowed them to use time at work to prepare their research results for publication in academic journals and to write books. Tek Labs even housed a couple of PhD students whose laboratory work became part of their dissertation research. These activities 'were just part of our work', one researcher recalled. 'We wanted to let people know what we are doing' (Hallen interview, 2001). In sum, Tek Labs' culture attracted researchers who were devoted more to advancing research and creating innovation than to serving the firm's markets. In this atmosphere, research in the Labs became an end in itself.

In its heyday, Tek Labs employed more than 400 researchers and occupied three floors at the Tektronix campus. The work there was very innovative, and patenting activity peaked in the mid- to late 1980s. But the Tek Labs suffered the same problems as Xerox PARC in Palo Alto: researchers were unsuccessful in turning innovations into products. Once the competitive environment changed, the limits of an academic culture within a high-tech corporation became obvious. Tektronix was forced to adopt a different organizational approach to R&D, and the company began to incorporate advanced research and development work within its product and business lines. As one R&D manager recalled:

> At about 1995, the decision was made that our laboratories were too far removed from our product development. Good technology was being developed there but we were not getting it into products . . . we basically abandoned Tek Labs. And the people were moved into the businesses they were most closely aligned to. (Hurt interview, 2001)

Table 4.2   Tektronix corporate changes and spin-offs

Period	Tektronix corporate changes	Number of first-generation spin-offs	Number of descendants/ subsequent-generation spin-offs	Total number of spin-offs
1946–70	Corporate growth and expansion	7		7
1971–83	Start of downturn and product diversification	18	5	23
1984–91	Vertical disintegration	27	15	42
1992–9	New corporate leadership	21	31	52
2000–7	Restructured and acquired by Danaher	4	21	25
Totals		**77**	**72**	**149**

Source: Author's analysis.

Entrepreneurship

The restructuring at Tektronix unleashed entrepreneurial dynamics in the Portland metropolitan region. The rate of entrepreneurial activity by Tektronix employees, however, differs by period and reflects the dynamics of firm building and corporate change (see Table 4.2). From the mid-1940s to the late 1970s, Tektronix employees founded only seven companies. They included firms such as Rodgers Organ, Selectron Technologies, and Wilbanks International. Starting with the first efforts to restructure the company in the early 1970s, spin-off activity increased. From 1971–1983 Tektronix spawned 18 companies. The period from the mid-1980s to the late 1990s was a dynamic one, accounting for 48 direct spin-offs. In recent years Tektronix ceased to be a wellspring of entrepreneurial dynamics: from 2000–7 only seven companies can trace their roots to the company. Figure 4.1 shows the number, nature, and range of Tektronix spin-offs for seven decades.

Three dynamics encouraged this entrepreneurial activity: the formation of the Tektronix Development Corporation (TDC), Tektronix's efforts to restructure, and employee frustration. In 1984 TDC was created as an internal venture capital arm of the company because management recognized the need to commercialize the innovative technology that was being created inside Tektronix. More than half the company's innovations did not get to the market, which represented an enormous loss of opportunities. In addition, key employees began to leave the firm to start

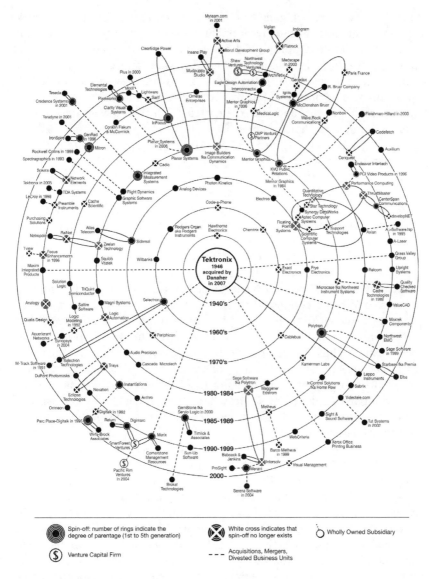

Source: Author's analysis.

Figure 4.1   Tektronix and its spin-offs

their own ventures. Management also believed that investments in these spin-off companies would give Tektronix the opportunity to gain insights into new technology areas not developed and commercialized within its own organization. The company wanted to stay connected with valuable employees who had great ideas but were frustrated with the company's unwillingness to pursue them. By financially supporting them, the hope was to maintain ties and stay connected to their new ventures. Silicon Forest companies that benefited from TDC's financial support include Planar Systems, ATEQ Corporation, Anthro Corporation, and TriQuint Semiconductors.

The second reason entrepreneurship increased over the years was rooted in Tektronix's efforts to restructure, especially those that transformed the company's vertical integration. The early 1990s was a time of corporate change in America and intensified international and inter-industry competition, and it was not unusual for firms to restructure and sell off some of their lines of business (Chandler, 1990; Mpoyi, 2000). In 1992, Tektronix recorded its lowest annual sales in nine years ($2.3 billion), and it became clear that the company had failed to exploit the commercial potential of the research being conducted in Tek Labs (Colby, 1992). To gain back its competitive advantage, Tektronix abandoned its tradition of doing everything in-house and began to sell business units or subsidiaries to new owners. Thus, the company's corporate crisis began to fuel regional high-tech growth. Most of the divisions that were sold or spun off retained their Portland presence and the majority of the workforce. Some of these new companies enjoyed rapid growth as independent units and became successful Silicon Forest companies such as Maxim Integrated Products or Merix (Barnett, 1994).

Employee frustration and dissatisfaction also motivated some Tektronix employees to start their own firms. Engineers were frustrated with the company's inability and unwillingness to exploit the research created in its labs. Various divisions, groups, and projects were often cancelled at the last minute. Tektronix struggled with these problems for years. Marshall Lee notes that 'over the years, engineers throughout the company have lamented the fact that on the whole Tektronix has been unreceptive to ideas outside the electronics-oscilloscope world' (Lee, 1986: 287). *Tekweek* noted similar resentment in 1979, and quoted a Tektronix engineer:

> These technological advances (many of which are new to Tek, not to the industry at large), have been, for the most part, ignored or delayed until critical by such production groups as ICM, Electrochem and Mechanical Products. New buildings, more equipment, additional employees are only excuses and will not solve what is widely considered an organization and management

attitude problem in these manufacturing service areas. This situation affects the company, as a whole, by adding time-to-market to every new instrument put into production. It is all too easy for many production service managers to push new technology aside because it does not fit exactly into their normal process flow or facilities. What is really distressing is when such areas refuse technical assistance from competent personnel that report through another management structure. It seems to me that this problem affects company morale, objectives and profits. (Tekweek, 1979: 3)

As a consequence, many engineers were frustrated enough to quit and start their own businesses. In some cases, Tektronix retained good relationships with these companies, and some entrepreneurs remember that Tektronix allowed them to use the company's resources, such as the machine shop. When Mentor Graphics was started by former Tektronix employees, Tektronix even offered the founders their old jobs back if their venture failed (Dodds and Wollner, 1991). Norm Winningstad, a former Tektronix engineer and the founder of Floating Point Systems, called Tektronix 'the Big Daddy' for its support to the companies that sprung up around it (Winningstad interview, 2001).

A SHORT HISTORY OF INTEL

Intel's growth in Oregon coincided with the diminishing importance of Tektronix. As Tektronix began to restructure, Intel started to flourish in the Silicon Forest. As outlined earlier, Tektronix began to downsize its local workforce and divest many business units. In doing so, Tektronix severely limited its impact as a surrogate university. In order to recover from this decline, the region's high-tech industry needed another corporation that would take on this role. However, Intel adopted a very different corporate model. In contrast to Tektronix, Intel is not vertically integrated. Rather, Intel closely integrates manufacturing with R&D and conducts parallel design efforts. The company also embeds innovation in the manufacturing process. In addition, Intel relies on a complex network of suppliers and contractors. Given these differences, how did Intel's evolution and maturation in Oregon contribute to regional high-tech growth?

Intel established its first branch plant outside of Silicon Valley in Portland in 1976. In 2009 Intel employed more than 15 500 people in the region, about 16.5 per cent of Intel's total workforce, making it one of the largest Intel branches and one of Intel's largest sites in the world. Today, Intel operates six campuses in Oregon and the company invested a total of approximately $18 billion from 1979–2009. These facilities are highly complex and comprehensive. They house Intel's most advanced manufacturing and R&D operations. The focus at the Oregon facilities is on computer, networking, and communication products. Key executives have chosen Oregon as their home, and various parts of Intel Capital, the world's largest venture capital investment fund, and the philanthropic Intel Foundation are located here. Intel's Oregon facilities have transitioned from being mere manufacturing branch plants to integrated manufacturing, research, and process development facilities, reflecting a general trend in the semiconductor industry (Angel, 1994).

Intel's Silicon Forest operations started out as semiconductor memory manufacturing plants. In 1974, Keith Thomson, Intel's facility manager in Santa Clara, was charged with finding an appropriate site for corporate expansion. One of the main requirements was that the new location had to be relatively close to the California headquarters, reachable by air in two hours. Portland appeared within the two-hour radius. After looking at two locations in Portland's suburban Washington County, Thomson recommended buying the 30-acre site in Aloha. At the time, Intel's location decision did not consider the local higher education infrastructure. Only closeness to the California headquarters and the availability and affordability of basic conditions for production were relevant. As Thomson remembers, 'there was no concern about having a major university . . . [W]e only wanted quality workers and availability of water and power because it was a production site' (Thomson interview, 2001).

Intel's start in Oregon was not smooth. After mothballing the facility for about six months because of economic uncertainties, Intel began the production of memory chips in 1976. This production was short-lived, because Intel exited the memory chip business in the early 1980s. By that time, however, the production facility had already started to reorient itself towards R&D in the field of microprocessors. This reorientation seems to have come about by serendipity: Bill Lattin, an Intel manager in California at the time, had visited the Oregon facility while on Christmas vacation (Lattin interview, 2001). He wanted to be closer to family and had the idea of moving his team to the Pacific Northwest. In March 1977, he and 17 engineers working on the iAPX 432 microprocessor moved to Portland. His decision fit the broader goals of Intel management. At the time, Intel started to move engineering groups (not just manufacturing) out of Silicon Valley. The impetus for this was an internal human resources study, which concluded that due to increasing costs of living in Silicon Valley, Intel's headquarters location had lost its appeal for attracting and retaining labour. At the time, Silicon Valley already had developed a bad reputation for employee retention. Young engineers who started to work with Intel would soon find alternative employment at other firms. During this time, heightened labour mobility was common in the Valley and affected many other high-tech firms (Angel, 2000). Therefore management thought that Oregon would be a more viable place to grow certain parts of the organization.

Work on the 432 microprocessor project had already started in 1975 in Santa Clara. The project was complex because it was an 'attempt to embrace the best theory of the time at every level of design – not just a new microprocessor architecture, but a new system architecture and new operating system software as well' (Intel, 1993: 14). Intel wanted to replace the minicomputer with this chip design, and the project represented a major departure from previous work. Albert Yu, then a senior vice president at Intel, recalls that 'Gordon Moore, the Intel CEO, finally decided that we should undertake a new architecture and fully fund the 432 project. He saw the 432 as a way to make Intel's microprocessor architecture truly world-class' (Yu, 1998: 121). This new architecture incorporated novel features such as fault tolerance, multiprocessing abilities for large-scale computations and object-oriented software. After the move to Oregon in 1977, the 432 team continuously worked on the design of the processor until its release in 1981.

To come up with new ideas for such a complex design, Lattin's team needed to be highly qualified (Lattin interview, 2001). Most of the key people working on the 432 project had received their academic credentials from the nation's leading institutions. Justin Rattner, who led the 432 engineering team and became an Intel Fellow, had attended Cornell University. One of the project's key software engineers was Kevin Kahn, an alumnus of Purdue University. Team member Clair Webb graduated from Utah State University. Several of these team members climbed the executive ranks of Intel. Rattner, for example, became vice president and chief technology officer and also head of Intel Labs. Kahn, an Intel Senior Fellow, became director of the Communications Technology Lab in Hillsboro, Oregon.

Even though the iAPX 432 microprocessor pushed the technical limits of the field, it proved to be a commercial failure because of a lack of demand. Its performance was below that of competing microprocessors such as the Intel 8088 microprocessor, which was introduced in 1979 with the IBM personal computer. Despite being one of the great 'disaster stories of modern computing', as *New York Times* journalist John Markoff (1998) called it, the 432 project had far-reaching implications for Intel's successive microprocessors because its features were directly incorporated into the Pentium processors, also developed in Hillsboro. Lattin's move to Oregon put Intel's Silicon Forest facilities at the centre of microprocessor design and development.

Despite the commercial failure of the iAPX 432, Intel kept engineers in Oregon working on refinements of the technology – this time, however, in a different organizational structure. Intel entered a joint venture with the German firm Siemens, which co-financed further developments of the 432 technology. The project, started in 1982, was called BiiN, and its engineers were based in the Silicon Forest. The goal was to build a computer that was resistant to catastrophic crashes and would appeal to the banking industry or military (Brandt et al., 1988). The two companies invested about $430 million in R&D, and work continued until the late 1980s. Conflicts over financing led to the termination of the project in 1989 (Northeast Parallel Architecture Center, 2002).

What happened to the 432/BiiN engineers when the project ceased? Portland's emerging high-tech industry provided them with enough employment opportunities to remain in the area. A large number went to Sequent Computer Systems, a local company that was started in 1983 by 17 ex-Intel employees. Others returned to Intel and worked on the 960 chip, a design that was based on the BiiN work, but was dropped by Intel in the mid-1990s. The 960 project was followed by work on the 486 processor. Although the chip had been developed in Santa Clara, Intel was looking for an available team to work on performance improvements and chose the Portland team for this task. As Yu recalls:

> It so happened that a team working on a microprocessor for embedded control, the 960 (a follow-on to the terminated BiiN project), in Portland, Oregon, was finishing up. Many experienced designers would soon be available. So, we decided to start-up a team in Portland to do the 486 clock-doubling part, later named the 486 DX2. Pat Gelsinger, who completed the 486 design, was running a platform architecture organization in 1989 to boost graphics and platform performance. Pat had long wanted to move his family out of Santa Clara in a country-like setting more like his hometown in Pennsylvania. Portland was just such a place. (1998: 147)

The iAPX 432, the BiiN project, Intel's 960 chip, and the performance improvements that resulted in the 486DX2 are among the landmarks in the evolution of Intel's Oregon facilities. All of these projects were based in Oregon and attracted highly qualified engineers and managers to the region. From the late 1970s until the early 1990s, Intel built a significant amount of microprocessor design expertise in the Portland region. This coincided with a change in the ways in which Intel organized innovation. Until the early 1990s, Intel traditionally waited to start the development of a new chip design until the old one was completed. However, this type of serial development was problematic in many ways. The design teams were too busy transferring their chips into production, and engineers who worked on novel designs naturally extended their old ideas into new projects (Yu, 1998). In addition, increasing competition pressed Intel to adopt parallel design efforts. Intel's Oregon-based engineers were in the right location at the right time.

While their counterparts in California were working on the Pentium microprocessor, management realized that in order to maintain its lead in the industry, the company needed to take up a new design effort in parallel to existing ones. The California team was already busy, but the Oregon team was both experienced and available to work on a new design. Yu notes that 'it was natural to ask that team to take on the next design, code-named P6, in parallel to the P5 development' (1998: 168). As Pat Gelsinger (Intel, 2002) remembers:

> Until now there was this belief that you couldn't do a new, major new architecture outside of Santa Clara, a major new successful one. Right? We had failed with the 960 and the 432 and stuff, so, we created the parallel design center up here in Oregon. Which was a big deal for the company at the time, a big new R&D investment. We started the design team up here, built the architectural expertise, really picked up some of the very qualified people out of the 960 efforts that were up here, and started to build the design capability here. And that kept growing, the P6, the Pentium Pro, it was a chip that resulted from that, ran that, started it up, recruited enormously, and got that effort underway. That design center today is an enormous asset to the company, as it's become one of our greatest sources of innovation in the IA32 family. (n.p.)

Over the next four years, the engineers at the Oregon design centre worked on the P6 microprocessor architecture. When the chip was introduced as the Pentium Pro in 1995, Portland's newspaper, *The Oregonian*, proudly announced that 'from start to finish, the P6 is a home-grown Oregon product' (Barnett, 1995). This chip and many subsequent designs had various code names that reflected the engineers' geographic roots: Klamath, Cascades, Tualatin, and Willamette are landmarks in the Pacific Northwest and indicate a strong connection between Intel's innovations and the company's presence in Oregon.

Intel's R&D efforts put Portland on the map for semiconductor design, development, and manufacturing. During the 1990s, Intel engineers in the Portland metropolitan region registered more than twice as many microprocessor design patents as their counterparts in Silicon Valley (see Table 4.3). In addition, from 1979–99 Intel's average annual patent growth in Portland (27 per cent) outpaced that of its inventors based in California (17 per cent). These trends illustrate the strategic importance of Intel's Portland location.

Table 4.3   Intel's microprocessor design patents, 1990–99[1]

Intel inventor's residence	Number of patents, 1990–9
Silicon Forest (Oregon)	684
Silicon Valley (California)	298
Sacramento (California)	271
Phoenix (Arizona)	105
Other regions in the US	68
Total no. patents	**1426**

Notes: 1. Analysis includes patent classes 708, 709, 710, 711, 712, and 714, which refer to electrical computers and digital data processing technologies. Silicon Forest refers to the Portland-Vancouver metropolitan region and Silicon Valley refers to the San Francisco-Oakland-San Jose metropolitan region.

Source: US Patent and Trademark Office.

INTEL FACILITATES CLUSTER DEVELOPMENT

Intel contributed in different ways from Tektronix to the growth of the Silicon Forest. Intel never employed a vertically integrated organizational model; rather, it integrated R&D into the manufacturing process. It used flexible teams and parallel design efforts to stay ahead of its competitors. While Tektronix sowed the seeds of the Silicon Forest through its contribution to entrepreneurship, Intel attracted suppliers and competitors to the region ensuring continued growth through the creation of an industry cluster. Intel anchors a network of suppliers, contractors, and competitors. In addition, like Tektronix, Intel functioned like a labour magnet.

Intel's Integrated Innovation Model

Intel's Oregon operations illustrate how the semiconductor industry integrates research and development with the manufacturing process. As noted in Chapter 3, the industry started to adopt new organizational models such as collaboration with external partners; closer integration of innovation with manufacturing instead of a bifurcated system; teams that combined key personnel from research, development, manufacturing, and marketing; and parallel design efforts. These organizational changes kept the industry competitive at a global level. They also played a pivotal role in the development of second tier high-tech regions like Portland. Portland is not simply the location for one of Intel's branch manufacturing plants. The organizational integration of R&D and manufacturing and the other changes transformed the Portland facilities from mere production sites to innovation hubs.

At Intel, research is closely connected to the development and manufacturing process. R&D labs are housed within product groups. Work on new microprocessor designs is closely integrated with manufacturing process development, which from its inception is geared towards mass production. Intel developed a unique model for integrating R&D and manufacturing by using process development facilities known in the industry as 'fabs'. Within these fabs Intel develops the manufacturing processes used for the production of new generation chips. New tools and systems are tested under the conditions of high-volume manufacturing. Once the processes and tools are set, they are copied exactly in a second fab at another location to save time and allow for a more efficient transfer of the technology and the manufacturing processes (McDonald, 1998). Once all the development work has finished, the fabs turn into manufacturing facilities. This process minimizes the gap between process development and high-volume manufacturing and the resulting problems. The results are high yields and better performance processes and products. In 1992, Intel established one of its first fabs in Aloha, Oregon and called it D1A. Over the years, Intel constructed other fabs in Oregon, including the latest fab, called D1D, which began construction in 2001 at the Ronler Acres campus in Hillsboro.

The decision to integrate R&D with manufacturing necessitated the co-location of manufacturing facilities with research, thereby turning branch plant locations like the Silicon Forest into important innovation sites. Intel's Research Pathfinding Lab (RP1), located in Hillsboro, illustrates this requirement: RP1 is dedicated to very advanced research on silicon technologies and equipment. The lab is adjacent to Intel's third fab, D1C, which currently produces the 300 mm wafers. This geographic co-location ensures the smooth and rapid transfer of knowledge created in the RP1 labs into the production processes.

By focusing research on manufacturing needs, innovations are not created for their own sake. As one business scholar (Chesbrough, 2001) states: 'Intel has structured and managed its labs with technology transfer to the fab foremost in mind' (n.p.). In that sense, Intel's efforts are a good example of how innovation works in an interactive way. Rather than relying on the supply of ideas and new knowledge created in a centralized lab – like Tek Labs – ideas are gained from a variety of sources: the manufacturing shop floor, the laboratory connected to the fab, customers, and suppliers. By avoiding the 'ivory tower' style, innovation at Intel is integrated, an approach that Tektronix only realized in recent decades.

Table 4.4   Intel corporate changes and spin-offs

Period	Intel corporate changes	Number of first-generation spin-offs	Number of descendants/ subsequent-generation spin-offs	Total number of spin-offs
1976–89	Branch plant: memory production; some design work	17	4	21
1990–9	Corporate expansion, development on Pentium Processor P5	18	22	40
2000–8	Various process development fabs opened	15	21	36
Since 1976		**50**	**47**	**97**

Source: Author's analysis.

Limited Impact on Entrepreneurship

In contrast to Tektronix, Intel has had fewer spin-offs, both in terms of first generation spin-offs and subsequent descendants (see Table 4.4). During Intel's early years in the Silicon Forest, the company spawned 17 firms. Among them was Sequent Computer Systems, founded by 17 ex-Intel employees. The 1990s marked a time of corporate expansion, primarily as a result of Intel Oregon's foray into the development of the Pentium Processor. This period saw 18 firms spin-off from Intel, with 22 subsequent descendants. From 2000–8, the number of Intel spin-offs decreased to 15, which spawned 21 descendants. Figure 4.2 shows the number, nature, and range of Intel spin-offs for four decades.

There are several explanations for why Intel has not had a greater impact on entrepreneurship in Portland. First, the company's corporate policies regarding equity ownership may have deterred potential entrepreneurs from leaving the company. Equity ownership may function like 'golden handcuffs' to undermine an employee's desire to start a new firm. Second, internal venture creation kept employees from leaving the company and creating their own business ventures. This is called intra-preneurship, and the practice may have retained valuable talent and ideas inside Intel. Intel provides financial support to employees interested in creating a company inside the corporation. Third, Intel's integrated innovation model tightly organizes knowledge creation and may limit knowledge spillovers. This integrated approach, however, seems to have limited opportunities for commercializing innovation outside of the corporation.

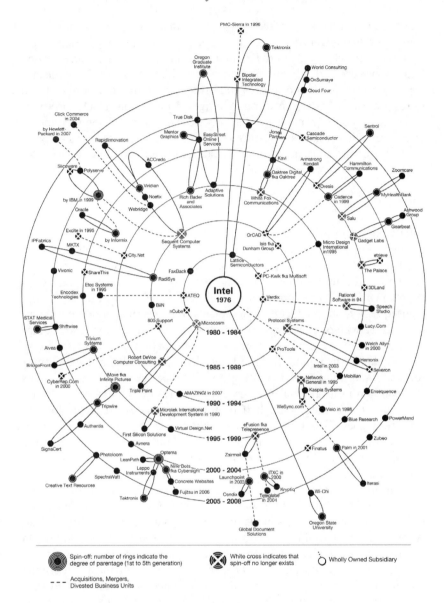

Source: Author's analysis.

Figure 4.2   Intel and its spin-offs

Knowledge is directly applied to the manufacturing process and rarely spills over through entrepreneurship. Consequently, knowledge spillovers to the region – especially in the form of spin-offs – have been more limited than in the case of Tektronix. In addition, unlike Tektronix, Intel has not experienced major corporate restructuring, preventing entrepreneurship in response to negative corporate changes. In addition, Intel's products are very different from those that Tektronix produced: semiconductor chips are high-volume, standardized products, and spin-off rates are generally lower in industries producing standardized products (Glasmeier, 1988).

Cluster Development

Intel's contribution to the growth of the Silicon Forest lies mainly in its function as an anchor firm in a semiconductor industry cluster. Intel attracted a range of specialized suppliers, subcontractors, and even competitors. Intel requires the local presence of a variety of specialized suppliers because the company deliberately avoids vertical integration. Consequently, supplier companies providing the semiconductor maker with silicon wafers, chemicals and gases, specialized manufacturing equipment and software, and other necessary production components, began to co-locate in the region. In 1995 Intel's local inter-industry expenditures totalled $456 million, representing about 55 per cent of Intel Oregon's $833 million in total inter-industry expenditures (ECONorthwest, 1998). This shows that more than half of Intel's purchases are made locally. The study goes further and concludes that 48 per cent of the local expenditures stayed within Washington County, indicating strong linkages to suppliers and subcontractors that are in close proximity to Intel's campuses.

In addition, Intel has attracted many competitor firms to the region. The presence of the world's most successful semiconductor manufacturer sent strong positive signals to other firms about the Silicon Forest. A local venture capitalist noted that 'Intel gave credibility to the Silicon Forest as a viable place to locate a high-tech company' (Shaw interview, 2001). Especially during the 1990s, as the high-tech market boomed and demand for chips surged, other semiconductor firms moved into the region and established a Portland presence. They took advantage of the region's labour pool and infrastructure of suppliers and benefited from training programmes Intel helped set up at local community colleges. In addition, the state's tax climate facilitated the location of firms, because it provided financial incentives for capital-intensive investments through the Oregon Strategic Investment Program. From 1994–6, new

Table 4.5   Announced new semiconductor investments in Oregon and SW Washington, 1994–6

Firm	Location	Investment (millions)	Projected jobs
LSI Logic	Gresham	$4000	2000
Intel (Ronler Acres)	Hillsboro	$2200	1400
Hyundai Electronics	Eugene	$1300	1000
Wafertech	Camas	$1200	800
Fujitsu Microelectronics	Gresham	$1032	445
Integrated Device Technology	Hillsboro	$800	975
Intel (Aloha D1E)	Hillsboro	$705	355
SEH America	Vancouver	$700	600
Komatsu Microelectronics	Hillsboro	$450	300
Mitsubishi Silicon	Salem	$340	400
Wacker Siltronic	Portland	$240	300
Totals		**$12967**	**8575**

Source: Portland Development Commission.

semiconductor investments were announced in the region totalling almost $13 billion (see Table 4.5). Foreign-based firms started to locate in the region during the mid-1980s. Japanese high-tech firms in particular took advantage of a favourable exchange rate, a more liberal tax climate in Oregon, and an expanding market for their products. Japanese semiconductor firms invested about $800 million between 1985 and 1999. Other than establishing a presence in the region, supplying other firms, and hiring local employees, these Japanese-owned firms have not influenced the region in terms of entrepreneurship, producing no significant spin-offs. They have truly functioned as branch plants. These firms took advantage of the presence of competitors and suppliers and they kept a close watch on these firms to stay competitive (Mia Gray et al., 1999: 305). They have been more interested in tapping Silicon Forest resources such as a specialized labour pool, a well developed supplier and customer infrastructure, and established distribution channels.

COMPARING TEKTRONIX AND INTEL

As the case studies illustrate, Tektronix and Intel have contributed to the growth of the Silicon Forest in very different ways. Table 4.6 compares the two firms in relation to various firm-building characteristics. Focusing on

Table 4.6   Comparing Tektronix and Intel

Feature	Tektronix	Intel
Industry	Measurement instruments	Semiconductors
Corporate changes	Disintegration Restructuring Refocus on core products	Continued corporate expansion in region; focus on process development
Linkages	Disintegration facilitated entrepreneurial opportunities	Expansion-induced clustering
Market connections	Industry leader Strong market connections	Intermediary supplier
Product type	Customized for industry use	Standardized commodity
Nature of production	Move towards integration of R&D and manufacturing	Integrated R&D and manufacturing Mass production
Innovation	Product innovation Tek Labs	Manufacturing process innovation
Corporate policies and culture	'Tek Culture' similar to 'HP Way' Strong culture of talent development 'Welcome mat' for entrepreneurs Divisionalization	Strategic orientation towards company goals Intrapreneurship
Assets	Mix of human and physical assets	Physical assets dominate Strong intellectual property assets
Labour	Engineer	Engineer Production worker

Source: Author's analysis.

these characteristics helps explain the different impacts of different firms on a region's entrepreneurial dynamics. This understanding is important if economic developers and policymakers want to know where new sources of economic growth come from.

One often-overlooked factor in entrepreneurship is the type of industry a firm operates in. The case studies of Tektronix and Intel indicate that firms operating in different industry sectors differ in terms of their influence on spin-off activity. Firms with a more varied product line show more variation internally and as a result generate more spin-offs. According to Klepper (1996) firms that operate in the early stage of a

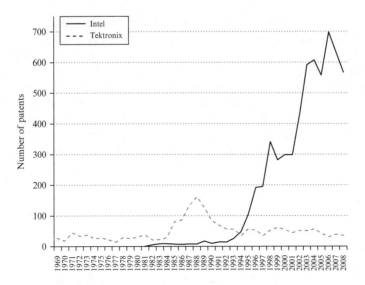

Source: US Patent and Trademark Office.

Figure 4.3   Patenting activity of Intel and Tektronix, 1969–2008

product cycle, such as product development and R&D, have a higher
spin-off rate than firms operating in a later stage, such as manufacturing. Although Tektronix's primary products were test and measurement
instruments like the oscilloscope, the firm also ventured into many other
product areas. During the 1970s when Tektronix started to diversify, the
spin-off rate increased, indicating that the level of product diversification
and R&D experimentation increased, allowing potential entrepreneurs
inside Tektronix to exploit new ideas and innovations. In contrast, Intel
has always operated in the field of semiconductors which is characterized
by a strong and narrow focus on manufacturing. Such a narrow focus
may have limited Intel's contribution to the region's entrepreneurial
dynamics.

Patenting activity is very important to the semiconductor industry
because firms are eager to protect knowledge about production processes
and chip design. Patenting data indicates that Tektronix's innovation
activity peaked in the mid- to late 1980s. This coincided with the firm's
impact on entrepreneurship, as it had the most first-generation spin-offs
during this time. Intel's patent activity peaked in 2006 when it registered
702 patents to Oregon-based inventors (see Figure 4.3). This spike may,
however, indicate that Intel was using patents to fend off competitors.

Such defensive or strategic patents may not translate into innovation capabilities that could be exploited by nascent entrepreneurs.

Corporate changes also influence the way in which firms impact a region's entrepreneurship. They create critical moments in which firms show higher rates of spin-off activity. Negative corporate changes affected Tektronix as it restructured, laid off employees, divested business units, and shut down Tek Labs during the 1980s and 1990s. Tektronix's corporate crises helped the region because it unleashed entrepreneurial potential. Corporate changes such as the reduction of vertical integration functioned as push factors for numerous employees to enter the economy as entrepreneurs. Intel, in contrast, has experienced continuous growth and expansion since it arrived in Portland in the late 1970s. Employees may not want to leave a growing firm, as it may still offer an exciting work environment.

Both Tektronix and Intel encouraged linkages with local high-tech firms and spin-offs. Former Tektronix employees were able to use the company's resources when they set up their entrepreneurial ventures. Intel's business practices fostered the development of an industrial cluster. Survey results (detailed in the next section) indicate that high-tech firms generally are more strongly related as suppliers and customers to Intel than to Tektronix.

Tektronix and Intel both have strong connections to their markets and they are both market leaders. This results in their ability to hire top talent. As labour magnets, both firms have attracted a workforce that provides the fodder for Portland's entrepreneurial community. They differ strongly, however, in terms of their corporate culture, their assets, and the ways in which each firm's products and manufacturing orientation may influence the type of labour they hire. Because Intel's focus is on improvements in its manufacturing process and the integration of R&D into production, its assets are expensive capital equipment, machinery, and tools, with human resources ranking second. Intel is also very strong in terms of intellectual property assets although, as noted above, these may not translate into human assets that could be exploited by would-be entrepreneurs. In addition, spin-off activity may also be limited by Intel's very strategically focused culture, which may not allow for resources that are available beyond the business's bottom line to be developed. In contrast, Tektronix's history is peppered with a lack of focus by management, which led to frustration among engineers and key personnel who would then venture out to set up their own firms. Tektronix is less capital intensive and has had a tradition of developing the engineer-manager.

ENTREPRENEURSHIP IN THE SILICON FOREST

Tektronix and Intel have both served as surrogate universities and contributed to the development of the emerging high-tech region known as the Silicon Forest. Both firms have made significant contributions to entrepreneurship. To understand the entrepreneurial dynamics in the Silicon Forest, in 2007 I conducted a survey of its high-tech firms, to which 204 companies responded. The survey gives a snapshot of the Silicon Forest and its entrepreneurial dynamics and helps us understand how firms operate in this region. Survey questions focused on the characteristics of founders and their start-ups as well as their relationship to anchor firms such as Tektronix and Intel. Respondents also gave information about the region as a business location and about the ways in which their firms interact with universities. The survey data was augmented with membership lists of industry groups to create a database of information about 645 firms. Figure 4.4 illustrates the pattern of emergence of these firms from 1894–2007.

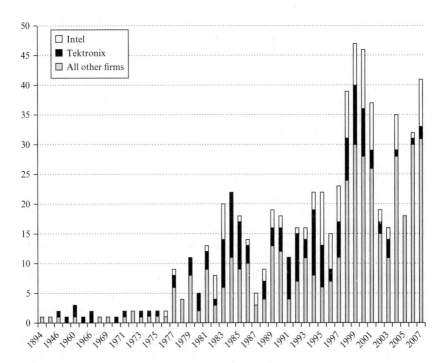

Source: Author's analysis.

Figure 4.4 High-tech firm emergence in the Silicon Forest, 1894–2007

Entrepreneurial dynamics in the Silicon Forest are characterized by three distinctive periods. The early to mid-1980s saw the emergence of a number of high-tech firms, including companies such as Mentor Graphics, InFocus, and Planar Systems – all spin-offs from Tektronix. Interviewees noted that entrepreneurs leveraged the numerous technology opportunities available at the time, such as display technology, new types of semiconductor technologies, and advances in electronic design automation systems. During this time, the Silicon Forest also saw an influx of capital as investors realized the potential of these technology opportunities. The second period in which entrepreneurial activities in the Silicon Forest peaked was the late 1990s and early 2000s. During this time the dot.com bubble grew and created numerous opportunities for entrepreneurial activities in the Internet sector and related fields. In contrast to the 1980s, venture capitalists searched for technology opportunities, not the other way around. With the bursting of the dot.com bubble, entrepreneurial activities also declined. In recent years (as illustrated by 2007, the last year for which we have data) entrepreneurial activities have picked up again. This may indicate a renewal of the Silicon Forest economy and a resurgence of entrepreneurial opportunities.

Entrepreneurs in the Silicon Forest

The firms that responded to the survey are on average ten years old, and the median founding year is 1997. The average number of founders of these firms was 2.38. About two-thirds of the responding firms (66.1 per cent) reported that more than two people started them. More than half of these founders (51.9 per cent) have had previous entrepreneurial experience and can thus be classified as serial entrepreneurs. Close to one-fifth (17.1 per cent) of these firms reported that former employees had left to start a new company, indicating that their firms had functioned as incubators for subsequent start-ups. The firms were primarily small high-tech firms, with 83.5 per cent having between one and 49 employees. These findings indicate that founding a firm in the Silicon Forest is typically a team effort, which echoes the literature on entrepreneurship (Shane, 2003). Generally, this literature indicates that team size is related to a firm's positive performance, primarily because a larger founding team allows firms to draw on a more diverse set of experiences and skill levels. The survey confirms the findings of the case study in terms of the importance of Tektronix and Intel as incubators of new start-ups. It is important to note here that the survey captures significantly fewer Tektronix and Intel spin-offs than the secondary research conducted to study the spin-off effects of these two firms.

Entrepreneurial firms in the Silicon Forest generally bootstrap their

Table 4.7   Characteristics of high-tech firms responding to Silicon Forest survey

Categories	Responses	Per cent
Survey descriptives		
Number of companies responding to survey	204	
Average age of firm (years; $N=204$)	10	
Median founding year	1997	
Average number of founders	2.38	
Serial entrepreneurs ($N=154$)	154	52.0%
Subsequent start-ups ($N=152$)	152	17.1%
Employment size		
1–4	46	31.5%
5–9	28	19.2%
10–19	25	17.1%
20–49	23	15.8%
50–99	8	5.5%
100–249	8	5.5%
250–499	5	3.4%
500–999	2	1.4%
1000 or more	1	0.7%
Valid N	146	100.0%
Source(s) of financing (multiple responses were allowed)		
Personal finances	104	51.0%
Friends and families	38	18.6%
Angel investments	37	18.1%
Other	31	15.2%
Venture capital	28	13.7%
Bank loan	25	12.3%

Source: Silicon Forest Survey.

ventures through the use of personal finances. Fifty-one per cent of the respondents indicated personal finances as one of their sources of funding. Friends and families provided financing for 18.6 per cent of the firms. The third most popular source of funding was angel investments, used by 18.1 per cent of the firms. Venture capital was used by 28 firms (13.7 per cent) and bank loans were used by 25 firms (12.3 per cent). Table 4.7 summarizes these characteristics of the survey respondents.

Prior employment was another aspect of Silicon Forest entrepreneurs captured by the survey. Among the 310 founders who responded, 11 worked for Intel and nine worked for Tektronix immediately before

Table 4.8   Founders' prior employment for Silicon Forest spin-offs

Parent type	Number of founders	Percent
Other firm	241	77.7%
University	27	8.7%
Intel	11	3.5%
Self-employed	10	3.2%
Tektronix	9	2.9%
Government, public agency, hospital	8	2.6%
Hewlett-Packard	4	1.3%
Valid *N*	310	100.0%

Source: Silicon Forest Survey.

starting their firms. The largest share of respondents (77.7 per cent) had worked for other firms. Employment in a university was the next most frequent origin (8.7 per cent). These findings are similar to other studies (Keeble et al., 1999) that have described local learning and diffusion processes. Incubating organizations such as other firms or anchor companies like Tektronix and Intel influence local entrepreneurship and economic growth. Entrepreneurs carry specialized skills and expertise, but they also help to diffuse culture and values as well as management and business models. The survey also revealed that 33.2 per cent of founders held a position in R&D/innovation. A significantly smaller share of the founders held sales (12.7 per cent), production (7.9 per cent) or marketing (7.6 per cent) positions. Keeble et al. (1999: 324) argue that entrepreneurship 'is an important process whereby technological and organizational expertise is diffused and a collective learning capability built up' within a region. Table 4.8 summarizes the prior employment data of the survey respondents.

Entrepreneurial Motivations of Spin-off Founders

We asked spin-off founders what prompted them to leave their previous employers (see Figure 4.5). Respondents ranked the need for independence and financial rewards highly (159 responses). Issues related to the incubator organization – such as frustration with the previous employer, or corporate changes – also ranked highly. These responses indicate that Silicon Forest entrepreneurs are not only motivated by pull factors such as their need for achievement, but also by push factors. A small number (37) indicated that when the founder had an idea and left the previous firm, the

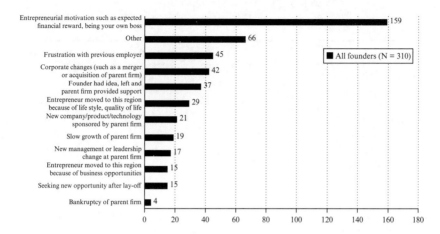

Source: Silicon Forest Survey.

Figure 4.5 Entrepreneurial motivations in the Silicon Forest. 'What prompted the founder to leave the previous employer to start this firm? (Please check all that apply)'

parent organization provided support. In addition, several (21) noted the parent firm's sponsorship of the new company/product/technology as a motivating factor.

The Parent-spin-off Relationship

Given the importance of firms as incubator organizations, the high-tech spin-offs were asked about how they relate to their parent firms (their imme-diate prior employers). We probed the types of linkages and relationships and asked about similarities in markets, technologies, and business models.

As Table 4.9 shows, most notably, Silicon Forest high-tech spin-offs generally do not interact with their parent firms. The majority of respond-ents (60.3 per cent) noted that their parent was not at all involved with their firm. Several spin-offs (19.9 per cent) reported that they have prod-ucts, technologies, or services that are of interest to the parents, who are their customers. In contrast, few reported parent firms being technology or product sponsors or financiers, investors, or suppliers.

Portland's high-tech firms diversify the regional economy. The majority of responding spin-offs (60.8 per cent) operate in a new market compared to their parents, while only 3.3 per cent operate in the same market. A little more than a third (35.9 per cent) noted that they work on a variant of their parent firm's product, technology, and/or service.

Table 4.9   Spin-offs' relationships with parent firms in the Silicon Forest

Category	Responses	Per cent
Linkages with parent firms (*'In what ways were or are the parent firms (the previous employer(s) of the founder(s)) involved with your firm?'*)		
Not at all	94	60.3%
Customer	31	19.9%
Other	16	10.3%
Technology/product sponsor	8	5.1%
Financier or investor	4	2.6%
Supplier	3	1.9%
Valid *N*	156	100.0%
Market similarity with parent firm (*'Is your company's product/technology/service in a similar or a new market compared to your parent firm's?'*)		
New market	93	60.8%
Variant of parent's product/technology/service	55	35.9%
Same as parent	5	3.3%
Valid *N*	153	100.0%
No answer	51	
Parent imprinting (*'Which of the following business practices are the most similar to your parent firm's? (Check all that apply)'*)		
Product/technology/service	60	53.1%
Innovation model	38	33.6%
Management style	35	31.0%
General business model	31	27.4%
Hiring practices	18	15.9%
Valid *N*	113	
Prior position of founder (*'What was the founder's position at his/her prior employer?'*)		
Marketing	24	7.6%
Production	25	7.9%
Sales	40	12.7%
R&D/innovation	105	33.2%
Other	137	43.4%
Total	331	100.0%

Source: Silicon Forest Survey.

Organizations employing nascent entrepreneurs can have a strong influence on their skills, capabilities, values, and work culture. The ways in which incubating organizations imprint on their spin-offs can describe the nature of knowledge spillovers. More than half of the survey respondents

Table 4.10   Silicon Forest high-tech firms' relationships with anchor firms 'In what ways does your company interact or has interacted with the following businesses in the region?'

Linkage type	Per cent of firms with linkages (number of responses)			
	Intel	**Tektronix**	**Hewlett-Packard**	**Electro Scientific Industries**
Customer	22.4% (33)	11.7% (17)	17.7% (26)	8.3% (12)
Supplier	15.6% (23)	6.9% (10)	14.3% (21)	3.5% (5)
Competitor	0.7% (1)	0% (0)	0.7% (1)	0% (0)
R&D partner	5.4% (8)	1.4% (2)	2.7% (4)	1.4% (2)
Not at all	55.8% (82)	80.0% (116)	64.6% (95)	86.8% (125)
Totals	**100.0% (147)**	**100.0% (145)**	**100.0% (147)**	**100.0% (144)**
No Answer	(57)	(59)	(57)	(60)

Source: Silicon Forest Survey.

(53.1 per cent) noted that their products/technology/services are most similar to those of their parents. About a third noted that they are following a similar innovation model (33.6 per cent) and management style (31 per cent). The general business model (27.4 per cent) and hiring practices (15.9 per cent) are other areas in which incubating organizations imprint their spin-offs.

Regional Advantages and Interactions

Portland's high-tech industry displays somewhat strong inter-firm linkages (see Table 4.10). Anchor firms like Intel, Tektronix, and Hewlett-Packard play an important role as customers to other high-tech firms. Tektronix was reported to be a customer by 11.7 per cent of respondents. Intel was reported to be a customer by 22.4 per cent of respondents. This latter finding supports the case study insights into Intel's role in forming the Silicon Forest semiconductor industry cluster. A small number of respondents (5.4 per cent) also noted that they are an R&D partner to Intel.

The high-tech firms in the region were asked about region-specific advantages and disadvantages of locating in the Silicon Forest (see Table 4.11). The results indicate that high-tech firms value the sort of location factors that are more intangible, such as quality of life and local access to innovative people, ideas, and technologies. The availability of managerial and professional talent was also ranked very highly.

Both the interviews and the survey indicate that quality of life has played

Table 4.11   Region-specific advantages for development in the Silicon Forest (by mean rating). 'How important have the following been for your firm's development? (Score from 1–5 with 1 indicating completely unimportant and 5 indicating extremely important)'

Advantage	Valid N	Mean rating	Per cent indicating somewhat and extremely important	Per cent indicating extremely important
Attractive local quality of life for staff and management	140	4.39	88.6%	56.4%
Informal local access to innovative people, ideas, technologies	137	4.23	86.1%	46.7%
Local availability of managerial/ professional staff	138	3.88	74.6%	26.8%
Availability of appropriate premises	137	3.42	54.0%	13.9%
Access to international airports	137	3.37	55.5%	19.0%
Access to local business services	137	3.35	52.6%	12.4%
Quality of local research staff	134	3.13	41.8%	17.2%
Local availability of research staff	134	3.13	41.8%	17.2%
Credibility, reputation and prestige of Silicon Forest as a high-tech location	136	3.08	41.2%	11.8%
Proximity to local customers	139	3.00	46.8%	15.8%
Proximity to local suppliers, subcontractors	137	2.98	41.6%	11.7%
Access to Silicon Valley	135	2.93	37.8%	9.6%
Local shareholders	135	2.84	37.0%	11.1%
Access to local sources of capital, finance	135	2.83	39.3%	14.8%
Supportive local government services	136	2.76	34.6%	8.1%
Research links with other firms or organizations in the region	135	2.72	34.8%	9.6%
Supportive local training organizations	135	2.70	27.4%	6.7%
Research links with OSU	136	2.34	22.1%	11.8%
Research links with other OR- or WA- based universities	132	2.15	19.7%	6.8%
Research links with PSU	134	2.10	15.7%	3.7%
Research links with U of O	132	2.02	13.6%	5.3%

Source: Silicon Forest Survey.

an important role in the growth of the Silicon Forest. Tektronix and Intel imported most of their employees to the Portland region. Imported workers found themselves in a unique cultural environment characterized by high quality of life and a more informal way of conducting work. These skilled workers are highly mobile (Florida, 2002a), and the Silicon Forest has implicitly leveraged its quality of life to attract and keep them.

About half of the respondents ranked factors such as the availability of appropriate premises (54.0 per cent), access to international airports (55.5 per cent) and business services (52.6 per cent), the quality and availability of local research staff (41.8 per cent each), and the proximity to local customers (46.8 per cent) and suppliers and subcontractors (41.6 per cent) as somewhat or extremely important. Interestingly, very few respondents ranked research links to local or other Oregon-based universities as extremely important.

Region-specific disadvantages may reveal weaknesses in the innovation systems of second tier high-tech regions (see Table 4.12). More than half of the survey respondents (54.1 per cent) noted the difficulty of accessing local sources of capital and financing as a somewhat or extremely important location disadvantage. This is particularly relevant for regional policymakers who are interested in building entrepreneurial high-tech regions.

Other location disadvantages that were ranked highly relate to the availability of labour. Even though Tektronix and Intel managed to build a specialized and skilled labour pool, the region's entrepreneurs notice a shortage of local skilled labour, particularly in marketing, sales, and management. The lack of a world-class research university was also seen as a significant location disadvantage and ranked as somewhat or extremely important by 27.4 per cent of respondents. Issues like the lack of subcontractors, lack of appropriate premises locally, housing problems, or an inadequate or costly environment for manufacturing ranked at the end of the list.

University-industry Linkages

We also asked survey respondents to note how their firms work with Oregon universities (see Figure 4.6). They indicated whether and how they collaborate with Portland State University or with other Oregon-based universities such as Oregon Health and Science University, Washington State University in Vancouver, Oregon State University in Corvallis and the University of Oregon in Eugene. Survey respondents identified hiring graduates as their most frequent type of relationships with local universities. Informal knowledge exchanges are other important mechanisms of university-industry interactions. For the respondents, collaborative research projects with universities and university staff acting as consultants

Table 4.12   *Region-specific disadvantages for development in the Silicon Forest (by mean rating). 'Have any of the following constrained your firm's development? (Score from 1–5 with 1 indicating completely unimportant and 5 indicating extremely important)'*

Disadvantage	Valid N	Mean rating	Per cent indicating somewhat and extremely important	Per cent indicating extremely important
Difficulty in accessing local sources of capital, financing	135	3.36	54.1%	30.4%
Shortage of local skilled labour	137	3.16	48.2%	16.8%
Shortage of local marketing and sales skills	134	3.15	43.3%	14.2%
Shortage of local managerial skills	136	2.89	33.8%	8.1%
Lack of world-class research university	135	2.67	27.4%	9.6%
Cost of premises locally	136	2.57	25.7%	2.9%
Shortage of research skills	137	2.49	16.1%	5.1%
Shortage of semiskilled labour	133	2.41	15.8%	3.8%
Inadequate local business services	135	2.36	17.8%	3.0%
Lack of local subcontractors	134	2.31	13.4%	1.5%
Lack of appropriate premises locally	135	2.18	13.3%	2.2%
Housing problems for staff	135	2.14	8.1%	0.7%
Inadequate/costly environment for manufacturing	135	2.11	10.4%	2.2%

Source: Silicon Forest Survey.

ranked second and third, while company staff teaching classes at universities ranked fourth. These rankings indicate that high-tech firms in the Silicon Forest prefer more informal ways of working with local universities. In contrast, licensing or patenting ranked very low. Interactions with specialized centres at the universities ranked lower too, primarily because these types of centres may serve a smaller share of Silicon Forest firms.

Although the Silicon Forest managed to grow in the absence of a world-class research university, the survey results indicate that nearby universities may play an important role in supporting the industry. They may not be the engine of growth in terms of spinning off companies, but they provide critical support to the innovative capacity of Portland's high-tech firms.

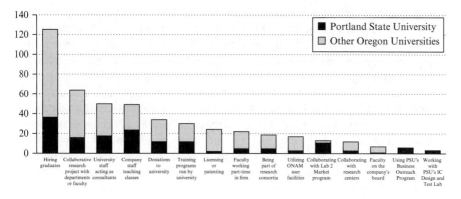

Source: Silicon Forest survey.

Figure 4.6 *High-tech firms' relationships with universities in the Silicon Forest. 'Since establishing your firm in this region, which of the following types of relationships has your firm had with the following universities? (Check all that apply)' (N=99)*

CLUSTER DEVELOPMENT AND PUBLIC POLICY

Tektronix and Intel formed the nucleus for Portland's high-tech industry cluster. Spin-offs forming around Tektronix helped diversify the region's high-tech industry and they offset the negative impacts of Tektronix's restructuring efforts. In contrast, Intel helped create a specialized semi-conductor industry cluster that is characterized by a diverse set of competitors, suppliers, specialized support services, and a supportive business environment.

Firms, not universities, led the evolution of the Silicon Forest making it a second tier high-tech cluster. Policymakers and politicians reacted to this growth and over time developed a set of initiatives to support the industry. Their efforts evolved from traditional cluster-based economic development practices to efforts geared towards increasing the innovativeness of firms. Economic development policies in Oregon evolved from initial activities geared towards improving the business environment through tax breaks and incentives, to more complex efforts that support industry clusters and innovative initiatives that connect universities and industries (Waits, 1998; Mayer, 2008, 2009b).

In recent years, policymakers, economic developers, and high-tech industry representatives have recognized the importance of investing in the higher education infrastructure and made tremendous progress in developing a unique science and technology strategy. Local leaders realized early on that the lack of a world-class higher education system would significantly limit the opportunities of the Silicon Forest. Lobbying efforts to improve higher education started in the late 1950s when then-Governor Mark Hatfield called for a report on science and engineering education and in 1959 appointed an industry-led advisory committee (Dodds and Wollner, 1990). As a result of these early collaborations, the region established a graduate-only engineering and science institute in Beaverton. Modelled after the Massachusetts Institute of Technology, it was called the Oregon Graduate Institute (OGI). Due to funding constraints, OGI (now part of Oregon Health and Science University) never achieved a standing similar to its famous East Coast model. Over the years, industry leaders kept complaining about the lack of an appropriate higher education infrastructure. While early efforts primarily focused on workforce development and education reforms, initiatives in the 1990s and 2000s began to emphasize the R&D infrastructure that a modern high-tech industry needs.

The push to improve the region's higher education infrastructure gained momentum in 1999 when an informally organized industry group, called the New Economy Coalition (NEC), emerged. NEC members, including high-level executives from firms like Intel and Tektronix, lobbied state legislators to support Oregon's higher education institutions. The group made clear that the future of the Silicon Forest depended on the quality of the state's research universities. However, the group was probably too narrowly focused on high-tech interests, and NEC never gained the momentum needed to sustain and implement its agenda within the political realm. Yet policy leaders realized the need to discuss the state's economic competitiveness. Parallel to NEC's efforts, the Oregon Council on Knowledge and Economic Development (OCKED) was formed by the governor in 2001. From 2001–5 this governor-appointed committee deliberated the best ways in which Oregon could improve its support for innovation, research, and development. OCKED members identified three goals: improved research capacity and technology transfer, improved capital and business formation, and workforce development. As a result of OCKED's work, the Oregon Innovation Council (Oregon InC) was created by the Governor and Legislature in 2005 to guide the state's innovation strategy and to oversee the implementation of the action items identified by OCKED. The resulting strategy built the foundation for a more focused approach to invest in so-called 'signature research' areas that built on the state's economic strengths in certain industry clusters, including, among others, high technology (Oregon Council for Knowledge and Economic Development, 2002). In 2003, the first such centre – the Oregon

Nanoscience and Microtechnologies Institute (ONAMI) – was created. ONAMI is a multi-institutional centre that facilitates research and commercialization of nanoscience and microtechnologies. It is a collaborative effort of the state's three public research universities, a federal research laboratory (Pacific Northwest National Laboratory), and more than 20 high-tech firms that function as research and commercialization partners. University and industry both have a stake in ONAMI's governance structure. In addition, there are tight cooperative links among the partners through research programmes, shared facilities, internship programmes, and commercialization agreements.

ONAMI's track record is strong, as it has had a significant impact on commercialization in the state (O'Connor et al., 2008): invention disclosures have increased (from 16 in 2002 to 30 in 2008), patent applications have more than tripled (nine in 2002 to 34 in 2008), licence income has increased, and the academic culture is changing. In addition, ONAMI's $2.5 million investment in proposal matching funds has leveraged an additional $15.2 million (for every dollar ONAMI invested, it received $6.08). ONAMI has secured $65 million in research funds, and it stimulated $1.8 million in cash inflows to Oregon businesses and universities from out-of-state donors. Oregon businesses contributed $29.7 million to ONAMI, and the total economic benefits from Oregon and non-Oregon sources are estimated at $107 million. ONAMI has also succeeded in recruiting talented researchers who not only focus on basic research but have an applied research agenda and market-oriented approach. This success story has several reasons, which might be insightful for other second tier high-tech regions that are characterized by a weak higher education infrastructure and the lack of critical mass in research and development. ONAMI maintains 'line of sight to industry' (Martin, 2008) through close collaboration and coordination with the region's high-tech firms. ONAMI also encourages and facilitates collaboration among the various universities and thereby helps the institutions develop critical mass. ONAMI is critically aligned with the state's innovation goals. Through ONAMI, policymakers, university presidents, and industry representatives work towards accomplishing the state's three high-tech goals (technology transfer, business formation, and workforce development). ONAMI also leverages a small amount of state funding through encouragement of matches and co-investments. In addition, ONAMI has an efficient and lean organizational structure, as it has no research staff of its own and only coordinates efforts between research institutions and industry. This type of network model encourages collaboration among all innovation actors. ONAMI also engages the venture capital community in evaluating funding for a commercialization gap fund.[2]

As Oregon continues its strategic approach to improving R&D in key sectors, the most recent innovation strategy targets a set of industries and technologies. Initiatives focus on ocean wave energy, food processing, and manufacturing. Signature research centre support will continue for ONAMI but also go towards an institute dedicated to biotechnology, infectious diseases, and drug development. In addition, several recommendations are made regarding a more supportive environment for innovation and entrepreneurship (such as angel and venture capital investments, innovation acceleration, and technology transfer).

The evolution of Oregon's R&D investment efforts illustrates how policy support can be strategically targeted to help boost a second tier high-tech economy. Being a resource-based economy, Oregon's political culture has traditionally not valued higher education, and therefore the state's policymakers have traditionally not invested to a great extent in their universities. With the efforts around Oregon InC and ONAMI, for example, the state's leaders have demonstrated commitment to new economy sectors. This leadership is needed because Oregon's economy has changed dramatically over the past decades. Knowledge-based industries such as high-tech are now driving the state's prosperity. Yet, most strategic efforts had to be initiated by industry, and public policy has been reactive.

CONCLUSIONS

This chapter traced the evolution of Portland's Silicon Forest, a second tier high-tech region. The analysis of its two anchor firms shows that Tektronix has contributed to a greater extent than Intel to the growth of Portland's high-tech industry. In that sense, Tektronix has fulfilled the role of a surrogate university, impacting the region in all three dimensions (talent, innovation, and entrepreneurship), while Intel has impacted regional economic growth mainly in the realm of labour and helping to grow an industrial cluster.

Portland's high-tech industry has continued to flourish, even with Intel's limited impact and the end of Tektronix's role as a surrogate university by the 1990s. Why did the region continue to evolve after Tektronix changed so dramatically? The seeds that the two high-tech companies created needed to fall on fertile ground to create additional high-tech growth. This fertile ground in turn was able to absorb the spillover effects created by Tektronix and Intel. Several important developments took place that shaped the Silicon Forest environment. First, through Tektronix's influence on entrepreneurship, a set of firms in related high-tech segments took root in the Silicon Forest. Tektronix spin-offs contributed to the diversification of the regional high-tech industry. In many cases, these firms have become viable and successful competitors to other firms in the region. Intel attracted labour skilled in semiconductor production, as well as a diverse set of subcontractors and suppliers critical to the company's local operations. Because of Intel's presence, semiconductor manufacturing equipment makers, semiconductor wafer manufacturers, and other highly specialized suppliers are part of today's Silicon Forest. Intel also attracted the attention of competitor firms. Taking advantage of the established supplier infrastructure and the specialized pool of labour, foreign-based semiconductor companies began to locate in the region. During the 1990s, the area attracted more than $8 billion in semiconductor investments. Over time the Silicon Forest was able to root a set of related and supporting industries that function as capable suppliers or stimulating competitors. Such related firms are a critical source for a region's competitive advantage, especially in regard to stimulating demand and further deepening the region's specialized labour market, as outlined in Porter's industry cluster theory (Porter, 1990, 1998, 2000a).

Second, the region was able to develop a set of support services that cater to the local high-tech industry. High-tech firms rely on specialized support services such as patent lawyers, public relations companies, management and consulting firms, employment agencies, and venture capitalists. Over the past two decades, a critical mass of such specialized services that companies can draw from developed in the Portland region.

Third, policymakers and economic developers reacted to the growth of the high-tech industry and developed effective policies that link local universities and the high-tech industry. Instead of being proactive, the political environment in the Silicon Forest is characterized as being reactive to high-tech growth. Motivated by the decline of the timber industry and the first signs of high-tech success, policymakers changed the state's tax structure to help recruit capital-intensive and foreign-based high-tech companies. Thus, in the mid-1980s, state legislators repealed the unitary tax, which was aimed at taxing multinational corporations on their worldwide revenues (Dodds and Wollner, 1990). As a result Japanese-owned high-tech corporations moved branch plants to the Silicon Forest. In the early 1990s, state legislatures instituted the Strategic Investment Program (SIP), which allowed Oregon counties to grant tax breaks to corporate capital investments. The passage of the SIP in the early 1990s was especially pivotal to Intel's evolution in the Silicon Forest because it came at a time when Intel made significant capital investments to expand its manufacturing facilities. The first SIP tax break was granted to Intel in 1994 (which covered $3.2 billion of investments). In 1999, Intel applied for the third SIP tax break. This time, the tax break covered $12.5 billion in investments for the next 15 years.

The absence of a world-class higher education infrastructure did not remain unnoticed by business leaders and policymakers. Over the years, efforts to improve education offerings were undertaken. In the early 1960s, the Oregon Graduate Institute (OGI) was established with substantial financial help from local industry (especially Tektronix). OGI was modelled on Stanford University, and its goal was to provide applied research and graduate education in engineering-related disciplines. However, OGI never received enough funding to grow into a Stanford- or MIT-like institution. Recent efforts have focused on technology-based economic development through the linking of universities with industry.

The final component of the Silicon Forest innovation infrastructure is the cultural environment. Portland is often heralded as a unique metropolitan area for its quality of life and it has been an essential component of Portland's economic development (Abbott, 2000, 2001; Abbott et al., 1994). It roots both individuals and businesses in the region and it functions as an important magnet for skilled labour. Silicon Forest entrepreneurs are reluctant to leave the region because they like to live there and conduct their business near their homes. In addition, Portland's high-tech firms benefit from collaboration through informal networking, in a corporate culture that is often thought to be less hierarchical than East Coast firms (Saxenian, 1994b). This informality promotes networking within the firm and between companies. This culture is believed to be an important component of the knowledge-based economy, because if people are networking with each other, knowledge is being transmitted. Such knowledge transfer is critical for the continued success of high-tech firms into the future.

NOTES

1. Many of these firms still operate independently in the Silicon Forest.
2. ONAMI's commercialization gap fund provides funding for early stage technology that is developed by researchers affiliated with the institute. The funding bridges the gap in funding between research result and products or services. For more information about this fund, see: http://www.onami.us/index.php/commercialization.

5. Boise: printers and semiconductors in the Treasure Valley

'If there was one primary item attracting us to this city, it would have to be the livability of Boise and the fact the people here wanted us.'

Ray Smelek, former HP General Manager, quoted in *The Idaho Statesman*, (June 14, 1973)

'Certainly for Boise, HP had a tremendous impact on developing the infrastructure to support high-tech companies. There wasn't much before HP started here.'

Steve Simpson, former general manager of HP's Boise Printer Division

BEGINNINGS OF HIGH-TECH DEVELOPMENT IN THE TREASURE VALLEY

Idaho may be an unlikely state for high-tech development, but its largest metropolitan area, Boise, has developed an entrepreneurial and innovative technology community. Boise is located in the Treasure Valley, an area where the Payette, Boise, Weiser, Malheur and Owyhee rivers drain into the Snake River. Idaho is widely known for growing potatoes, but a large part of its economic power comes not from the agricultural sector but from exporting semiconductor chips and computer printers. In 2008 computer and electronic products manufacturing accounted for 41.9 per cent of Boise's export activity (Muro et al., 2010). The Boise area's most prominent technology firms are Micron Technology, the only company that still manufactures semiconductor memory chips in the US, and Hewlett-Packard (HP), the Silicon Valley-based high-tech firm. Both HP and Micron Technology started their operations in Boise in the 1970s. At the time, Boise was a small city located in the midst of a largely rural state on the periphery of the Pacific Northwest. Back then, the region's higher education infrastructure was not sufficient to support a budding high-tech economy. Boise State University, for example, gained university status in 1974 and granted its first doctoral degree 18 years later in 1992. Over time, Micron and HP helped build and expand higher education offerings in the state, and today Boise State University is the largest university in Idaho.

Yet Boise's emergence as a high-tech region is anything but university-based. Like in Portland, Boise's two major technology firms engage in cutting edge innovation processes; they attracted talented employees, and spin-off companies formed around them, compensating for the missing higher education capacities.

High-tech employment in Boise is considerably lower than in Portland. In 2005, the Boise area's 18 969 high-tech employees worked for 1335 firms, of which 77 per cent employed fewer than nine people and a mere 3.4 per cent employed more than 100. Micron and HP are the largest high-tech employers in the area. In 2007, Micron employed about 10 600 people, and HP had 3340 people on its Idaho payroll. Despite the dominance of the two firms, other Boise-based companies have found their niches and specialize in semiconductor manufacturing, computer and electronic products, software publishing, and engineering services. Boise's high-tech economy does not display strong industry clustering dynamics, but there is a small number of semiconductor firms. Some were attracted by Micron. SCP Global Technologies, for example, relocated to Boise in 1981. ZiLOG, Cypress Semiconductors, Marvell Semiconductors, Applied Materials, Avago, and Inapac have branch facilities in Boise. There are also a few semiconductor start-up firms that were founded by local entrepreneurs (such as American Semiconductor and Ovonyx). Other local companies include semiconductor equipment makers Anestel Corporation and JST Manufacturing. In addition, there are several firms that specialize in information technology services, Internet services, networking, and electronic products that integrate hardware and software (particularly as it relates to embedded software and firmware). The last technology traces its roots to the capabilities HP developed in Boise, and many of the firms in these industry segments are spin-offs from HP or provide contracting services to HP. The cluster of high-tech firms is complemented by a small number of service firms such as public relations and marketing agencies, accounting firms, and engineering service firms. In recent years, the region has seen the emergence of a few angel and venture capital funds.

Boise's high-tech industry is cyclical due to its small size and dependence on manufacturing-oriented and market-sensitive sectors such as semiconductors and computer peripherals. Some have argued that Boise's economy is especially vulnerable because firms like Micron and HP are engaged in low-cost competition and because the economy does not specialize in higher value services such as consulting or engineering (Muro, 2010). Total high-tech employment significantly increased from 1999–2003, but then declined from 2003–5. This may be the result of the ups and downs characteristic of the semiconductor industry and the fact that Micron has had a series of lay-offs in recent years.

Boise is clearly a second tier high-tech region. Compared to pioneering high-tech regions like Silicon Valley or Boston and to other second tier high-tech regions like Portland, Boise's high-tech industry is rather small. Yet specialization measures such as the high-tech location quotient demonstrate that Boise's high-tech industry is highly concentrated and specialized. Looking at entrepreneurial dynamics, along with R&D funding, we can see that Boise developed an entrepreneurial and innovative streak. This is not surprising given the region's tradition in fostering well-known firms such as Albertsons, Morrison Knudsen Corporation, Ore-Ida, Boise Cascade, and the JR Simplot Company. Entrepreneurial dynamics peaked briefly in the early 1990s. The number of firms founded started to pick up again in the late 1990s and early 2000s. While entrepreneurial activities dropped during the most recent recession period from 2007 to 2009, it has picked up again in the last couple of years. These entrepreneurial dynamics are reflected in indicators of entrepreneurial churning: the percentages of firm births and deaths are similarly high, as in other high-tech regions. This churning is important for the creation and renewal of a high-tech economy and it seems to be an important driver of Boise's emergence as a second tier high-tech region. Estimates for R&D funding show that expenditures increased from $37 million in 1999 to $130 million in 2004. The increase was significant, even though the Boise region lags behind other metropolitan areas in terms of the actual amount of funding.

Despite the ups and downs in the high-tech industry, the development of a knowledge-based economy has helped fuel the region's general growth. The region has been one of the fastest growing metropolitan areas in the country. This growth has been fuelled by the influx of residents from neighbouring states. Californians especially have taken advantage of low housing costs and moved to Idaho during the past decades. As a result, from 1970–2000 the Boise metropolitan area has grown fivefold, from 115000 to about 532000 residents (Blanchard, 2005). This residential growth is not without its problems, and has left marks on the Treasure Valley landscape: The region is facing challenges such as unplanned, exurban sprawl and leapfrog development. Despite high quality of life and efforts to strengthen Boise's downtown, housing developments outside the metro area and along the mountain ridges threaten future sustainable development.

Boise's high-tech roots go back to 1973 when HP decided to establish a branch operation there to manufacture computer peripherals – printers and magnetic tape drives. When the firm entered the laser printer market in the early 1980s, the focus of HP's Boise operation evolved from manufacturing to R&D in computer peripherals. A few years after HP moved to Idaho, Micron Technology was founded in Boise by entrepreneurs who were native to the state. Boise's high-tech community grew despite the lack of a world-class research university. Like in Portland, the two dominant firms (HP and Micron) functioned as 'surrogate universities'. The firms in Boise, however, differed in important ways, as this chapter will show. In the following, I trace the history of HP and Micron and compare their influence on talent, innovation and entrepreneurship dynamics in the region. I use survey results to illustrate current dynamics among Boise-based high-tech entrepreneurs. I finish the chapter with a critical discussion of the efforts to advance public policy in support of high-tech development.

HEWLETT-PACKARD COMES TO BOISE

No other high-tech firm is so intimately connected with the evolution of Silicon Valley than HP. The founders of HP started their business in 1938 in the legendary garage of a suburban home along a tree-lined street in Palo Alto, California, and this garage is widely known as the birthplace of Silicon Valley. Less known, however, is the fact that HP influenced the growth of many other high-tech regions in the US, including Boise, and that many significant innovations that HP developed originated in these second tier regions. The most prominent example is HP's most successful product, the laser printer, which was developed in Boise and manufactured by Canon in Japan. As a result of HP's market successes and subsequent expansions, several regions, including Boise, flourished because HP's presence and evolution turned them into nodes of high-tech activity. Understanding how HP evolved from a company that developed and produced test and measurement instruments to a successful computer products firm, and one of the world's largest high-tech firms, is critical for understanding the evolution of Boise as a high-tech region.

HP was founded by two graduates of Stanford University. Bill Hewlett and Dave Packard met while studying electrical engineering at Stanford University, and their entrepreneurial efforts were supported by Stanford's Dean of the School of Engineering, Frederic Terman. From its modest beginnings in Palo Alto, HP quickly grew into one of Silicon Valley's most important electronics firms. The company began with the production of audio oscillators, instruments that are used to test sound equipment. Demand for test and measurement instruments grew during and after the Second World War, and HP had expanded from three employees in 1940 to 3021 employees in 1960. Spurred by the rapid growth of the electronics industry, HP was among the first US high-tech companies to expand into Asia, with a joint venture in Japan in 1963. During the 1960s, HP also began to locate manufacturing plants outside of Palo Alto. Its first branch facility opened in 1960 in Loveland, Colorado. HP's first computer was developed in the 1960s and initially used to programme its test and measurement products. It was during this time that HP entered the field of computing. In 1966, the company launched its first computer, the HP 2116A. Several innovations in computing followed as HP started to develop its own line of computer products: the first desktop scientific calculator in 1968 and the handheld calculator in 1972. HP produced its first minicomputer in 1974 and its first personal computer in 1980. As a result of its entry into computing, HP began to develop peripheral devices such as memory storage devices and printers. In 1980 HP introduced the first laser printer that was 'fast and inexpensive enough to use outside a central computer room' (Hewlett-Packard, 2007). This innovation ushered in HP's most successful product – the LaserJet printer – which was designed and developed in collaboration with Canon in Japan. The alliance with Canon marked a milestone for HP, breaking its tradition of only developing products in-house, often called the 'Not Invented Here' (NIH) culture. HP was not only known for its technical innovations, but also for its innovations in corporate culture and management. Its founders developed the 'HP Way' (Packard, 1995). This unique company culture is based on a set of values, objectives, strategies, and practices that focus on an open and trusting work environment, a high level of individual achievement and contribution, teamwork, flexibility, growth, passion for the customer, and good corporate citizenship, among others. By 2006 HP had become one of the most important firms in the laser printer industry and has consistently maintained a market share between 45 and 65 per cent (deFigueiredo and Kyle, 2006). In 2006 HP shipped its 100 millionth laser printer, had $91.6 billion in revenue, and employed 156 000 people worldwide.

HP's Decision to Locate in Boise

As it entered into the computing business, HP saw the opportunity to manufacture and sell computer peripheral products such as printers and storage devices. As a result, HP expanded into this fast-growing area. In 1972, one of HP's manufacturing managers at the Mountain View Division in California, Ray Smelek, was put in charge of planning and organizing the set-up of a new printer peripherals business to support the emerging minicomputer market (Smelek interview, 2007). This decision had far-reaching geographic implications: Smelek, who would later become the first general manager of HP's Boise Division, was informed by Bill Hewlett that the new peripherals business should be set up in a completely new location. HP executives and managers felt that HP already had a strong presence at its headquarters in Silicon Valley and its branch in Loveland, Colorado. They did not want to put 'too many eggs into one basket' (Smelek interview, 2007) and felt the need to geographically branch out. The new division should be a US location within easy reach of HP's headquarters in Silicon Valley and its Computer Division in Cupertino, California, so Smelek would need to find a spot within a two-hour flight from Palo Alto with excellent air connections. This is strikingly similar to the location requirements Intel had when it located its first manufacturing branch plant in Oregon (see Chapter 4). Recall that at the time, high-tech firms like HP were fairly young and still located within the US. In addition, these firms had a strong tradition of vertical integration, and manufacturing was primarily in-house. Establishing new branch locations close to Silicon Valley may have been a strategy to reduce risks and uncertainties. In choosing a location for HP's second branch plant, Smelek also had to consider other requirements, including quality of life concerns such as low crime and reasonable housing costs, a welcoming attitude towards a new high-tech firm, an adequate supply of power, and a good labour force (Guerber, 1973).

A cursory review put 11 cities in the western US on their map. All of them had a flight connection within the two-hour limit. Knowing that he would need to move his family so that he could establish the new division, Smelek talked to his wife and children about where they wanted to live. From these conversations it became clear that the family preferred the northwest over the southwest, and he narrowed his selection to three cities in the Pacific Northwest. In February 1973, Smelek and his colleagues visited Boise, Idaho; Spokane, Washington; and Corvallis, Oregon. They talked to policymakers and economic developers in each community and felt that any of them would fit the bill. When he returned, Smelek asked his family which city they would prefer (Smelek interview, 2007). The final vote came down to his children's preference for Boise, because it had amenities such as nearby winter recreation, horseback riding, and even a driving age of 15. In a newspaper article, Smelek notes that 'in May 1973 I made the decision to go with Boise and we started the division in September of that year' (Howard, 2003).

Boise, however, did not fulfil one of HP's requirements: it lacked a sufficient and well developed educational infrastructure. Boise State College (as it was then) did not offer a four-year programme in engineering. Indeed, its College of Engineering was established much later, in the 1990s. Smelek and his colleagues talked to the University of Idaho located in Moscow, about 300 miles north of Boise, but the university did not have much interest in engineering. This deficiency, however, did not deter HP from locating in Boise. HP was able to compensate because it had already established a long-distance education programme with Stanford University on closed circuit television that could be transmitted to Boise. In addition, the Boise Division was primarily a manufacturing site in the beginning, and the majority of its first engineers were recruited from outside the state, while labour for the manufacturing process was hired locally. Only later, when HP's Boise Division took on product development, would a better higher education infrastructure become a pressing issue. In terms of education, Boise stood in striking contrast to one of the other finalists, Corvallis, Oregon, home to Oregon State University, a large land grant university. Smelek, however, remembers that Oregon's 'anti-growth attitude' unsettled HP, so they took Corvallis out of consideration (Smelek interview, 2007). Oregon's then-Governor, Tom McCall, had commented on national television that people who were not from Oregon could visit, but should not stay (Mayer and Provo, 2004). Interestingly, HP later also established a presence in both Corvallis and Spokane.

HP's Early Years in Boise: 1973–89

HP began operations in a leased building in downtown Boise in 1973. This new operation was not yet its own division, but part of the Data Systems Division based in Cupertino, California. HP had purchased manufacturing rights from Tally Corporation based in Kent, Washington, for the so-called 2000 printer series, which would become HP's first printer manufactured in-house, the HP 2607 printer (HP Computer Museum, 2010). The purchase of manufacturing rights from Tally allowed HP to enter the printer business at once. A year after HP set up shop in Boise, the operation became its own formal division, and Ray Smelek was named its first general manager. In 1978, HP issued the first printers that were fully designed and manufactured by HP (the HP 2608 and 2631). Becoming a division critically shaped HP's influence on the Boise economy. In 1958 HP had established a division structure for its internal organization, giving each product group full responsibility for developing, manufacturing, and marketing its own portfolio. With these responsibilities came accountability for any losses or gains. Overall, divisionalization allowed HP to focus on specific products and to be more flexible by avoiding bureaucratic structures. Another important result was the development of an entrepreneurial culture within HP divisions that would affect the employees. Divisionalization gave Boise sufficient independence from HP headquarters, so that managers and engineers were able to make many decisions without consulting executives in California. Therefore, from the beginning HP's Boise Division was anything but an ordinary branch plant. Instead, it operated like an independent company.

Set up to manufacture line impact dot matrix printers, the Boise branch plant quickly diversified and added new products. In 1974 manufacturing of tape drives was moved to Boise, and about 80 engineers and designers transferred there from Cupertino. Two years later, disk drive manufacturing was shifted to the new Disk Memory Division in Boise, along with disk drive marketing functions. The Disk Memory Division grew rapidly and had to be split into two groups (the Disk Mechanisms Division and the Disk Storage Systems Division). With each transfer, the Boise site gained more skills and capabilities as well as additional responsibilities for new product introduction. When HP introduced a new line of disk memories, a local manufacturing manager was quoted in the local newspaper, saying 'these products were conceived and designed in Boise by Treasure Valley people' (Keltz, 1981). During the late 1970s, line printers also grew more complex, and HP introduced the first microprocessor printer in 1977. Product diversification continued, and in 1980 HP introduced its first laser printer; it was developed in cooperation with Canon and used an engine developed by Ricoh. By 1983 the Boise operation manufactured 14 different products ranging from printers to disk drives, and the branch operation represented an important part of HP's overall organization. The greater number and variety of products necessitated organizational restructuring. In 1988 HP split its operations in Boise into three units: publishing products, hardcopy technology, and mass storage. Together these three units accounted for more than 25 per cent of HP's total business, indicating that the Boise site grew in importance for the overall HP operation (Beebe, 1988).

Boise's evolution as a high-tech location and HP's success as a computer peripherals company are intimately connected with the success of HP's laser printer and, in particular, HP's most successful product, the LaserJet, introduced in 1984. Developed by Boise engineers in cooperation with their counterparts at Canon in Japan, the LaserJet exemplified a shift in the way HP was developing and manufacturing computer equipment. Canon developed a low-cost printer engine and assembled the printer in Japan. HP's Boise Division was responsible for marketing and manufacturing the type fonts and the electronics (firmware, drivers, controllers, and so on) used in the printer. This was a big departure from HP's long-standing tradition of vertical integration and in-house manufacturing.

The partnership between HP and Canon goes back to 1975, when Bill Hewlett was introduced to Canon's prototype laser beam printer at an industry trade show (HP Computer Museum, 2010). HP managers negotiated an agreement to develop products in cooperation with Canon, and Canon engaged in joint development with HP of floor-model printer technology (De Figueiredo and Teece, 1996). Later on Canon started to supply the engine for the laser printer and also manufactured the laser printer. At times, HP's purchases of printer engines represented nearly 50 per cent of Canon's printer output (De Figueiredo and Teece, 1996).

The LaserJet introduced important technical innovations, such as the electro-photographic laser. Unlike the daisy wheel impact printer or the dot matrix printer, the laser printer was faster and less noisy. The printer represented what Christensen (1997) calls a discontinuous improvement over previous products. In addition, the first LaserJet was not limited to a number of character sets; it was compatible with computer software developed by HP and IBM, and – something that would entice consumers – it could fit on a desk. The first LaserJet printer HP developed in Boise had a price tag of $3495 and was able to print eight pages per minute (*The Idaho Statesman*, 1984). David Packard notes that the LaserJet 'created a totally new printer market' (Packard, 1995: 115). And indeed, by 1986 the LaserJet had captured 85 per cent of the market for laser printers (Friend, 1986) – with HP selling its one millionth LaserJet within two years (Pewitt, 1988).

HP's strategy for the LaserJet printer was to constantly improve the printer's capabilities while at the same time lowering the cost for the consumer (Packard, 1995). Over the years, subsequent models of the LaserJet introduced new features, such as improved print quality and paper handling, graphic capabilities, colour features, and so on. Such improvements meant continuous investments in R&D at the Boise operation, ensuring its evolution from a mere manufacturing branch plant to one focused on innovation and R&D. In addition, HP concentrated on the end consumer and made marketing a central component of the operation. Compared to disk drive manufacturing, the laser printer operation in Boise was quite small in the beginning. A Boise-based executive notes that the laser printer operation was very different from the disk drive:

> The disk drive [division] was a lot more mechanical, pretty hard core electrical engineers, very little marketing. It was driven by R&D, it was your, what I would consider a pretty typical, HP organization. When you walked over to the LaserJets the first thing I noticed was there was a lot more marketing people, [things were] much more marketing focused. There were a lot more women and very few mechanical engineers. Not many even electrical engineers. It was very different. We were building a small controller board, it was pretty standard parts. And there was a lot more computer science. (Spohn interview, 2007)

Apart from engaging in innovative activities related to products such as printers and memory storage, HP's Boise operation also pioneered important manufacturing process innovations. In 1982 the Boise site opened a highly automated assembly operation and two years later added a brand new automated materials distribution and manufacturing centre. These manufacturing process innovations happened within the context of vertical integration. At the time, HP already had a long tradition of manufacturing critical components in-house. The Boise Division was engaged in printed circuit board manufacturing; it also ran a surface mount centre; and later on HP manufactured its own formatter boards for the laser printers.[1] One of the reasons for this integrating manufacturing of critical components was HP's desire to control product quality.

Vertical integration, market leadership, and successful new product introductions translated into the rapid growth of the Boise operation. By 1980, within the first seven years, employment increased to 2600. HP's Boise workforce significantly expanded in the 1980s, and by 1989 HP counted 3500 workers on its Boise payroll. HP's Boise Division also influenced the growth and development of other HP sites. In an effort to relieve and focus the Boise operation, tape drive manufacturing was shifted to Greeley, Colorado, in 1983. Several other business units were created from the Boise operation, including the inkjet division in Vancouver in Washington State, the San Diego division and the division in Bristol, UK. The division in Vancouver was established in 1979 and grew into HP's inkjet printer division. Shifting the inkjet printer division to Vancouver allowed parallel development of the two competing printing technologies and gave room for each site to pursue improvements and innovations independently of each other (Christensen, 1997).

Boise's inadequate education infrastructure did not harm HP's growth. Boise-based managers projected employment to climb to about 10 000 workers at the local site. This, however, never materialized because major restructuring efforts influenced HP's evolution in Boise; these will be discussed in the next section.

Corporate Restructuring: 1990–2009

After continuous growth during the 1970s and 1980s, HP's development in Boise was shaped by corporate restructuring. During the 1990s, HP started to turn to outside suppliers for critical printer and computer components. As a result, the Boise Division started to shift from an operation primarily focused on manufacturing to one that develops and tests laser printers. These changes had far-reaching implications for the Boise economy. Promising growth projections that were made by HP executives never materialized. Instead employment growth slowed and over time even shrank. Large manufacturing units shifted to other locations, primarily in Southeast Asia. In addition, some functions were spun off as business divisions or were sold to other firms.

One example showcases HP's restructuring efforts. As noted earlier, HP transferred disk drive manufacturing from California to Boise in 1977.

Over the years HP introduced new types of disk drives, and the division grew rapidly to the point that in 1981, it generated about $200 million in revenue, having grown by 90 per cent per year since its move to Boise. Growth continued, and in 1991 HP's Disk Memory Division (DMD) generated about $600 million, a significant share of HP's overall revenues of about $20 billion. DMD accounted for about 10 per cent to 15 per cent of the capacity of the Boise-based manufacturing operation. Manufacturing disk drives was not an easy undertaking. Technological developments such as shrinking the size of the drives required rapid adjustments to the manufacturing process. In 1991 HP decided to move its disk drive manufacturing to Malaysia. At the time competition had increased, especially because small US-based start-up companies (such as California-based Seagate) entered the market and were quite successful in lowering costs by moving production abroad (McKendrick et al., 2000). About five years later in 1996, HP closed its Disk Memory Division in Boise and exited this market.

HP also closed or transferred other Boise manufacturing operations. When HP introduced the laser printer, manufacturing of the line impact printer went overseas (first to Japan, then China). In 1990 HP phased out the ten-year-old printed circuit board fabrication operation. About four years later in 1994, the Surface Mount Centre was closed, and HP turned to outside suppliers. With the closing of all these operations, Boise's manufacturing share declined substantially. While in 1994, manufacturing activities accounted for about 30 per cent of the Boise operation, in 1998 that share was a mere 10 per cent. In addition to closing and transferring manufacturing operations, HP also sold some of its operations to other firms. In 1998, Jabil Circuit, Inc. acquired HP's LaserJet Formatter Manufacturing Organization (FMO). Jabil continued to produce for HP and manufactured locally. In 2002, however, Jabil closed its Boise facility, and the region lost about 500 jobs. In 1999 HP spun off the test and measurement business and created Agilent Technologies, an independent company focused on manufacturing test and measurement products, semiconductors, and other electronic products. Boise's HP operations were affected because the local semiconductor production facilities became those of Agilent Technologies (later sold to Marvell Technology Group).

The nature of HP's Boise operations completely changed in a matter of a decade. By the mid-1990s the shift away from manufacturing was in full swing. Today, HP employees at the Boise site engage primarily in R&D, marketing, and customer service. Whatever is left of manufacturing is supportive of these efforts, including prototype development, product testing, and quality assurance. Table 5.1 shows the history of HP's operations in Boise from 1973 to 2005.

Table 5.1   History of Hewlett-Packard in Boise, 1973–2005

Year	Activities
1973	HP starts Boise operation to manufacture line printers
1974	Manufacturing of magnetic tape drives moves to Boise
1975	HP begins cooperation with Canon
1976	Disk drive activities were shifted to Boise
1977	Introduction of first microprocessor printer
1980	Boise Division developed laser printing system for computers (HP 2680A)
1983	Manufacturing of tape drives is moved to Greeley, Colorado
1984	Introduction of LaserJet printer, cooperation with Canon
1986	Introduction of new generation of disk drives
1987	HP creates LaserJet printer division with worldwide R&D, marketing, and manufacturing responsibilities HP Boise develops HP's first scanner
1988	Reorganization of peripherals group into three units: publishing products, hardcopy technology, and mass storage HP Boise operation starts to manufacture formatter boards for laser printer HP sold 1 million laser printers
1989	Introduction of HP's first personal laser printer
1990	HP phases out printed circuit board fabrication
1991	HP transfers disk memory production to Malaysia
1994	HP phases out surface mount centre
1994	Introduction of colour laser printer
1996	Closing of Disk Memory Division Introduction of the 'mopier'
1998	Formatter board operation sold to Jabil
1999	HP spins off Agilent as a new company
2005	HP opens sales centre hpshopping.com as an online consumer-shopping subsidiary

Source: Author's analysis.

HEWLETT-PACKARD'S ROLE AS A SURROGATE UNIVERSITY

Hewlett-Packard's arrival in 1973 set Boise on a path to become a second tier high-tech region. Like Tektronix, HP played the role of a surrogate university in the Boise economy. HP attracted and developed talent. Though its corporate restructuring efforts during the 1990s and 2000s, HP changed from a manufacturing-oriented firm to one focused on developing consumer-oriented innovations. It also functioned as an incubator for spin-off companies which diversified the Boise economy. HP's influence, especially in the realms of talent, innovation, and entrepreneurship, shows striking similarities to Tektronix's role in the Silicon Forest.

Talent

When HP came to Boise, the company had to create its own labour pool. At the time, there were no other high-tech firms in the area. Many skilled employees – engineers and managers – had to be imported from other regions. Attracting talent from outside Idaho was not difficult for HP. On the one hand, Boise offered a high quality of life. On the other hand the major draw was HP itself. For many young engineers and recent college graduates looking for interesting work, a good income, and a nice place to live, HP represented an exciting company to work for. As one high-tech entrepreneur who came to Boise in the late 1970s to work for HP right out of college notes, HP was a 'pole of attraction . . . It isn't just about the money,' he notes. 'It is about doing interesting work in a place that seems appealing to live' (Lundt interview, 2007). Boise offered all of the above, and that made it easy for HP to convince talented people to come to Idaho. 'I did not even know where Boise was', the engineer remarked. 'HP was the catalyst for me to look at a different part of the country. I saw that it is really nice, and I liked recreation; I learned to ski. There are a lot of wonderful things about the area, but HP was very much the catalyst' (Lundt interview 2007).

HP's management valued the ease with which they could attract talent to Boise. HP also did not have any difficulties with recruiting locally. This attractiveness facilitated the set-up of a high-tech manufacturing operation within a short time. In 1976 HP's general manager in Boise was quoted in the local paper: 'Hewlett-Packard has been able to attract "extremely trainable" employees to the Boise area' (*The Idaho Statesman*, 1976). He went on to highlight the loyalty of the employees and the fact that HP had a very low staff turnover rate. Low turnover rates represented an advantage over Silicon Valley where labour poaching was already happening. A former employee who joined HP in 1978 and left the company six years later to start his own venture noted that HP

> was a good place to work. In those days it was a real booming time, there was lots of hiring, and so there were lots of job openings. And Hewlett and Packard were still around, and everybody was very happy with their jobs then. It was very rare for anyone to leave in those days. It was a really great place to work. (Hodges interview, 2007)

HP compensated for Boise's lack of a world-class research university through distance education, and the company developed two programmes with California-based universities. One of these was a long-distance education effort in cooperation with Chico State University, located about 100 miles north of Sacramento, California. In the late 1970s, Chico State developed a computer science master's degree programme that was offered to HP employees at the Roseville, California branch facility. The programme was developed to help engineers move from hardware engineering to software engineering. It was expanded to other locations, including Idaho, Oregon, Washington, and Colorado, reaching HP employees in these states via satellite links (Chico State University, 2000). Another distance education programme allowed HP employees to earn a master's degree from Stanford University while working at HP in Boise. The programme used videotapes and peer mentoring through programme alumni. As part of the programme, HP employees had to spend one semester at Stanford University in California. They often lived in dorm rooms and quite enjoyed their experience on campus. Unlike Tektronix where educational programmes were offered in-house, HP drew on outside resources to ensure continuing education of its employees. Over time, the local education system improved and helped to meet HP's need for education, but until then the long-distance offerings helped replace the missing opportunities.

One particular aspect of the HP work culture that facilitated the development of talent was the tradition of moving engineers into management positions. Several current and former HP employees explained how they were able not only to develop their engineering skills but also to gain important insights into how to manage a project, how to oversee staff, and how to market a product. In short, they were also able to gain important managerial skills. One former HP employee who worked as an engineer and then as a manager notes that

> at HP I learned how to develop technology into a product that could actually make money and sustain a business. I was a program manager for two programs, which means I led a team of peers – other project managers who were in manufacturing, finance, marketing, Q&A, all the other R&D areas, software, hardware, mechanical. So I got to do that and that helped a lot because you get into finance, the planning for the future, and you have to present the data to those higher up. And you see the process going on. So that helped quite a bit. (Riskey interview, 2007)

It was also common for engineers to switch from one product group to another. Some started out as engineers in the disk drive operation and later became managers in the emerging laser printer group. These engineer-managers often were able to climb the ranks into senior executive positions at HP, and it was not unusual to have a general manager or a vice president who had advanced their entire career at HP's Boise operation. HP helped develop engineer-managers who possessed both technical and managerial skills. The development of managerial human capital proved to be especially important for the spin-offs that would develop around HP. The literature on the emergence of industry clusters highlights the importance of managerial labour and the combination of scientific and managerial skills (Bresnahan, et al., 2001; Goldstone, 2009). Breshnahan et al. (2001) describe the process of developing an indigenous supply of engineer-managers for Silicon Valley. The case of Boise was not much different, with HP helping develop talent with a dual skill set.

The shift from manufacturing to product development involved significant transformations of the labour force. During the 1970s and 1980s, HP's labour force in Boise was dominated by mechanical engineers. The development and manufacturing of products such as disk drives involved tasks that revolved around complex mechanical systems, and the skill sets of mechanical engineers were especially appropriate. When HP began to outsource most manufacturing activities – including the manufacturing of the printer engine and the assembly of the printers – its focus shifted from mechanical systems to software development. With this shift, a significant change in the nature of the labour force took place, and over time it became dominated by computer scientists. In addition, the focus on consumer products required greater attention to marketing and sales. Today, two-thirds of HP's Boise labour force is engaged with R&D, and about one-third works in marketing and sales (Spohn interview, 2007).

Innovation

HP's role as a surrogate university differed from Tektronix's in terms of innovation and entrepreneurship. Unlike Tektronix, HP never established a separate R&D lab in the Boise region. Interactions between the Boise operation and the centralized HP Labs that were established in 1966 in Palo Alto were limited to individual projects. HP Labs in Palo Alto were created to advance innovations that would help HP enter new markets, and their work was critical in the development of innovations such as the pocket scientific calculator and thermal inkjet printing. In Boise, however, R&D was always integrated with the division's group and was mostly done in support of product development. HP's innovation activities in Boise have been oriented on consumer needs and focus on improving products (such as the LaserJet printer). Engineers and marketing experts worked closely together to incorporate these product innovations. In this way, innovative activities at HP in Boise are very different from those that would be undertaken in a research laboratory. With the laser printer, for example, improvements encompassed technical changes such as the ability to interrupt printing jobs, networking printers, digital printing, and so on. Unlike coming up with a new invention, the laser printer represented a consumer commodity whose features were continuously improved.

Boise's innovation culture evolved in a distinctly different way than the overall HP operation had, and it deviated from the traditional HP culture. With the introduction of the LaserJet printer, the Boise operation set an example in terms of collaborating with industry partners such as Canon in Japan. HP's traditional way of operating was focused on the in-house development of innovations rather than sourcing new ideas outside. HP engineers believed that ideas 'not invented here' were inferior. In Boise, however, a culture of openness was encouraged and fostered. This meant that engineers were encouraged to incorporate innovations developed outside of HP and to focus on open systems. For example, HP managers in Boise decided to incorporate serial printer interfaces that were compatible with other computer systems, such as those developed by IBM. Managers based in Boise felt strongly that proprietary systems would limit them, especially as operating systems such as DOS and UNIX were emerging. The development of an innovation culture in which engineers and managers were open to outside ideas represented something new for HP. Interviewees noted that being located in a second tier high-tech region such as Boise and being at a distance from the HP headquarters in California probably facilitated the evolution of this culture – which eventually would take root in the overall organization – because engineers and managers had more freedom in making decisions about product development and innovation. As a result of this shift to open systems, HP also began to engage outside suppliers, thereby starting the transformation of HP into a vertically specialized company (Lazonick, 2009). In addition, smaller start-up firms in the Boise region were often given the opportunity to work with HP in developing new ideas. This was the case with the HP spin-off Extended System, as I will describe below.

Entrepreneurship

Hewlett-Packard was not only the first major high-tech employer and innovator in the Boise metropolitan area, but also the region's most important incubator for spin-off companies. Especially in the years following restructuring and the introduction of the laser printer, HP unleashed great entrepreneurial potential. From 1973 to 1989, seven spin-off companies can directly trace their roots to HP. Among these firms were companies such as Computrol and Extended Systems, two early high-tech pioneers

Table 5.2   Hewlett-Packard corporate changes and spin-offs

Period	HP corporate changes	Number of first-generation spin-offs	Number of descendants/ subsequent generation spin-offs	Total number of spin-offs
1973–89	Corporate change and expansion	7	1	8
1990– 2007	HP restructures operations in Boise	27	23	50
Totals				**58**

Source: Author's analysis.

in Boise. In addition, several machine shops (Loya Machine, Advanced Precision Machining, and Metalcraft) were founded during that time, spun off in an effort to refocus HP's operations and outsource production efforts that were not directly related to HP's core products. Another spin-off was the IT services firm CRI Advantage, which contracted with HP. Between 1990 and 2007, former HP employees founded a total of 27 companies, which then served as incubators for an additional 23 start-ups. Altogether, HP's Boise operation spawned 58 new companies (see Table 5.2 above and Figure 5.1 on p. 147).

Two aspects of the HP culture encouraged entrepreneurship. First, HP provided talented and entrepreneurially oriented employees an ideal work environment, in which they could gain managerial skills that they would need when starting a new company. Second, HP's Boise operation provided numerous technology and market opportunities for small start-up companies. Together, these factors influenced the nature and extent to which HP employees formed entrepreneurial ventures.

Former HP employees who left the Boise Division to start their own companies described HP as very supportive of their entrepreneurial endeavours. Not only did they gain important managerial expertise when they worked as engineer-managers, but they were also able to use HP equipment and parts to develop their own projects. Often these projects were not related to their immediate work tasks. In some cases, this freedom helped HP employees to get a head start on their entrepreneurial ventures. One entrepreneur who left HP to found a firm that developed computer controls notes that

all HP divisions have a thing called 'lab stock'. They have every kind of electronic component that you can find. Engineers were encouraged to use lab stock for their own purposes, mostly for hobbies. A lot of engineers are sort of techies or nerds, and they like to invent or play with things after hours. So we were encouraged to use the equipment, you know, the development equipment, the computers, and parts, to make toys or projects or whatever. And of course most people don't leave, so it is a really good idea because you are in there on the weekends and learning how to do things new on your own time, and a lot of times that gets carried over to the work hours. But for our first couple of models, we used a lot of the development equipment that we didn't own ourselves. I had a partner helping me, and we used a lot of parts and things, and so that helped a lot. (Hodges interview, 2007)

Besides providing a supportive and experimental work environment, HP helped its former employees to manage entrepreneurial risks. Several former HP employees managed to return to work for HP when their ventures failed or came to a dead end. As one engineer who left HP to be part of a start-up noted,

HP was pretty good about taking people back. Some firms, like Micron, if you leave, you are out, but for HP at that time it was the thought that people went out and got this entrepreneurial experience. So if you left on good terms, going back was never a problem. . . . there usually is a welcome mat for you if you screw up, as long as you leave on good terms. (Haney interview, 2007)

Others were able to remain employed by HP while they started their ventures. If the venture failed, many HP employees knew that they could return to their former employer in some capacity. HP's 'welcome mat' lowered the entrepreneurial risk, and this seemed especially important in a second tier high-tech region like Boise. Unlike Silicon Valley, Boise does not possess a diverse industrial environment and a deep and wide pool of employment opportunities. Boise-based entrepreneurs take a higher risk than their Silicon Valley counterparts when they leave stable employment because they might not be able to find alternative employment if their venture fails.

HP also provided numerous technology and market opportunities, especially through subcontracting and outsourcing. Several start-up firms that were founded by ex-HP employees maintained contracts with HP for tasks such as machine shop services, IT services, and higher level activities such as the development of technological improvements and innovations for the printer. With the introduction of new products such as the laser printer, HP also offered new technological opportunities for small start-up companies. One HP spin-off that benefited from new products developed by HP is Extended Systems, Inc. (ESI), founded in 1984. Initially the founders wanted to develop database servers, but the need for revenues to keep the fledging company afloat during the first years forced them

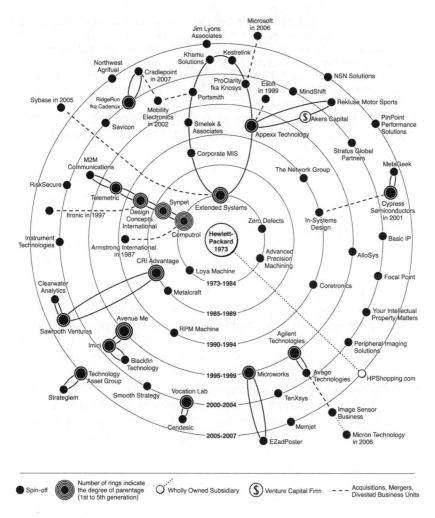

Source: Author's analysis.

Figure 5.1 Companies with founders from Hewlett-Packard's Boise operation

into other business activities. During the same year as ESI was founded, HP introduced the LaserJet printer, and ESI developed a technology that would allow one single printer to be connected to multiple computers (a spooler system). This allowed a single laser printer, which was very expensive at that time, to be shared by several computer users. The technology was co-marketed by HP. A former HP and current ESI employee notes,

I was involved with marketing the LaserJet at that time, and we did not have all the pieces at HP. So we heavily relied on smaller companies to help us provide the complete solution. So what happened is the HP sales team effectively was selling share pools for Extended Systems. Even though HP didn't technically do it, they were the ones that always pointed and said, here is what you need to share this stuff. (Simpson interview, 2007)

Over time, ESI moved away from printer products and entered the realm of mobile software and devices. HP, however, had allowed ESI to develop into a viable business.

THE DEVELOPMENT OF MICRON TECHNOLOGY

Micron Technology is a semiconductor manufacturing company that specializes in the production of computer memory chips, a key component of most electronic devices. It is one of a few companies that still manufacture memory chips in the US, after most firms exited this industry segment in the 1980s (Leachman and Leachman, 2004). Nowadays, most Micron competitors are foreign, and manufacturing takes place in lower cost countries such as Taiwan and China. Having a firm produce memory chips in the US is unusual. Locating such a firm in Idaho is even more unusual, because the clusters for semiconductor design and production are in California, Oregon, Texas, and Arizona. Yet Micron Technology successfully leveraged Boise as a second tier high-tech region. In 2007 Micron was the largest high-tech employer in Boise, with about 10 600 workers on the Idaho payroll. Micron's worldwide employment at the time stood at about 20 000. Micron is a locally grown high-tech firm whose influence on the evolution of Boise's high-tech economy has been limited compared to that of Hewlett-Packard.

Micron Technology was founded by three design engineers who had been working for Mostek Corporation in Dallas, Texas. The three engineers – Ward Parkinson, Dennis Wilson, and Douglas Pitman – developed new chip designs of Mostek which was one of the most important firms in the field of memory semiconductor design and production at the time. Ward Parkinson was approached by Mostek's former head of research, Paul Schroeder, and recruited to work for the British-financed semiconductor start-up company Inmos Limited (Parkinson interview, 2007). The firm was funded by the British government to help diversify the UK economy into new sectors such as semiconductors. When a legal battle ensued between Mostek and Inmos about poaching and trade secrets, the three engineers left Inmos and started their own venture that was initially financed through a contract with Mostek. The firm was started in Ward

Parkinson's house in Texas, but none of the engineers liked living in Texas, so they started to look for an alternative location. Ward Parkinson asked Doug Pitman, a fellow Idaho native, to explore possible locations for the new firm. Possible sites included Logan, Utah; Bozeman, Montana; and Boise, Idaho (Parkinson interview, 2007). Pitman visited all three cities but favoured Boise since he was originally from Idaho. Even though Parkinson thought that staying near their customers in Texas would be better for the fledgling company, he okayed Pitman's location for the new firm. Eager to return to Idaho, Pitman quickly found appropriate premises and, feeling confident about the move, even bought a house in Boise. Following Pitman's successful trip to Idaho, Micron Technology started its operation in the basement of a dentist's office in Boise.

In the dentist's basement, the three Micron engineers worked for about a year on the design of a new memory chip for Mostek, then the leader in the market for dynamic random access memory (DRAM) chips. While the Micron engineers were working on the chip design, Mostek was acquired by United Technologies Corporation to avoid an unfriendly takeover. The acquisition put a hold on the work Micron did for Mostek. Then United Technologies breached the contract and took the unfinished chip design, leaving Micron with no business and no income. Micron's founders, however, wanted to continue to work on semiconductor chip design and manufacturing. To do that, they had to look for alternative funding sources. Ward Parkinson had helped some entrepreneurial farmers (Allen Noble, Ron Yanke, and Tom Nicholson) repair their sprinkler system. All three had made their fortunes in Idaho's agricultural economy as a potato farmer, a machine shop operator, and a sheep rancher, respectively. Parkinson invited them to lunch to discuss a finance proposal for Micron Technology, and they put up the first round of funding. This financing, however, was not enough to fund the construction of a semiconductor fabrication facility, which Parkinson estimated would take another $1 million. The three investors put Micron in touch with Scott Simplot, the son of JR Simplot, one of Idaho's wealthiest potato farmers. JR Simplot had made his fortune by supplying potatoes to the military during the Second World War and later on to fast food chains like McDonald's. Scott Simplot was convinced that Micron Technology would be successful, given the emerging computer industry and the founders' track records (Attebery, 2000). Equally convinced that the venture would work out, his father, JR Simplot, initially invested $1 million. With this support, they were able to build a manufacturing facility in Boise. Over the years, JR Simplot invested another $20 million in the company.

Boise, Idaho, was probably the best location for Micron Technology to get started. The initial capital from local investors represented 'patient capital', an investment that gave Micron some time to turn a profit. Low costs in the Treasure Valley helped Micron to build a large-scale manufacturing facility for well below what other high-tech locations would have cost. And in a sector that is highly sensitive to price fluctuations, success also depended on low labour and electricity costs. Parkinson notes that 'Boise was always at an enormous cost advantage to every place in the world. . . . It probably had a 30–50 per cent cost advantage' (Parkinson interview, 2007).

Early Growth Phase, 1978–89

Micron Technology was founded during a period when the US semiconductor industry experienced significant changes: during the 1980s, US semiconductor firms lost their leadership position to their Japanese competitors. As noted in Chapter 3, the US share of worldwide semiconductor sales fell from 58 per cent to 37 per cent, while the Japanese share rose from 26 per cent to 49 per cent (Angel, 1994). Japanese firms were able to gain this market leadership because they were able to lower prices, primarily by adopting high-quality, high-volume production methods, especially in the commodity device market, producing dynamic random access memory (DRAM) devices.[2] Japanese investments in process technology and manufacturing equipment allowed them to match the quality of US products and to avoid delivery shortages. In addition, Japanese firms were able to ride out declining sales and price reductions because their large, integrated organizational structures helped them compensate for short-term losses. These developments adversely affected US firms and completely changed the industry's structure. Several large US semiconductor makers (including Intel, Advanced Micro Devices, and Motorola) exited the DRAM market segment and began to focus on more design-intensive and higher value semiconductors such as microprocessors (Angel, 1994). In addition, many new US firms adopted a business model that separated R&D from production. These firms became known as 'fabless semiconductor companies'. They were concentrated in Silicon Valley and heavily dependent on manufacturers abroad.

At the same time, however, lower-cost regions like Portland's Silicon Forest and Boise's Treasure Valley were able to gain a foothold as locations for large, vertically integrated semiconductor manufacturers like Intel and Micron. During a time of great market volatility, Micron carved out a niche in the DRAM market primarily because innovations were focused on the production process. By closely integrating design and production in the same facility, it was able to produce smaller and more reliable chips than its competitors. Even though fabless chip design firms emerged, the production and the design of commodity memory devices stayed within integrated device manufacturers (IDMs) like Micron Technology. Leachman and Leachman (2004) note that

> for such high-volume commodity products, it is essential to strive for the lowest possible manufacturing cost. This requires the development and refinement of a fabrication process technology optimized for the specific product. The number of process steps must be reduced wherever and whenever possible, certain process machines may need to be dedicated and tuned to perform specific process steps, and frequent relatively small modifications of the process technology enabling smaller design rules ('shrinks') likely will be advantageous (p. 224).

Micron Technology's innovation environment may be characterized as high-volume manufacturing driven by considerations to decrease costs and retain control over each step in the design and manufacturing process, with less concern for the customer. This stands in contrast to the nature and type of products that HP produces and markets from its Boise operations. Table 5.3 shows the history of Micron Technology in Boise.

During the 1980s Micron introduced two new DRAM chips, the 64K DRAM and the 256K DRAM. Within only a few years, the company was able to scale up two fabrication plants. In addition the firm set up Micron Custom Manufacturing, a wholly-owned subsidiary that produced modules for Micron's memory chips. During this time Micron also advanced its chip design, primarily by reducing the size. This was important because smaller chips implied lower manufacturing costs, which gave Micron an advantage over its US and Japanese competitors.

Diversification, Strategic Alliances, and Global Presence: 1990–2009

Since 1990 Micron Technology has emphasized product diversification, the formation of strategic alliances with other, mostly non-local, semiconductor firms, and the expansion of its global manufacturing presence. In 1991, Micron entered the personal computer business and created Edge Technology, which later would be known as Micron Computer or Micron PC. In 1994 Micron acquired Minneapolis-based personal computer manufacturer ZEOS International, Inc. and two years later merged it with Micron Custom Manufacturing and Micron Computer to form Micron Electronics.[3] Other wholly-owned subsidiaries or divisions that were started during the early 1990s included Micron Custom Manufacturing Services, Micron Internet Services, the Memory Applications Group, Micron Systems Integration, and Micron Investments. Micron's diversification strategy during these years may represent an attempt to offset the

Table 5.3   History of Micron Technology in Boise, 1978–2010

Year	Activities
1978	Micron Technology is founded in Boise, Idaho
1981	Manufacturing of the 64K DRAM product starts in Micron's first fabrication facility
1984	256K DRAM is introduced and produced in second fabrication plant
	Micron Custom Manufacturing is started to build modules for Micron Technology's memory chips
1985	Prices for memory chips fall
	Other leading US-based semiconductor makers exit DRAM market
1986	US and Japan enter into a semiconductor trade agreement
1991	Edge Technology is started as a subsidiary to manufacture memory-intensive personal computers (later named Micron Electronics and Micron PC)
1994	Micron acquires personal computer manufacturer ZEOS International, Inc.
	Micron announces plans to build a manufacturing facility in Lehi, Utah
	Steve Appleton becomes Micron's president, chairman, and CEO
1996	Crucial Technology is created as a division to market and sell memory upgrades
	ZEOS International, Micron Computer, and Micron Custom Manufacturing Services merge to become Micron Electronics
1998	Micron acquires Texas Instrument's worldwide memory operations
	Micron Custom Manufacturing Services sold to Cornerstone Equity Investors
	Intel invests $500 million in Micron to co-develop memory products
2000	Micron expands in Lehi (Utah) and in the United Kingdom
2001	Micron Electronics acquired by Gores Technology Group, renamed MicronPC (shut down in 2008)
2002	Micron acquires Toshiba's commodity DRAM operations and gains manufacturing presence in Virginia
2006	Micron expands assembly and testing in Singapore
	Micron partners with Intel to form IM Flash Technologies, a new company to manufacture NAND flash memory
	Micron partners with Photronics to develop photomasks
2007	Opening of new manufacturing facility in China
2009	Micron phases out 200 mm wafer manufacturing operations in Boise
2010	Micron partners with Australian Energy Limited to develop photovoltaic technology

Source: Author's analysis.

*Table 5.4   Micron Technology corporate changes and spin-offs,
1978–2009*

Period	Corporate changes	Number of first generation spin-offs	Number of descendants/ subsequent generation spin-offs	Total spin-offs spawned
1978–89	Corporate growth	1		1
1990–2009	Diversification and expansion	6	15	21
Since 1978		**7**	**15**	**22**

Source: Author's analyis.

cyclical nature of the memory chip market. All new subsidiaries started their operations in Boise.

Interestingly, only Micron Electronics had a significant impact on local entrepreneurship through its function as an incubator, producing more spin-offs than its parent firm (see Figure 5.1 and Table 5.4). From 1978–2007, only six companies were founded by former Micron Technology employees. In contrast, Micron Electronics had ten spin-offs, from which another five were created between 1995 and 2007.

Micron Electronics spin-offs specialize in Internet and networking services, software, information technology services, and business and professional services. The reasons for Micron Electronics' impact on entrepreneurship in the Boise region may lie in the different nature of its products and its general work culture. For one thing, Micron Electronics produced high-performance personal computers, and innovation was oriented towards the consumer product. In contrast, at Micron Technology innovation has been oriented towards the manufacturing process. The difference between product and process innovation might influence entrepreneurship through the type of labour force each firm attracts and the nature of the entrepreneurial opportunities that present themselves to employees. In addition, interviewees noted that Micron Electronics offered an exciting work environment and that they 'learned how to develop a product better than anybody' (Moesner interview, 2007). Lastly, entrepreneurial abilities were fostered because Micron Electronics operated as a completely separate business from its parent firm.

In recent years Micron has engaged in strategic partnerships with other semiconductor firms that are geared towards the development of new capabilities and the opening of new markets. Most of these activities are with non-local companies and reach beyond Boise's borders. In 2006,

Micron and Intel formed a new company – IM Flash Technologies – to jointly develop and manufacture NAND flash memory, a type that does not need a constant power supply to retain data and is used in a variety of consumer electronics. Production takes place at Micron's Lehi, Utah, facility. Other partnerships include a 2006 joint venture with Connecticut-based Photronics to develop photomasks used in the manufacturing process and a 2010 joint venture with the Australian company Energy Limited to develop photovoltaic technology.

Similarly, Micron has adopted a global strategy to expand its manufacturing capacities. Through the acquisition of Texas Instruments' memory business in 1998, Micron scaled up its manufacturing operation and added wafer fabrication assembly and testing facilities in Italy, Texas, and Singapore. Leachman and Leachman note that through this purchase, Micron changed 'overnight from a company with 100 per cent of its fabrication performed within the US to a company operating large fabs in Europe, Japan, and Singapore as well as the US' (2004: 217). In 2002 Micron acquired Toshiba's commodity DRAM operations and gained a manufacturing presence in Virginia. In February 2010 Micron acquired the Intel memory spin-off Numonyx for $1.27 billion. Headquartered in Switzerland, Numonyx has a global manufacturing presence which was added to Micron's portfolio. These acquisitions not only put Micron into a leadership position in markets such as flash memories, but they also created a greater global presence for Micron. Boise, Idaho, is now only one of many locations. Figure 5.2 shows Micron's spin-offs and wholly-owned subsidiaries.

COMPARING HEWLETT-PACKARD AND MICRON TECHNOLOGY

Differences in firm building between Micron Technology and HP are important in explaining the firms' divergent contributions to entrepreneurial activities. We have to open the black box of each firm and examine the ways in which its industry sector, corporate changes, linkages, market connections, product type, nature of production, innovation culture, corporate policies and culture, assets, and labour type play a role in spin-off dynamics (see Table 5.5).

Micron and HP differ in significant ways. HP's Boise operations are part of the consumer electronics market, while Micron produces memory semiconductors, a commodity product. HP's customers are consumers, so its technologies and products are characterized by a high degree of variation and customization, and lower sensitivity to price variations. HP has a rich

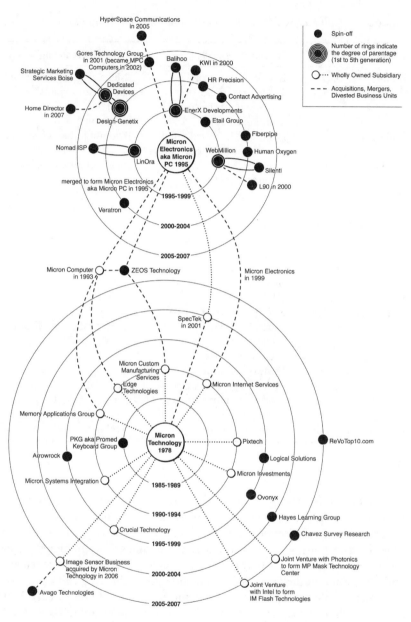

Source: Author's analysis.

Figure 5.2 Micron Technology spin-offs and wholly-owned subsidiaries, 1978–2007

Table 5.5   Comparing Hewlett-Packard and Micron Technology

Feature	Hewlett-Packard	Micron Technology
Industry sector	Consumer electronics	Memory semiconductor
Corporate changes	Transformation from manufacturing to R&D and marketing	Corporate expansion mainly outside of region
Linkages	Disintegration facilitated contracting opportunities	Did not induce clustering
Market connections	Industry leader Strong market connections	Intermediary supplier
Product type	Customized for end consumers	Standardized commodity 'Just making chips'
Nature of production	Move away from manufacturing to prototyping, design, marketing	Vertically integrated mass production
Innovation culture	Product innovation Break with 'NIH' syndrome	Manufacturing process innovation
Corporate policies and culture	HP Way Strong culture of talent development 'Welcome mat' for entrepreneurs Divisionalization	'Secretive' 'Frugal' Limited divisionalization (MicronPC)
Assets	Move away from physical assets to more human asset-based	Physical assets dominate Strong IP assets
Labour type	Engineer manager	Technical production

Source: Author's analysis.

history of developing innovations based on the type of product, such as the laser printer, and its Boise operations are more focused on the product conception and development phases. In contrast, Micron's customers are other high-tech firms. Its products are commodities that are highly sensitive to price variations. Micron is focused more on process improvement and innovation in the execution/production phase than the conception or development phase (How can we make more chips at a lower price?). This focus may not allow for much creativity on the shop floor. HP's Boise operations have also evolved from focusing on vertical integration with R&D and manufacturing of various components in-house to outsourcing to other countries. Micron Technology in contrast, has only recently expanded to other geographic areas and retains a strong tradition of

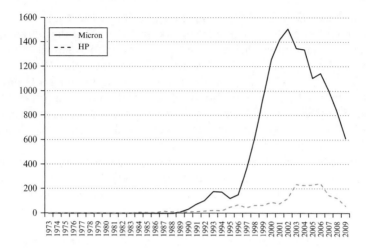

Source: US Patent and Trademark Office.

Figure 5.3   Patenting activity of Micron Technology and Hewlett-Packard, 1973–2009

integrating the various R&D and manufacturing processes. Opportunities for backward and forward linkages do exist for both firms. However, more firms indicated that they have developed backward linkages (as suppliers) with HP than with Micron (see discussion below). These linkages may also give rise to entrepreneurial opportunities, as many spin-offs use their parent firms as customers.

HP's Boise operations have also evolved from vertical integration, with R&D and manufacturing of various components in-house, to outsourcing to other countries. Micron Technology, in contrast, retains a strong tradition of vertical integration and has only recently expanded to other geographic areas.

Micron and HP also differ in terms of patenting (see Figure 5.3). Micron and its subsidiaries are very active patentees, and from the latter half of the 1990s until the early 2000s, patenting activity increased rapidly. Since the early 2000s, the company has typically ranked among the top 20 patent holders in the US. Micron's patenting activity peaked in 2002, when the company registered 1512 patents in Idaho. In recent years, however, Micron has registered fewer patents in Idaho. This may be the result of Micron's expansion into other geographic regions such as Virginia and Utah. Patenting activity at HP's Boise operation increased from 2003–2006, but is still significantly lower than Micron's.

Several of the entrepreneurs interviewed for this research indicated that

HP provided them with a learning environment in which they not only honed their technical skills but also their knowledge about the market they operate in. In addition, their experience in working for a global company enabled them to access global markets, something that Breshnahan and Gambardella (2004) emphasize is important in building a high-tech cluster. In addition, HP's tradition of decentralization and the creation of small business units allowed employees to gain entrepreneurial experience which gave them important managerial and business skills. A more in-depth discussion follows.

Corporate policies play an important role in encouraging or hindering entrepreneurial activities. The interviewees indicated a sharp contrast between HP and Micron. As mentioned earlier, HP was often labelled as a 'great place to work', a 'very supportive environment', 'cutting edge', and 'innovative'. HP provided an open door policy to employees who left to start a business or work for another firm and wanted to come back. This 'welcome mat' offered employees the chance to take entrepreneurial risks knowing that they would have a fall back. In some cases, entrepreneurs were able to work part-time for HP while they were developing their business. HP also allowed employees to work with so-called 'lab stock', electronic supplies in their spare time. Some used HP equipment and tools to built prototypes of their venture's products and technologies. Qualitative insights into Micron's culture present a different picture. Interviewees noted that Micron was 'secretive,' 'frugal', and not very diversified in terms of its products ('Micron is just a chip manufacturer'), and many had a sense that the firm was not well connected to the local business community. This confirms other research on the global semiconductor industry showing that this type of high-tech industry does not exhibit industrial clustering (McCann and Arita, 2006).

The ways in which these two firms have organized themselves and the differences between them explain some of the variation in entrepreneurial dynamics. HP and Micron function as anchor tenants (Feldman, 2003) in Boise's regional economy. Anchor firms that spawn many spin-offs create externalities that benefit entrepreneurs. Feldman notes that a 'large firm may be a better anchor, in terms of economic success, for a developing industry than an equivalent number of small firms. Even if the stock of skilled employees were equal under each regime, the large firm may exert a stronger influence' (2003: 323). In the case of Boise, firm size is not a sufficient variable to explain the different spin-off dynamics for HP and Micron. Rather, it is the ways in which these firms built their organizations; the types of products, innovations, and production processes they use; and their corporate cultures.

ENTREPRENEURSHIP IN BOISE

HP and Micron Technology shaped Boise's high-tech economy in important ways. Both firms contributed to entrepreneurship through spin-offs
that were created by former employees. Local entrepreneurship in general
has been critical to Boise's success as a second tier high-tech region. Figure
5.4 illustrates the emergence of 358 high-tech firms in the Treasure Valley.
Two periods stand out: the late 1970s to early 1980s were marked by the
establishment of HP and Micron. The two firms triggered modest entrepreneurial development during this time. The early 1990s to the mid-2000s
were marked by a higher level of entrepreneurial activity. Throughout
the years HP and Micron contributed to this development either through
spin-offs or through the establishment of subsidiaries.

High-tech Entrepreneurs in Boise

What are the characteristics of entrepreneurial high-tech firms in Boise?
Where do the entrepreneurs come from and what motivates them? How
have they financed their firms? And what kind of relationships do these
entrepreneurs have with their parent firms? The survey of high-tech firms

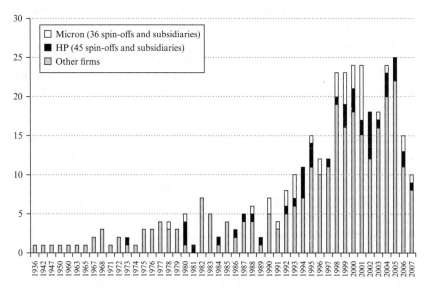

Source: Author's analysis.

Figure 5.4 High-tech firm emergence in Boise, 1936–2007

Table 5.6   Founders' prior employment for Boise spin–offs

Parent type	Founders	Per cent
Other firms	112	62.57%
Hewlett-Packard	26	14.53%
Government, public agency, hospital	15	8.38%
Micron Technology	9	5.03%
Self-employed	9	5.03%
University	8	4.47%
Total	**179**	**100%**

Source: Boise Survey.

in Boise reveals some interesting trends and development patterns. We collected email addresses for 215 firms and sent them the online survey. In addition, local groups such as Kickstand (a statewide non-profit entrepreneur support organization) and the Idaho Office of Science and Technology, advertised the survey through their newsletters and membership lists. Given this snowball method, it is not possible to assess the response rate, but altogether 135 firms responded to the survey. Most of the firms responding to the survey are small and generally representative of Boise's high-tech economy: 40.2 per cent employed one to five people and 25 per cent employed five to nine (see Table 5.6). Unfortunately, none of the large firms such as HP or Micron responded to the survey.

On average firms responding to the survey are 8.8 years old. The median founding year was 1999. There were 293 individuals involved in starting the 135 firms. As in Portland, founding a high-tech firm was a team effort, and on average 2.2 entrepreneurs were engaged in starting each venture, and 53 per cent of them note that they have founded a firm before. This confirms Boise's entrepreneurial culture and indicates that the local high-tech economy provides a welcoming environment for serial entrepreneurs. Only nine firms (compared to 26 in Portland) report that they have generated subsequent spin-offs. This may be because the entrepreneurial firms in Boise remain small and may therefore provide only a limited source of subsequent entrepreneurship. This might represent a serious limitation to Boise's growth as a second tier high-tech region.

The survey results indicate that HP and Micron functioned as incubators for a significant number of start-ups in Boise. Of the founders of these new ventures, 26 were employed by HP immediately prior to starting their firms, and nine came from Micron. Other companies were the prior employers of 112 founders, and 15 founders had worked for government, a public agency, or a hospital. Nine founders had been self-employed and eight had worked at a university. The majority of these founders worked for corporations, indicating that firms, not universities, are important for the growth of a second tier high-tech region. This finding stands in contrast to claims often made by policymakers about the role of universities as engines of growth. The importance of the corporate sector as a source of entrepreneurship is also confirmed by studies of regions where universities have played prominent roles, such as Cambridge, UK, and Silicon Valley (Cooper, 1971; Keeble, et al., 1999).

The survey included a question about the ways in which entrepreneurs financed their ventures. Assessing funding sources is important because, as a second tier emerging high-tech region, Boise has not been able to attract large amounts of venture capital. The lack of venture capital is typical for emerging high-tech regions. These investments usually go to more prominent regions such as Silicon Valley or Boston (Kenney and Florida, 2000). During the third quarter of 2007, for example, Silicon Valley, received 35 per cent of the $7.1 billion invested in companies and the New England region claimed a 14 per cent share (PricewaterhouseCoopers and National Venture Capital Association, 2007). As a result, almost 50 per cent of venture capital investments were made in only two regions of the US.

The survey results illustrate the ways in which entrepreneurs cope with the lack of funding and how they bootstrap their ventures. A large majority of respondents (82 per cent) indicated that they used personal finances. This was followed by bank loans and financial support from friends and family (20 per cent). Angel investments were also a source of financing (15.2 per cent), while venture capital was only selected by a few (6.5 per cent). This 'bootstrapping mentality' may reflect the status of Boise as a second tier region. The difficulty in accessing local sources of capital and financing was echoed when entrepreneurs were asked to rate the factors that constrain the development of their firms in the Boise region. Financing ranked second, after the shortage of local skilled labour (see Table 5.7).

There is also a large debate in the literature about whether venture capital investments spur entrepreneurial development, or promising deals (technologies, business ideas, and so on.) attract venture capital investments. This so-called 'chicken or egg' problem might also have a unique local dimension. In Portland, for example, venture capital investments followed the availability of deals and ideas (Mayer, 2005b). This may also be the case in Boise: promising ideas may have developed more in recent years, as reflected by increasing entrepreneurial activities. In addition, Boise's local investment community has been maturing. Starting in the late 1990s, a small venture capital and angel investor community began to form in the Boise metropolitan region. Akers Capital, one of the

Table 5.7   Characteristics of high-tech firms responding to Boise survey

Categories	Responses	Per cent
Survey descriptives		
Number of firms responding to survey	135	
Average age of firm (years; N=135)	8.2	
Median founding year	1999	
Average number of founders	2.2	
Serial entrepreneurs (N=100)	53	53.0%
Subsequent start-ups (N=97)	9	9.3%
Employment size		
1 to 5	37	40.2%
5 to 9	23	25.0%
10 to 19	8	8.7%
20 to 49	14	15.2%
50 to 99	5	5.4%
100 to 249	5	5.4%
250–499	0	0.0%
500–999	0	0.0%
1000 or more	0	0.0%
Valid N	92	100.0%
Source(s) of financing (multiple responses were allowed)		
Personal finances	76	82.6%
Friends and family	19	20.7%
Bank loan	19	20.7%
Angel investments	14	15.2%
Other	10	10.9%
Venture capital	6	6.5%

Source: Boise Survey.

first locally based venture capital firms, was founded in 1999. Another, Highway 12, opened its office in downtown Boise in 2001. The Boise Angel Alliance formed in 2004, and some of its members started the $800 000 Boise Angel Fund in 2007. That same year, Boise investors formed a local chapter of the Keiretsu Forum. Several Seattle-based venture capital firms have recognized the potential of the Boise region and keep tabs on the high-tech community: Frazier Technology Ventures and Buerk Dale Victor have established offices in the Treasure Valley. The emergence of an investment community indicates that Boise's entrepreneurial and small business community may have more local capital available than in the past.

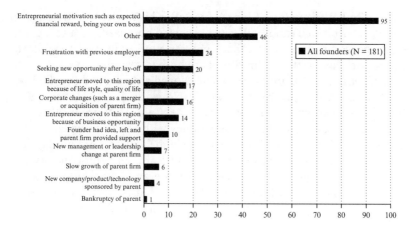

Source: Boise Survey.

Figure 5.5 Entrepreneurial motivations in Boise 'What prompted the founder to leave the previous employer to start this firm? (Check all that apply)'

Entrepreneurial Motivations of Spin–off Founders

Figure 5.5 illustrates the reasons why entrepreneurs left their previous employer to start their own firms. Asked what motivated them, the majority (52.5 per cent) indicated that it was the desire to become entrepreneurial, to expect financial rewards, and to be your own boss – in short, the entrepreneurial motivation was a pull factor. However, it is interesting to see that frustration with the previous employer (13.3 per cent), lay-offs (11 per cent), and corporate changes (8.8 per cent) rank high as well. This may indicate that corporate changes – especially those that have negative implications for anchor employees – may function as important push factors. As we have seen, both HP and Micron have changed significantly since they started in Boise in the 1970s. Several of the interviewees noted that HP's restructuring also influenced its business model, management, and innovation culture. Micron added new subsidiaries, which in turn were acquired or closed (for example, MicronPC). These corporate changes may have influenced employees in their decision to become entrepreneurs. The findings demonstrate that both pull factors and push factors play an important role in the entrepreneurial process.

Boise's quality of life also attracted entrepreneurs: 9.4 per cent reported that they moved to Boise for lifestyle reasons. One example illustrates this development. In 1996 Caleb Chung moved to Boise from California in search of a better quality of life. A year after his move, he developed the Furby, an electronic robot that quickly gained popularity as a toy. Chung was engaged in numerous other ventures until 2002 when he started Ugobe with his partner John Sosoka, who had also moved to Boise for lifestyle reasons. At Ugobe, the two developed an animated toy dinosaur, the Pleo. Even though the Pleo was developed in Boise, Ugobe's CEO, Bob Christopher, was located in Emeryville, California, primarily, Chung notes, because of 'his ability to raise money with people in Silicon Valley' (Chung interview, 2007). Unfortunately Ugobe's success did not last, and the company consolidated its operation in Boise and subsequently filed bankruptcy in 2009. Chung remains in Boise and is working on a new venture together with a local artist. The case illustrates the efforts of an entrepreneur who picked Boise for its lifestyle and quality of life.

The Parent-spin–off Relationship

Entrepreneurial firms in Boise diversify the local high-tech economy. From the survey, 68.7 per cent of founders indicated that their firm's product, technology, or service is in a new market compared to their parent firms. This indicates that entrepreneurial firms in Boise engage in the Schumpeterian process of creative destruction. Less than a third of the responding firms (27.3 per cent) indicated that their products, technologies, or services represent variants of those of their parent firms. Only 4 per cent are in the same market as their parents.

A large majority of the firms responding to the survey (71 per cent) indicated that their parent firms are not involved with their ventures. A small subset, however, indicated that the parent firm is a customer (11 per cent). Only 3 per cent indicated that the parent firm is a financier/investor, and another 3 per cent indicated that the parent firm is a sponsor of their technologies or products. Additionally, 2 per cent indicated that the parent firms are suppliers to their firms. These results indicate that if a parent firm is involved with an employee's start-up, then it is most likely as a customer. This relationship is similar to the experience Extended Systems had with HP in Boise.

The parent organization leaves a large imprint on the start-up company in terms of business practices such as technology, management style, and innovation model (see Table 5.8). Almost a quarter (24.4 per cent) of respondents indicated that they organize business practices around production, technology, or services similarly to their parent firms, while 17 per cent have a similar management style, and 15.6 per cent a similar innovation model. Similar hiring practices were reported by 10.4 per cent, and 8.1 per cent indicated similar general business practices. Technological affinity with the parent firm seems to be most important. There are some

Table 5.8 Spin-offs' relationships with parent firms in Boise

Categories	Responses	Per cent
Linkages with parent firms ('In what ways were or are the parent firms (the previous employer(s) of the founder(s)) involved with your firm?')		
Not at all	71	71.0%
As a customer	11	11.0%
Other	10	10.0%
As a financier/investor	3	3.0%
As a sponsor of technologies or products	3	3.0%
As a supplier	2	2.0%
Valid N	100	100.0%
Market similarity with parent firm ('Is your company's product/technology/service in a similar or a new market compared to your parent firms?')		
New market	68	68.7%
Variant of parent's product/technology/service	27	27.3%
Same as parent	4	4.0%
Valid N	99	100.0%
Parent imprinting ('Which of the following business practices are the most similar to your parent firms (Check all that apply)?')		
Production/technology/services	33	24.4%
Management style	23	17.0%
Innovation model	21	15.6%
Hiring practices	14	10.4%
General business model	11	8.1%
Valid N	64	
Prior position of founder ('What was the founder's position at his/her prior employer?')		
Other	100	55.2%
R&D	48	26.5%
Production	7	3.9%
Marketing	16	8.8%
Sales	10	5.5%
Valid N	181	100.0%

Source: Boise Survey.

striking differences between HP and Micron: the majority of the firms in the HP family indicated that their management style, innovation model, and hiring practices were similar to their parent firm; this was true for only two Micron-related start-ups. This suggests that the 'HP Way' (Packard, 1995) diffuses to local start-up companies.

Table 5.9   Boise high-tech firms' relationships with anchor firms. 'In what ways does your company interact with the following businesses in the region?' (N= 98)

Linkage type	Percentage of firms with linkages (No. of responses)	
	Micron Technology	Hewlett-Packard
Customer	13.3% (13)	15.2% (15)
Supplier	9.2% (9)	16.2% (16)
Competitor	0% (0)	1.0% (1)
R&D partner	2.0% (2)	0% (0)
Not at all	75.5% (74)	67.7% (67)
Totals	**100% (98)**	**100% (99)**
No answer	37	36

Source: Boise Survey.

Many founders in this study reported a strong background in R&D (26.5 per cent), and only a few in marketing (8.8 per cent) or sales (5.5 per cent). Open-ended answers in the 'other' category (55.2 per cent) indicated that many have a technical or managerial background. This finding from the survey is supported by the interviews for this research, in which a majority indicated that they had held positions in R&D before starting their ventures. Those who worked for HP experienced similar career paths: they generally started as engineers (electrical, software, or mechanical) and progressed to managing groups within the company. There seems to be a strong likelihood that the engineer-manager is the type of person most likely to enter entrepreneurship (Breshnahan and Gambardella, 2004).

Regional Networking and Interaction

Does the presence of anchor firms like HP and Micron facilitate the development of an industrial cluster? Do high-tech firms in Boise engage with these anchor firms via customer or supplier relationships? As Table 5.9 shows, while most firms indicated that they do not engage with Micron or HP (68.4 per cent and 75.5 per cent respectively), a small subset do. We can see clear differences in these interactions. HP seems to have developed a larger set of backward (supplier) and forward (customer) linkages with locally based firms than Micron Technology: 15.3 per cent indicate that they are HP customers, while 13.3 per cent are Micron customers; and 16.3 per cent indicate that they are HP suppliers, while only 9.2 per cent are Micron suppliers. It seems that HP is more strongly connected than

Table 5.10   *Functional linkages of firm operations to other regions. 'Is the firm's manufacturing, R&D, or management located outside of Boise?' (N=94)*

Operations outside Boise	Yes	No
R&D	25.5% (24)	74.5% (70)
Manufacturing	20.2% (19)	79.8% (75)
Management	20.2% (19)	79.8% (75)

Source: Boise Survey.

Micron with the local high-tech economy via both backward and forward linkages. Apart from a few competitor firms, Micron has not attracted a large set of suppliers. This stands in contrast to the case of Portland where Intel, as described in Chapter 4, facilitated cluster development through the attraction of numerous suppliers and competitors. Neither Micron nor HP plays a role as R&D partner.

A significant number of firms in this sample indicated that their firm's manufacturing, R&D, or management operation was located outside of the Boise metropolitan region (see Table 5.10). About 25 per cent noted that their R&D staff were located somewhere else. Often these linkages were to California (Silicon Valley) or the Pacific Northwest (Portland and Seattle). About 20 per cent noted that their manufacturing and management were both located somewhere else. For manufacturing, the open-ended answers were split between Asian locations and other US locations. Interestingly, many of the firms with management in other regions mentioned that their executives lived in high-tech regions such as Silicon Valley. In the interviews, entrepreneurs noted that it was beneficial to have contacts in these regions because of the market connections they provide. This may indicate how Boise's high-tech entrepreneurs are connected to other high-tech economies. On the flip side, however, some entrepreneurs mentioned that Boise's high-tech economy does not provide alternative employment options for executives if a spin-off does not work out. Therefore, working with executives in other high-tech regions offers them a safety net.

Doing Business in Boise

As in Portland, Boise-based entrepreneurs ranked the most important region-specific advantages as quality of life for staff and management; informal local access to innovative people, ideas, and technologies; and local availability of managerial/professional staff (see Table 5.11). This

Table 5.11   Region-specific advantages for development in Boise (by mean rating). 'How important have the following been for your firm's development? (Score from 1-5 with 1 indicating completely unimportant and 5 indicating extremely important)'

Advantages	Valid N	Mean rating	Per cent indicating somewhat and extremely important	Per cent indicating extremely important
Attractive local quality of life for staff and management	96	4.28	84.38%	51.04%
Informal local access to innovative people, ideas, technologies	95	4.16	88.42%	37.89%
Local availability of managerial/ professional staff	96	3.57	56.25%	26.04%
Access to local business services	95	3.49	58.95%	9.47%
Availability of appropriate local premises	96	3.39	47.92%	13.54%
Credibility, reputation and prestige of Boise as a high-tech location	95	3.34	50.53%	13.68%
Proximity to local customers	96	3.21	51.04%	21.88%
Access to local sources of capital, finance	95	3.12	38.95%	17.89%
Access to international airports	94	3.11	42.55%	13.83%
Supportive local government services	96	3.09	43.75%	9.38%
Proximity to local suppliers, subcontractors	96	3.09	42.71%	10.42%
Quality of local research staff	95	3.04	33.68%	11.58%
Supportive local training organizations	96	3.04	41.67%	9.38%
Local availability of research staff	96	2.98	33.33%	8.33%
Local shareholders	96	2.78	30.21%	10.42%
Research links with other firms or organizations in region	96	2.70	33.33%	9.38%
Access to Silicon Valley	95	2.61	28.42%	6.32%
Research links with BSU	96	2.58	29.17%	6.25%
Research links with other ID-based universities	95	2.22	16.84%	3.16%

Source: Boise Survey.

Table 5.12   *Region-specific disadvantages for development in Boise
(by mean rating). 'Have any of the following constrained
your firm's development? (Score from 1-5 with 1 indicating
completely unimportant and 5 indicating extremely
important)'*

Disadvantages	Valid N	Mean rating	Per cent indicating somewhat and extremely important	Per cent indicating extremely important
Shortage of local skilled labour	91	3.66	62.6%	29.7%
Shortage of local marketing and sales skills	91	3.00	33.0%	13.2%
Difficulty in accessing local sources of capital, financing	91	2.90	34.1%	16.5%
Shortage of local managerial skills	91	2.85	28.6%	7.7%
Lack of local subcontractors	91	2.82	28.6%	3.3%
Lack of world-class research university	91	2.75	25.3%	7.7%
Shortage of local semiskilled labour	91	2.70	26.4%	5.5%
Shortage of research skills	91	2.70	23.1%	7.7%
Cost of premises locally	91	2.42	16.5%	4.4%
Inadequate local business services	91	2.40	12.1%	3.3%
Inadequate/costly environment for manufacturing	91	2.16	7.7%	1.1%
Lack of appropriate premises locally	91	2.07	6.6%	0.0%
Housing problems for staff	91	1.99	5.5%	0.0%

Source: Boise Survey.

survey finding corroborates the interview results. The majority of interviewees highlighted the fact that Boise offers a high quality of life, enabling
firms like HP and Micron to attract and retain knowledge workers. Firms
also rate the availability of managerial and professional staff as an important advantage. The development of anchor firms such as HP and Micron
may have been significant in this regard because these firms were able to
attract talent from outside the region. Boise respondents ranked research
links with universities lower than all the other factors. These rankings echo
the survey results for Portland, where this factor was also less important.

The survey also asked entrepreneurs about region-specific disadvantages (see Table 5.12). Respondents ranked a shortage of skilled labour
very highly, with 62.6 per cent indicating this was somewhat or extremely

important. Shortages in local marketing and sales skills were ranked as somewhat or extremely important by 33 per cent of the respondents. In addition, 28.6 per cent of respondents viewed the shortage of managerial skills as another important disadvantage, and 34.1 per cent noted the difficulty in accessing local sources of capital and financing as an important disadvantage.

The findings for both advantages and disadvantages parallel the results from the Portland survey. Second tier high-tech regions seem to trump with quality of life. They are also places where it is easy to access innovative ideas. Due to the presence of large anchor firms that often are market leaders in their respective industries, these regions have managed to create a labour pool of highly qualified professional, managerial, and research staff from which small start-up firms can draw. Research linkages with universities seem to play less of a role than the university's role in educating students who are then hired by the industry. The results for Portland and Boise also indicate a few problems for second tier high-tech regions: firms face severe local labour shortages and have a hard time accessing appropriate local sources of capital.

University-industry Linkages

Like Portland's Silicon Forest, Boise's does not host a large research university. Nevertheless, Boise's higher education system has come a long way. With about 20 000 students in 2010, Boise State University has become the largest university in the state. In recent years, the university has strategically focused on improving admission standards, striving for research excellence, and connecting with local industry. The BSU College of Engineering, founded in 1996, has been able to build close relationships with local industry. The BSU Technology and Entrepreneurial Centre (TECenter) was started in 2003 and assists with the development of start-up companies through business incubation and acceleration programmes.

How does the local high-tech industry interact with Boise State University? What role does the university play in helping local industry? What is the nature of university-industry relationships? As Table 5.13 shows, educating students is the most used function of the university, with 48.9 per cent of the respondents reporting that they hire BSU graduates. The second most important relationship is in the realm of small business development and support services, with 40 per cent of the respondents reporting that they have worked with the BSU TECenter. In addition, 36.7 per cent have used the Idaho Small Business Development Center (Idaho SBDC), a university-based organization offering consulting and training

Table 5.13   High-tech firms' relationships with Boise State University.
'Which of the following types of relationships has your firm
had with Boise State University? (Check all that apply)'
(N=90)

Type of relationship	Responses	Per cent
Hiring graduates	44	48.9%
Working with TECenter	36	40.0%
Using services from Idaho SBDC	33	36.7%
Other	29	32.2%
University staff as consultants	25	27.8%
Collaborative research project	16	17.8%
Company staff teaching classes	14	15.6%
Donations to university	13	14.4%
Using services offered by TechHelp	13	14.4%
Training programmes run by university	12	13.3%
Faculty working part-time with company	9	10.0%
Faculty on company's board	7	7.8%
Being part of research consortia involving university	3	3.3%
Licensing or patenting	1	1.1%

Source: Boise Survey.

to small businesses and entrepreneurs since 1986. And 27.8 per cent report
that they have used university staff as consultants. It is interesting to note
that more formal types of interaction between university and industry,
such as being part of a research consortium or through licensing and
patenting, occur less often.

CLUSTER DEVELOPMENT AND PUBLIC POLICY

Even though Boise has a highly innovative and entrepreneurial high-tech
community, the high-tech economy does not display strong clustering
dynamics (see Table 5.9 above). Unlike hub-and-spoke industrial districts
like Seattle (Gray, et al., 1996, 1999), HP and Micron do not engage in
extensive backward and forward linkages with the regional high-tech
economy. Neither firm has attracted many suppliers or competitors. The
survey results illustrate this: three quarters of the respondents have no
relationships with these two anchor firms. Boise also has relatively few
firms that specialize in servicing the high-tech industry (such as intellectual
property lawyers, human resource agencies, and specialized accountants).

While the region offers a set of generic support factors such as a competitive cost structure (labour, electricity, water, and so on) and high quality of life, specific aspects such as a strong business services industry or a specialized workforce and education infrastructure that support the industry are missing. For example, the region still does not have a community college system that would support the development of a specialized labour pool. Overall, certain aspects of cluster development are missing: strong inter-firm relationships, local demand conditions that encourage industry upgrading, specialized factor conditions, and a critical mass of related and supporting industries.

Boise also lags behind other high-tech regions in terms of a proactive public policy environment that would support the high-tech industry. This is illustrated by the efforts that have been underway in support of higher education. Traditionally the state has not invested heavily in R&D, and major policy programmes aimed at advancing a knowledge-based economy were repeatedly rejected by the legislature. Beginning in the late 1990s, state leaders – primarily business and higher education representatives – started to pay attention to the needs of a technology-based economy. Several planning efforts have been undertaken since then, but so far most legislative proposals have failed because of opposition from rural interests.

In 1999, Governor Dirk Kempthorne announced the formation of the Idaho Science and Technology Advisory Council (STAC) in the Idaho Department of Commerce (Idaho Department of Commerce, 2011). The council developed Idaho's first strategic plan for science and technology development which was released in early 2001. Underlying the strategy was the connection of various innovation actors and institutional frameworks that would guide the exchange of ideas and innovation. The plan called for investments in science and technology education, R&D, university-industry-research collaborations (including a so-called Research Excellence Initiative), commercialization and technology transfer, entrepreneurship, technology infrastructure, and marketing of Idaho as a location for technology firms (Office of Science and Technology, 2004). The report recommended the creation of a science and technology corporation. It also recommended establishing a commercialization and technology transfer system to leverage resources at Idaho's universities and the Idaho National Laboratory, which is located about four and a half hours east of Boise in Idaho Falls. The governor incorporated the STAC's recommendations in his 2001 budget. However, most of these proposals failed to get the support of the legislature due to the politicians' bias towards rural interests, and so were not funded.

As a result of the STAC's first round of deliberations, in 2004 the state created the Office of Science and Technology (OST) within the Idaho Commerce and Labor Department to focus on high-tech industries and their potential to contribute to economic development in the state. Also in 2004, the STAC was reconstituted to assess the state's progress in science and technology and to provide an update to the strategic plan. The action plan priorities the council prepared this time were similar to those of 2001 (Office of Science and Technology and Idaho Commerce and Labor, 2004). In addition to the update, the council prepared an assessment of Idaho's core competencies and developed a commercialization concept for the state. The council continued with its work towards strengthening collaboration and innovation among universities, laboratories, and industry within the state by creating innovation centres and hiring key professors. This work provided the basis for Governor Kempthorne's 2007 budget request in 2006, but it too was rejected by the legislature, when lawmakers considered how to disburse a $214 million surplus. The only budget requests legislators funded at the time were rural initiatives such as a $5 million investment in rural broadband services.

During 2006, the council made a third attempt and proposed a $48.8 million economic stimulus package. The recommendations included $10 million in tax credits for investments in technology and bioscience companies and $38.8 million for investments in education, R&D, marketing, business incubators, and infrastructure. It is interesting to note that the proposal did not include a focus on funding collaboration, university-industry partnerships, or commercialization activities, as the earlier one did. Perhaps the numerous failed attempts discouraged the council to include these items. A small amount was incorporated in the proposal to provide $1.4 million in funding for the Research Matching Grant Program which would meet the 1:2 match requirement of the federal National Science Foundation's 2008 EPSCoR Research Infrastructure Improvement grant. The majority of investment recommendations were focused on tax credits, small business assistance, postsecondary education, and investments in Idaho's TechConnect office, a state-wide organization that focuses on assisting entrepreneurs which was founded in 2002.

When the council's third set of proposals were presented, Idaho had a new governor. In 2007, CL 'Butch' Otter did not consider the council's recommendation in his 2008 budget request. Instead, he included $38 million for a needs-based scholarship endowment fund, $5 million for community colleges, a one-time increase of $15 million for the Higher Education Research Council (HERC) for research projects that facilitated economic development (this included research being conducted by the three universities at the Center for Advanced Energy Studies, a joint venture between the universities and the Idaho National Laboratory

(Otter, 2007)), and $10.9 million for a dairy and animal research and education facility. Otter's proposal to invest $15 million in the HERC topped the council's recommendation of a $1.4 million investment in this programme. According to the HERC's policies and procedures, the money could be allocated to infrastructure and research, but there were no specific requirements on how universities interact with industry. The HERC operates the Technology Incentive Grant Program which was developed by the State Board of Education to enhance instruction and to increase faculty productivity. There is no indication that the HERC funds university-industry partnerships, technology transfer, or commercialization of research.

Battles over science and technology funding continued into 2008. The state's budget allocated some funding to TechConnect and $1.6 million for the Center for Advanced Energy Studies in Idaho Falls, $1.4 million for the HERC, a one-time appropriation of $1.6 million for competitive research grants, and $1.5 million to foster innovative learning. That year, the governor also disbanded the Science and Technology Advisory Council. As a response to the retreating gubernatorial leadership, Idaho's technology businesses self-organized and created the Idaho Technology Council, a private-sector membership group interested in advancing the high-tech economy and science and technology issues in the state.

Still Idaho's governor Otter seems to be sceptical of state investments in R&D. In the *Idaho Business Review*, he said that 'some states making investments aren't getting a return on investments' (Kovsky, 2007). STAC members seem to be disappointed about the lack of gubernatorial support. One former STAC member noted in the interview: 'if you don't have support of the governor, it is challenging to initiate recommendations. The only way to measure our effectiveness is to give us the ability to try something' (Crawforth interview, 2007). Some interviewees in this study (Reed interview, 2007; Solon interview, 2007) lamented that Idaho's legislature and governor are more supportive of rural interests than the needs of the emerging technology economy based in the state's largest urban areas. While some sectors that receive investments (such as those related to agriculture, bioscience, and energy) may connect well with rural interests, others that would be more relevant to the state's urban high-tech economies (such as the semiconductor and software industries in Boise) have not benefited from state investments. The strong urban-rural divide may be responsible for the lack of support, despite the need to invest in a knowledge-based economy in urban areas like Boise.

While large firms such as Micron Technology and HP have successfully shaped public policy (especially as it relates to higher education and corporate tax breaks), they have not been as vocal in the discussions about a statewide science and technology strategy that would foster innovation, commercialization, and technology transfer. These large firms may have 'long arms' that can reach to sources of innovation outside of the state, and therefore they may not be as interested in state policies in support of innovation. In contrast, small start-up firms would have benefited more from the proposed science and technology programmes and investments. It remains to be seen if private-sector coalitions – as organized in the Idaho Technology Council – will continue to lobby for these initiatives.

CONCLUSIONS

This chapter traced the evolution of Boise as a second tier high-tech region. The research highlights the following key observations. First, Boise's high-tech economy evolved because of the presence of two anchor firms, HP and Micron Technology. These anchor firms served the region as 'surrogate universities' through the development of talent, creation of innovation, and the formation of spin-off companies. Second, while both firms recruited and developed talent, they influenced regional economic development differently in terms of innovation and entrepreneurship. The firms differed in terms of their innovation model. While HP focuses on product innovations, Micron engages in process innovation. These differences influence the extent to which each firm engages with the local economy through backward and forward linkages. Third, entrepreneurship is a driving force in Boise's high-tech economy. Even though the two anchor firms are the region's largest employers, HP had a greater influence on entrepreneurship than Micron. Entrepreneurial firms diversify the economy through their entry into new markets. Fourth, Boise's high-tech economy represents a cluster that is growing and evolving rather than mature and specialized. Fifth and lastly, public policy efforts in Idaho have not been as forceful as in Portland's Silicon Forest, and the state's policymakers have so far shown limited support for urban industries such as high-tech. In contrast, the various grassroots activities by the private sector show promising engagement by entrepreneurs and high-tech representatives.

What is the future of Boise as a second tier high-tech region? There are several aspects of the Boise economy that indicate that the region is standing on shaky ground. Unlike Portland, where the high-tech community was able to diversify through the creation of larger firms and evolve beyond its anchor firms Intel and Tektronix, Boise has not been able to grow much beyond its largest employers, HP and Micron. The region's other firms are primarily small businesses. More than three quarters (77 per cent) employ fewer than nine people, and a mere 3.4 per cent employ more than 100. None of the spin-offs has reached employment levels beyond a small-to-medium-sized enterprise (more than 250 employees). This creates a strong dependency on the fate of the two anchor firms. During their growth phase, these two firms shaped Boise's technology community in positive ways. Yet in recent years, they have shed employment and undertaken significant restructuring efforts to focus on core activities. Micron, for example, has dropped about 3500 jobs between 2008 and 2009. These lay-offs included about 500 employees who worked in Micron's 200 mm wafer fabrication operation, which was shut down in 2009. The cyclical nature of the memory semiconductor market was partially responsible for the lay-offs, reflected in Micron's dismal bottom line. After three years of significant losses, Micron moved back into profit again during the first quarter of 2010. Market fluctuation is not the only reason Micron has had such a dismal record. More important are the corporate changes and resulting geographic shifts the company has undergone in recent years. While Micron will continue to operate R&D facilities and corporate functions such as product design, quality assurance, and systems integration in Boise, in recent years the firm has created additional manufacturing capacities in distant locations, opening a manufacturing facility in Utah and acquiring the assets of other firms in regions like Virginia, Italy and Singapore. Micron's recent move into China indicates an increased emphasis on adding capacities in low-cost environments, and these developments might represent a new type of business model that other large integrated semiconductor manufacturing operations are following. As a result, the Boise economy is much more vulnerable to changes nowadays than it used to be. Micron's lay-offs and the general downturn in the economy following the 2008 global financial crisis led to a significant increase in the region's unemployment rate, which climbed to 9.1 per cent in August 2010 from a low of 2.7 per cent in 2006.

These developments should alarm the state's policymakers and politicians. Yet neither Idaho nor the Boise region has developed a coherent strategy to support the high-tech industry cluster. This vacuum is currently being filled by various grassroots efforts. In 2009, a group of high-tech industry professionals formed the Idaho Technology Council. This member-driven, non-governmental professional association is modelled after its successful counterpart in Utah. In contrast to Utah, however, where Republican governors partnered with the state's business community to develop various programmes in support of the technology community, including funding for higher education and the development of local sources of funding for entrepreneurs, Idaho's politicians still cling to resource-based sectors and traditional location factors such as taxes and regulations.

NOTES

1. The surface mount centre was a manufacturing division that produced electronic circuits for which components were mounted on the surface of a printed circuit board.
2. Commodity semiconductors are mass produced chips that are used in a variety of consumer products. They are called commodity because they can be produced in a standardized fashion and in high volumes.
3. Micron Electronics was acquired by Gores Technology Group in 2001 and from then on was known as MicronPC. MicronPC did not survive and shut down in 2008.

6. Kansas City: growing a second tier life sciences region in the heartland

'There are times in the lives of great cities when they seem caught, almost suspended, between their past and their future. This is such a time for Kansas City. The city stands with one leg planted in an old economy of manufacturing, rail transportation and low-skill jobs, while the other leg is striding briskly into the knowledge economy of high-tech jobs, complex information systems and the dazzling intellectual revolution of the life sciences. Can Kansas City be a center of excellence in the relentless competition of the global knowledge economy?'

Greater Kansas City Community Foundation (2005: 3)

INTRODUCTION TO THE ECONOMY IN KANSAS CITY

The previous chapters described the growth of regional high-tech economies. Portland's Silicon Forest was seeded by firms that produce test and measurement instruments and semiconductors. Boise's high-tech economy is similarly specialized. In both regions, firms such as Tektronix, Intel, HP, and Micron Technology helped shape their surroundings through their innovation efforts and entrepreneurial activities. Can the dynamics of growth in these high-tech economies be generalized to regions that host a different set of knowledge-based industries such as biotechnology or life sciences? Are second tier life sciences regions similar to second tier high-tech regions? In this chapter I explore the case of a second tier life sciences region: the evolution and growth of the life sciences economy in Kansas City.

The quotation at the start of this chapter hints at the changes the Kansas City economy is facing. Located at the confluence of the Kansas and Missouri rivers, Kansas City's economy traditionally specialized in transportation, warehousing, and distribution. Yet the region is experiencing significant economic changes, and its leaders are focusing on the potentials of an emerging life sciences economy. Kansas City is a mid-size city in the Midwest of the US. Its population stands at about 1.9 million, and the metropolitan region is divided between the states of Kansas and Missouri. Kansas City is known for its rich cultural and culinary history (the jazz style Bebop was developed in Kansas City and Kansas City-style barbeque is widely known for its slow smoked meat) and also for its grand boulevards that shape the urban landscape – and has an economy that is surprisingly diverse and robust. The region is home to three Fortune 500 headquarters (the telecommunication firm Sprint Nextel Corporation, the tax preparation company H&R Block, and the transportation service provider YRC Worldwide) and also hosts the headquarters of nationally known firms such as Applebee's, Hallmark Cards, and Garmin International, among others. The region has weathered economic recessions better than similar cities, primarily due to its diversified economic structure. In recent years, Kansas City also has experienced inner-city revitalization and a downtown development boom.

While Kansas City boasts a relatively diverse and stable economy, the region is not performing well on a variety of measures related to innovative research and entrepreneurialism. Kansas City-based inventors are registering patents well below the national average; the region ranks very low in terms of the amount of research and development funding it receives; its colleges and universities award a relatively small number of advanced academic degrees each year; and regional entrepreneurs have not been able to obtain many federal small business grants or venture capital deals (Vey, 2006). Like Portland and Boise, Kansas City lacks a world-class research university, a shortcoming regional leaders have repeatedly lamented (Greater Kansas City Community Foundation, 2005, 2010). Despite these challenges, the region's economy is – as the quote above suggests – 'striding briskly into the knowledge economy' (Greater Kansas City Community Foundation, 2005: 3). A variety of firms in sectors as diverse as life sciences, telecommunications, and information technology are playing an important role in reshaping the economy, attracting and developing talent, and functioning as entrepreneurial seedbeds. In addition, significant investments have been made in area research institutions and universities, and the region's policymakers have developed programmes to boost technology transfer and commercialization. While the goal of becoming the next Silicon Valley or the hottest new biotechnology centre is likely out of reach, Kansas City has significant potential to emerge as a second tier location for firms in the life sciences sector.

KANSAS CITY'S LIFE SCIENCES ECONOMY

Kansas City region's life sciences industries specialize in a number of subsectors including clinical research, drug development and delivery, animal health and nutrition, and basic biomedical research about genes and proteins. The industry is rather small, especially compared to metropolitan areas that lead the field. However, a closer look at the specialization and industrial structure of certain sub-sectors reveals that Kansas City has some unique competitive strengths and advantages.

In 2004 the region's 330 life sciences firms employed a total of 10473 people.[1] The life sciences industry is anchored by firms engaged in pharmaceutical manufacturing and in clinical trials and drug development. Kansas City's strength in pharmaceutical manufacturing goes back to the establishment of Marion Laboratories, a pharmaceutical manufacturing company that was founded in 1950 in Kansas City by Ewing Marion Kauffman. What is left of Marion today are the manufacturing operations of Sanofi-Aventis, a pharmaceutical firm headquartered in France, and Quintiles Transnational Corporation, a clinical research organization headquartered in North Carolina's Research Triangle Park. Sanofi's Kansas City operations are among the firm's primary manufacturing sites, where approximately 370 employees manufacture drugs such as Allegra, Amaryl, and Ketek. In 2010, however, Sanofi announced that it will phase out manufacturing in Kansas City. The presence of Marion Laboratories and later its subsequent operations, including Sanofi-Aventis, triggered the development of several clinical research organizations and small life sciences companies. Today Kansas City is home to firms such as LabOne (now Quest Diagnostics), Clinical Reference Laboratory, Laboratory Corporation of America, Regular Clinical Consultants (now PRA International), Phylogenetix Laboratories, and Quintiles.

Kansas City ranks second in the nation behind the Research Triangle Park area in hosting firms that perform contract research for pharmaceutical purposes. Contract research organizations provide pharmaceutical research, testing, development, clinical trials, and associated services to other pharmaceutical and biotechnology companies. According to a 2003 study (Thomas Miller and Associates, 2003), half of all Kansas City life sciences firms are classified as clinical research organizations (75 firms). In addition, Kansas City-based life sciences firms specialize in the development and commercialization of pharmaceutical products and drugs, employing an estimated 4000 people (Thomas Miller and Associates, 2003). Companies such as Teva Neuroscience, CyDex, Proteon Therapeutics, and Pharmion (now Celgene Corporation) are part of this sub-sector. Many firms doing contract research or drug development are spin-offs from Marion Laboratories. In addition, Kansas City hosts one of the nation's best-funded biological and molecular research organizations, the Stowers Institute for Medical Research.

Most life sciences firms are located within the Kansas City metropolitan region. While the cities of St Joseph, Missouri, and Lawrence, Kansas, are

Table 6.1   Major industry sectors in Kansas City MSA, 2004

Industry sector	Total employment	Number of firms	Average annual wages
Life sciences[1]	10473	330	$52735
Telecommunications	25471	375	$72014
Information technology	12498	1321	$71995

Notes: 1. The life sciences industry was defined using the NAICS codes listed in the Kansas Economic Growth Act. We excluded NAICS 54194 since this category primarily includes licensed veterinary practitioners who are typically not associated with life sciences research and innovation.

Source: Bureau of Labor Statistics, Quarterly Census of Employment and Wages.

not included in the official US Census definition of the Kansas City MSA, the majority of interviewees acknowledged their economic importance to the region's life sciences sector. Several studies have included these two areas in their assessments of the industry (Burress et al., 2004; Thomas Miller and Associates, 2003). The St Joseph area is home to a vibrant cluster of companies working in the fields of animal health and nutrition, as well as agricultural chemicals. The local chamber of commerce estimates employment in this sub-sector at 4600 and lists 16 companies. The broader Kansas City region is known as the 'Animal Health Corridor' (Animal Health Corridor, 2007) where firms such as Boehringer Ingelheim, Vetmedica, Friskies PetCare, and Phoenix Scientific are located. Together the animal health and nutrition industry located in this corridor captures about 40 per cent of the North American animal health and nutrition market (New Economy Strategies, 2004).

Over the past couple of years nearby Douglas County, Kansas, and its urban centre Lawrence have become the location of choice for a handful of bioscience firms, a trend due in large part to the presence of the University of Kansas and its expanding life sciences research programme. A 2004 study for the Lawrence Chamber of Commerce estimates that there are about eight bioscience firms in the area employing an estimated 170 people (Rosenbloom et al., 2004). Table 6.1 shows the major industry sectors in the Kansas City metropolitan area.

Compared to other regions, Kansas City's life sciences economy is rather small and less powerful in terms of its research and commercialization potential. Table 6.2 compares Kansas City's biotech industry to that of San Francisco and Raleigh-Durham (also known as Research Triangle Park). The San Francisco region counts as one of the most important biotechnology regions in the US, ranking just behind Boston in terms of

Table 6.2   Comparing Kansas City's biotech industry to San Francisco and Raleigh-Durham

Feature	Kansas City	San Francisco	Raleigh-Durham
Biomedical research infrastructure			
Life scientists (1998)	220	3090	910
Number of institutions granting PhDs (1999)	1	3	3
Number of PhDs granted (1999)	11	215	166
Top-ranked research universities (1982)	0	3	1
NIH funding (2000)	$27 921 183	$703 529 044	$469 119 754
NIH funding share to top 100 cities (2000)	0.20%	6.0%	4.0%
NIH funding change in share for medical schools (1985–2000)	0.10%	–1.2%	0.7%
Number of biotechnology-related patents (1975–99)	183	5578	1027
Biotechnology commercialization infrastructure			
Venture capital investments, number of deals (1995–2001)	1	261	54
Venture capital investments, amount (1995–2001)	$12 000 000	$3 028 917 500	$379 687 000
Highly active venture capital firms (1995–2001)	0	21	2
Initial public offerings (1998–2001)	0	31	1
Value of R&D alliances (millions, until 2001)	0	$2792	$225

Source: Cortright and Mayer, 2002.

biomedical research infrastructure capacity and National Institutes of Health funding. San Francisco stands out among biotechnology centres for its ability to commercialize biotechnology innovations. This success is indicated by high levels of venture capital funding, a large number of active venture capital firms, and a large number of established and newly emerging biotech firms. Raleigh-Durham has emerged in recent years as a so-called biotechnology challenger region (Cortright and Mayer, 2002). Its firms specialize in biomanufacturing and pharmaceutical manufacturing, contract manufacturing, and medical device manufacturing (Lowe,

2007). Cortright and Mayer (2002) count both regions among the top nine biotechnology centres in the US.

As Table 6.2 indicates, Kansas City does not belong to this premier league of biotechnology regions. It ranks low on measures of both bio-medical research infrastructure and biotechnology commercialization. Other measures of biotechnology industry activity also show a wide gap in terms of research and commercialization capacity between Kansas City and the two leading biotech centres.

DYNAMICS OF GROWTH: FIRM BUILDING AND ENTREPRENEURSHIP

Kansas City's emergence as a second tier life sciences region is rooted in similar processes of firm building and entrepreneurship as we observed for Portland and Boise. The region's life sciences economy started in 1950 with the founding of Marion Laboratories, a firm that specializes in bring-ing pharmaceutical products through the regulatory approval process and into the market, but never developed a significant research capacity. Marion Laboratories' influence was primarily the development of a labour pool with specialized expertise in drug development, testing, regulatory approval, and market research. It also functioned as an incubator for a handful of spin-off companies (see Table 6.3). As a result, Kansas City was able to establish a strong track record in clinical research and drug development and testing. The mere presence of Marion Laboratories and its spin-offs, however, was not sufficient to propel Kansas City into a second tier life science region from the outset. Several other developments shaped this evolution. In 2000 Kansas City's life sciences industry received an extraordinary boost: a philanthropic gift of $2 billion by local entre-preneurs, which established the Stowers Institute for Medical Research. The Institute's endowment is the largest endowment in the world solely devoted to basic life sciences research (Greater Kansas City Community Foundation, 2005). After the Stowers Institute was established, local industry representatives and policymakers started to become proactive. They created the Kansas City Area Life Sciences Institute (KCALSI), an organization that encourages networking and collaboration between life sciences firms, hospitals, and universities. These industry-based efforts to grow a life sciences economy triggered a significant public policy response, which I describe in the following sections. I begin by tracing the evolution of firms and research organizations in the region and illustrate their con-tribution in the realm of firm building, human capital development, and entrepreneurship.

The Legacy of Marion Laboratories

Kansas City's strength in contract research and pharmaceutical development goes back to the establishment of Marion Laboratories, founded by Ewing Marion Kauffman in 1950. Kauffman, who grew up in Missouri, started his career as a pharmaceutical salesman working for Illinois-based Lincoln Laboratories. Lacking a formal education in medicine or pharmacy, Kauffman acquired his knowledge of the industry through reading industry journals and talking to the doctors whom he visited on his sales tours (Morgan, 1995). Kauffman founded Marion Laboratories to sell injectables and prescription drugs to doctors in the Kansas City region. As an entrepreneurial sales person, he developed a business model based on development and marketing of pharmaceutical products, for which basic research was done by other companies, often firms outside the US. Marion Labs never developed an in-house basic research capacity. Instead, it established a business model known as 'search and develop' (a model that uses research breakthroughs developed by other firms and turns them into marketable products), through which it attracted and developed a labour force that became highly skilled in clinical testing and in regulatory matters of drug development, sales, and marketing (Skodack, 1992).

Using this business model, Marion Laboratories grew into a flourishing company. During the 1950s Marion's most successful product was Os-Cal, a bone strengthening supplement, and by the late 1950s its sales stood at $1 million. Pavabid, a drug that increases the blood flow throughout the body, helped propel Marion's sales to more than $30 million by 1970. The company had an initial public offering on the New York Stock Exchange in 1965, and in an effort to diversify during the late 1960s and early 1970s began a series of acquisitions of related companies (Morgan, 1995). During the late 1970s the firm's performance sagged because of difficulties with federal drug approval, spurring it to divest non-core business units and begin to license and market new drugs (Keenan, 1985). By the 1980s, however, Marion belonged to the group of leading pharmaceutical companies in the US, and its success was based on the development and marketing of a few key drugs. By the mid-1980s, Marion employed about 2100 people in Kansas City to develop, test, manufacture, and market pharmaceutical products. Marion's success helped embed the firm deeply in the Kansas City region. In addition, Kauffman's philanthropic activities, such as his efforts to establish the Kansas City Royals as a major league baseball team and the founding of the Ewing Marion Kauffman Foundation as a grant-maker focused on entrepreneurship and education, further deepened Marion Labs' commitment to the region.

The late 1980s brought a series of changes to Marion's ownership structure and ultimately also to Marion's regional commitment. To keep Marion Laboratories growing and profitable by adding strengths in basic research, the company's executives decided to merge with Merrell Dow Pharmaceuticals, a division of the Dow Chemical Company, to form Marion Merrell Dow in 1989 (Heaster, 1989). Kansas City became the headquarters location of the newly created company, which continued to expand over the coming years. Merrell Dow complemented Marion's strengths in development and marketing, and enhanced the firm's emphasis on the discovery phase in the R&D process. Additional changes occurred in the early 1990s. In 1993 a broad restructuring process led to the first lay-offs, and in 1995 German-based Hoechst acquired Marion Merrell Dow and formed Hoechst Marion Roussel. The firm remained headquartered in Kansas City. The merger with Hoechst created the world's third largest pharmaceutical company, tripled Marion's sales, and catapulted the Kansas City-based firm into the global pharmaceutical market. In 1995, Hoechst Marion Roussel had $3.1 billion in sales and $438 million in net profits (Morgan, 1995). Kansas City remained a strategic manufacturing site, and all new products were introduced from there. Additional ownership changes, however, were on the horizon. In 1998 the North Carolina company Quintiles Transnational bought the drug development and approval operation of Hoechst Marion Roussel. This division is still operating in Kansas City as a contract facility and it has partnered with Marion's successor firms and with other local pharmaceutical drug manufacturers. In 1999, Hoechst merged with Rhone-Poulenc to form Aventis, and this time the Kansas City-based operation lost its headquarters status. As a result, 900 administrative jobs were moved to New Jersey, of which about 130 were filled by Kansas City employees. The remaining 770 employees preferred to stay and look for alternative employment opportunities in the region (Karash, 1999; Stafford, 2001). Hoechst had decided to move the North American headquarters despite a large incentive package offered by state and local authorities. One reason was the attraction of the New Jersey area as the premier location for pharmaceutical companies, improving the company's ability to hire qualified talent and to be close to other research-oriented large pharmaceutical companies. A small manufacturing operation remained in Kansas and by 2001 it employed about 900 people and manufactured drugs such as Allegra, Cardizem and Ketec. The mergers and acquisitions, however, continued, and in 2004 Sanofi acquired Aventis and the new firm became known as Sanofi-Aventis. In 2010, however, Sanofi announced that it would phase out manufacturing in Kansas City.

Marion Laboratories' business model influenced the evolution of Kansas City's life sciences economy in important ways. Marion Laboratories never developed strengths in basic research and therefore did not contribute to the formation of a strong research base in the Kansas City life sciences community. Marion Laboratories never developed drugs from scratch. Instead, the firm formed partnerships with pharmaceutical research companies outside of the Kansas City region (Etkin, 1979). Kauffman biographer Anne Morgan writes that in the early years:

> the company had neither the funds nor the personnel to conduct basic research, so Kauffman added to the standard offerings with new products which he licensed from other pharmaceutical houses or drug manufacturers. By the mid-sixties, purchasing marketing rights of a specific product for a specified term and territory would become standard practice for Marion. Recognizing that the company lacked the resources to develop an in-house scientific research program, Marion Laboratories became dependent on locating, licensing, and bringing to market the discoveries of others. (Morgan, 1995: 85)

New product development initially took place informally and later was expanded to include more formal searches for licensing partners. In the 1960s Marion Laboratories established a new products committee and its members scanned the literature for promising medical developments. After Marion Laboratories went public in 1969, the search for new products became more important, so it was formalized, and the geographic focus was widened. Marion Laboratories formed licensing agreements with firms in Panama, Sweden, and Japan, among others, and was able to find new bestselling drugs without in-house research. Once a product was identified for licensing, Marion employees in Kansas City analysed the product's characteristics and information, including patents, samples, and clinical data. Various in-house departments (technical, medical, marketing, and so on) were involved in assessing market potential. In some cases, Marion's R&D team altered a product's appearance (for example transforming Gaviscon, Marion's first foreign licensed product, into a more chewable tablet). Often universities across the US were involved in conducting tests of the products with patients. This widespread search-and-develop method had significant advantages: without the need to make large investments in basic research, Marion could focus on developing its marketing and sales expertise. This set Marion apart from its competitors such as Merck, Lilly, or Hoffman-LaRoche. The process was also less time consuming: licensing products and bringing them to market often took less than a year, while new product development could take many years.

Marion's business model and the company's evolution, as described above, had important implications for the Kansas City regional economy. Marion never developed strong in-house research capacities. Marion employees engaged in applied research primarily as it related to optimizing drugs for the US market. Marion developed expertise in licensing products, bringing drugs through the regulatory approval process, as well as testing and optimizing the drugs. Marion's orientation towards applied research however never helped build a strong industrial research capacity in the Kansas City region and Marion never functioned as an innovation hub for the region – with limited entrepreneurial spin-off activity. Unlike leading biotech or life sciences regions, Kansas City was not able to leverage the presence of Marion Labs to spur significant growth in life sciences. This is an important point because research on biotech and life science regions has shown that the presence of research-intensive institutions (firms, universities, research institutes, and so on) is critical for the development and growth of the industry. Zucker and Darby (1996), for example, have shown that the involvement of star scientists in research and commercialization is a key determinant of where and when new biotech firms emerge

The lack of a research-intensive institution that could spur additional development, especially in the form of entrepreneurial spin-offs, limited the ability of Kansas City to develop its life sciences industry. Spin-off activities around Marion Laboratories were limited to a few firms that emerged primarily as a result of Marion's mergers and acquisitions in the late 1980s. These corporate changes spurred an exodus of valuable Marion employees. One interviewee, a former management executive for Marion, noted that the first merger (with Dow) affected upper management more than other levels and recalled that 12 out of 14 executive officers left the firm (Herman interview, 2005).

The upside of these changes was that they created the impetus for entrepreneurial activities, including the formation of new companies. Most former Marion employees did not leave the region because they were rooted in Kansas City. They either found another local job or became entrepreneurs themselves. This location inertia facilitated Kansas City's initial development as a second tier life sciences region.

One example of a Marion spin-off illustrates the effects of location inertia. Pharmion, a pharmaceutical company focused on hematology and oncology, was started in 1999 by former Marion employee Judith Hemberger and Colorado-based Patrick Mahaffy. From the start the company operated in two locations: its headquarters in Boulder, Colorado, and Overland Park in Kansas City. Pharmion's presence in Kansas City reflects the region's expertise in regulatory affairs, drug development, and clinical testing because about 40 employees – many of whom are former Marion employees – work in these areas at the Kansas City facility. The founders were able to tap their Marion networks in Kansas City for both readily available labour and specialized support services (Strohmeier interview, 2005). Drawing on these resources was important for a spin-off company like Pharmion.

Altogether, former Marion Laboratories employees are involved with at least 17 other firms (see Table 6.3). These firms are either direct spin-offs from Marion or, like Pharmion, have set up part of their operations in the Kansas City region. Most of them have adopted Marion's business model of licensing from biotechnology companies and specialize in developing and marketing pharmaceutical products. Some, like ImmunoGenetix Therapeutic, partner with local university researchers.

Marion's legacy went beyond the creation of a specialized labour pool to significantly influence the corporate practices and organizational principles of many Kansas City-based life sciences firms. Several Marion spin-offs – including RxCCI, CyDex, and Medi-Flex – adopted Marion's business practices, including the culture of meritocracy and profit sharing programmes. Other home-grown firms, such as Cerner Corporation, a health care information technology company, consciously copied the Marion model and call their employees associates. In addition, corporate (that is human resources) practices have been adopted by entrepreneurs who experienced them first-hand during their time at Marion. It was often these ex-Marion employees who were instrumental in shaping the cultures of their new firms.

In sum, Marion contributed significantly to the creation of a specialized labour pool in Kansas City, as well as to the founding of new firms that often specialized in the same industry and in some cases even adopted the Marion business model. There is not much left of Marion Laboratories after all the mergers and acquisitions. What remains are strong networks of former Marion employees and new start-up companies working in closely related fields. Still, while Marion's legacy is important, the company did not profoundly influence the region's capacity to innovate and create knowledge. Marion Laboratories' research efforts focused primarily on developing and testing pharmaceutical compounds. Marion employees knew how to test, package, and market pharmaceutical products, but basic research was done elsewhere, mostly at laboratories outside the region. As a result, this model of 'small R and big D' (Laufenberg interview, 2005) did not produce spillover effects in the form of path-breaking research areas and new ideas that would be commercialized by entrepreneurs. Coupled with the lack of a world-class research university, Kansas City has thus not been able to match the success of other life sciences or biotech regions where the commercialization of research and ideas benefited from the presence of institutions that engage in research and scientific discovery.

Table 6.3   History of Marion Laboratories and its spin-off companies,
1950–2005

Events associated with Marion Laboratories	Year	Companies founded by ex-Marion Lab employees
Marion Laboratories founded by Ewing Marion Kauffman	1950	
Marion Labs goes public	1965	
Marion Labs receives licence for Carafate	1975	
	1976	Beckloff & Associates founded
Marion Labs has bad economic performance	Late 1970s	
Marion Labs divests several business units to refocus	Early 1980s	Spin-offs: American Stair-Glide, Kalo Laboratories, Marion Scientific, Rockwill Safety & Health
Marion Labs begins to sell Cardizem	1982	
	1983	CyDex founded by ex-Marion employee Peter Higuchi
Marion Labs employs 2148, with about 500 in R&D	1985	Medi-Flex formed through a leveraged buyout by Joe Brandemeyer
Marion Labs expands R&D staff and grows by about 100	1987	
	1988	EPIQ Systems (formerly known as Electronic Processing, Inc. – EPI)
Marion Labs merges with Dow Chemical to form **Marion Merrell Dow**, headquartered in Kansas City	1989	
Marion Merrell Dow is expanding	1990	
Marion Merrell Dow employs 2500	1992	Rip Grossman & Associates
Marion Merrell Dow announces 1300 job cuts, first lay-offs in history; R&D is spared	1993	
German-based Hoechst acquires Marion Merrell Dow and forms **Hoechst Marion Roussel**; Kansas City is US headquarters	1995	

Table 6.3   (continued)

Events associated with Marion Laboratories	Year	Companies founded by ex-Marion Lab employees
	1997	IMTCI sold to PRA International; operation stays in Lenexa, KS
Quintiles Transnational Corp. buys drug development and approval operation from Hoechst Marion Roussel; works with them as a contract research organization, keeping 500 employees	1998	Regulatory/Clinical Consultants, Inc. (RxCCI) founded by Diane Saif
Hoechst merges with Rhone-Poulenc to form *Aventis*; headquarters and 130 people moved to New Jersey; loss of 900 white-collar jobs	1999	InTouch Solution founded by Faruk Capan
Aventis employs about 1300 in Kansas City, mainly industrial and distribution-related jobs	2000	Cultural Horizons founded Ex-Marion employees found Pharmion in Kansas City
	2001	Teva Neuroscience formed from Teva Marion Partner
	2002	ImmunoGenetix Therapeutic founded by Jim Lauffenberg
Hostile takeover of Aventis	2004	
by Sanofi Synthelabo forms *Sanofi-Aventis* to manufacture Allegra and Ketek; 850 employed	2005	Regulatory/Clinical Consultants (RxCCI) sold to PRA International

Source: Author's analysis.

BUILDING RESEARCH CAPACITY: THE STOWERS INSTITUTE

Although Marion Laboratories never completely fulfilled the role of a surrogate university, the region's research infrastructure got a boost when the Stowers Institute for Medical Research (Stowers) opened its facility in November 2000. It was established by a philanthropic endowment of $2 billion by Jim and Virginia Stowers, local entrepreneurs who had founded American Century Investments. In contrast to the region's commercial firms, Stowers conducts high-level basic research in biological and molecular sciences. Stowers 'seeks more effective means of preventing and curing disease through basic research on genes and proteins that control fundamental processes of cellular life' and aspires to be 'the most innovative biomedical research organization in the world' (The Stowers Institute for Medical Research, 2011), supporting its researchers to achieve world-class excellence in their respective areas. Its facilities and laboratories are designed to provide a high-quality research environment for a maximum of about 30 research groups. To date, Stowers employs about 500 people and runs about 24 independent research programmes, and plans are in place to expand its facilities. The establishment of the Stowers Institute and the size of the endowment put Kansas City on the map for global biomedical research. Its endowment is already larger than all the biomedical research institutions in San Diego combined, and it has been called 'the largest endowment in the world devoted to basic life sciences research' (Greater Kansas City Community Foundation, 2005: 37).

Planning for Stowers goes back to the early 1990s when its founders began thinking about their estate and making a philanthropic contribution to their hometown. Initially they were confronted with a lot of scepticism regarding the location. As the co-chairman of the Stowers' Board of Directors recalls, 'some advisors told Jim Stowers that he could not build a world-class research facility in Kansas City' (Brown interview, 2005). Jim Stowers had heard such criticism before when he founded his mutual fund management company in Kansas City and had proven a lot of sceptics wrong. He was determined to prove them wrong one more time.

During the planning phase, Stowers travelled across the country to gather information about how to best set up a research institute. These conversations with researchers led the institute to adopt a philosophy based on excellence in basic research. To achieve excellence, the institute built a high-quality research facility, created a supportive and collaborative environment, and attracted researchers who are among the best in their respective fields. The incentives Stowers can offer to researchers, as well as its budding national and international reputation, have contributed to a high rate of success in recruiting leading scientists from all around the world to come to work in Kansas City.

As a premier research institution Stowers can play an important role in the Kansas City economy, even though direct economic effects (such as a large number of spin-offs) have yet to materialize. By 2006 Stowers researchers had not spun off any start-up companies and linkages to local firms had not been developed. Small impacts, however, can be observed.

Some local life sciences firms have been able to recruit trailing spouses of researchers who moved to the region to work for Stowers. The institute's presence also helps the region's universities to recruit scientists and researchers who see potential in working with their colleagues at Stowers. In turn, Stowers benefits from the universities in the region, because most of its researchers hold joint appointments at area institutions. The establishment of the Stowers Institute catalysed relationships among the region's institutions, such as universities, hospitals, research institutes, and community colleges.

Several observers, however, question the local economic impact the Stowers Institute will have. They remain fearful that the ideas and innovations created locally will be commercialized in other regions. To address these concerns, the Stowers Institute formed the BioMed Valley Discoveries, a systematic effort to address the commercialization of research created at Stowers and its research partners, the University of Missouri in Kansas City and the University of Kansas. BioMed Valley Discoveries is a for-profit venture dedicated to the development of discoveries through intellectual property licensing. Income generated through these activities will be channelled back to the research partners and will fund further research in life sciences.

KANSAS CITY'S EMERGING INNOVATION MILIEU

The mere presence of an anchor research institution such Stowers, or a pharmaceutical manufacturing firm such as Marion Laboratories, does not guarantee the emergence of a life sciences region. Successful life sciences regions have also developed a supportive environment in which innovation and knowledge created at firms and research institutions is translated into real economic benefits through entrepreneurial actions and commercialization activities (Bagchi-Sen, et al., 2004; Cortright and Mayer, 2002; Powell, et al., 2002). The literature refers to such an environment as an innovation milieu (Crevoisier and Maillat, 1991). An innovation milieu creates the conditions for the growth of companies, which in turn leads to a self-sustaining mechanism that ultimately produces an industry cluster in which firms specialize in certain segments and complement each other. A successful innovation milieu has several components, including firms that do work and network with each other, specialized support services and supplier companies, and a strong and specialized labour market. It also supports and encourages active networking among businesses and higher education institutions. Finally, an innovation milieu necessarily supports risk taking and entrepreneurship (Feldman and Francis, 2001; S. M. Walcott, 2002). For example, as a source of risk financing and of management and business advice, venture capitalists and angel investors play a fundamental role in building high-technology and life sciences regions (Florida and Samber, 1999).

The innovation milieu in Kansas City has several significant strengths but also significant weaknesses (see Table 6.4). Among the strengths are the availability of good business support services and a strong labour market – both linked to the Marion Laboratories legacy – and a high quality of life and low cost of doing business, important factors in retaining skilled employees and starting new businesses. While still weak compared to life sciences hotspots around the country, the region's research infrastructure is improving, and there are some signs of entrepreneurial activity.

The region's industrial legacy has helped to create locally available support services, a strong labour pool, and some entrepreneurial activity. Support services – market research firms, drug testing and clinical trials firms, regulatory affairs consultants, and so on – are critical, especially for young companies. As discussed above, the region also has a specialized labour pool from which firms can draw. For example, the labour force of some Marion-related start-ups consists predominately of ex-Marion employees. Finally, major firms such as Marion have spurred the growth of several new firms, while a handful of serial entrepreneurs have also created companies within existing industry sectors. Together these factors indicate the increasing maturity of the Kansas City economy and the ability for local entrepreneurs to conceptualize new opportunities while staying in the same region or city.

Until recently Kansas City's academic sector lagged behind many other biotechnology regions, and its R&D investments had been made primarily in the private sector without many spillover effects to the region. However, the investments at Stowers are addressing this shortcoming and are enhancing the region's research activities. In addition, local universities such as the University of Kansas Medical Center and the University of Missouri-Kansas City have made a significant commitment to become more important players in life sciences research.

Besides increased investments in research, several interviewees mentioned that the collaboration among the research institutions in the area has significantly improved with the inception of the Kansas City Area Life Sciences Institute (KCALSI) in 2000. A non-profit umbrella organization, KCALSI represents the life sciences research community and functions as its voice (Kansas City Area Life Sciences Institute, 2011). KCALSI consists of ten stakeholder institutions, comprising the region's medical hospitals and research institutions, and its main task is to facilitate collaboration among them, especially for joint research proposals and obtaining external funding. From the outset, KCALSI was charged with the goal of increasing the amount of research expenditures at its stakeholder institutions to $500 million annually over a period of 10–12 years. In its fifth year, 2005, research expenditures amounted to $275 million, almost twice the amount expended five years earlier. Local economic development leaders and entrepreneurs interviewed for this project credit the institute for successfully raising the level of research funding and also bringing the various research institutions together and facilitating their collaboration.

Several interviewees credited Kansas City's quality of life for helping to retain entrepreneurs and employees (Kessinger interview, 2005; Dispensa interview, 2005; Franano interview, 2005). The low cost of living – especially house prices – facilitates the retention of a highly qualified labour pool. Some interviewees indicated that low costs of doing business may have helped young start-up companies with limited budgets. For pharmaceutical development companies, costs for materials used in clinical trials and for using facilities at the region's research institutions are significantly lower than in the most prominent biotechnology or life sciences centres such as Boston or San Francisco. Several interviewees also mentioned that the small size of the Kansas City region facilitates collaboration among the research institutions.

The Kansas City region also has significant shortcomings, particularly in its entrepreneurial support system. Kansas City entrepreneurs experience difficulty in attracting venture capital or obtaining angel investments. Its organizational support for entrepreneurship is highly fragmented, and the level of networking among entrepreneurs and between industry and academia appears to be low. Addressing these issues is essential if the region wants to move forward as a life sciences and information technology hub. While most cities and regions in the US are improving their research infrastructure, only the regions that are best equipped for leveraging new ideas and turning them into commercial ventures will realize the economic benefits. In other words, regions have to build entrepreneurial pipelines: mechanisms to commercialize ideas and knowledge into tangible economic outcomes.

The majority of entrepreneurs interviewed for this research mentioned that it was difficult to raise venture capital or find angel investments in Kansas City (Kessinger interview, 2005; Cowden interview, 2005; Song interview, 2005; Strohmeier interview, 2005), a finding supported by a 2004 study conducted by the Policy Research Institute at the University of Kansas (Burress, et al., 2004). The interviewees felt that there was a lack of understanding locally about financial investments in high-risk industry sectors such as life sciences. Entrepreneurs also mentioned that they had a very difficult time convincing venture capitalists and other outside investors – primarily those based on the East and West Coasts – to pay attention to their business plans. In fact, several were asked whether they would be willing to relocate their firms closer to the venture capitalists. Interviewees cited two reasons for these trends. Some felt that Kansas City's location in the heartland, combined with the fact that the region is not known as a high-tech or life sciences centre, creates obstacles in attracting venture financing. Others thought that the region is lacking the deal flow (as measured by the number of opportunities for venture capitalists to invest in creative ideas) which would attract risk financing. There are several efforts underway in the region to address the lack of locally-based venture capital. Overall, however, efforts to increase the amount of capital flowing to the region seem to be fragmented, focused on just one industry sector or one state, and some initiatives have ceased because of a lack of funds or management problems. All of the nine venture capital firms listed in the 2004 Kansas City Book of Lists (*The Business Journal*, 2004) have made the majority of their investments in companies located outside the region. In addition, some of these firms have run out of funding and are not making new investments. These trends may be a result of the overall downturn in the economy and may not be a specific Kansas City problem.

Organizational or institutional support for entrepreneurs can make a significant difference in growing a high-tech economy. Trade associations, industry support groups, and professional associations can facilitate networking that leads to sharing of new ideas and cross-fertilization within the industry. The Kansas City region has a good endowment of entrepreneurial support services such as coaching and mentoring, but their efforts are not well coordinated and for the most part they do not strategically target the growth of knowledge-based firms. For example, while KCALSI, as noted above, is considering ideas about how best to approach entrepreneurial support and commercialization in the life sciences sector, these ideas have yet to materialize. Stowers' efforts to establish a corporation that deals with intellectual property and licensing include partners such as the region's two main universities, but are focused primarily on licensing and not on entrepreneurial development. KCSourceLink (KCSourceLink, 2011), a small business resource centre that serves the whole region, provides support for small businesses, but it does not have a clear specialization in high-growth entrepreneurs in sectors such as life sciences or information technology. In early 2006, the Kansas Technology Enterprise Corporation (KTEC) initiated a new programme to mentor entrepreneurs and link them to technology and innovation creation. The programme, called KTEC Pipeline (KTEC, 2011), is a good start at nurturing entrepreneurial talent but is still, of course, in its nascent stage of development.

And though nationally and internationally known for its philanthropic support of entrepreneurship, the Kauffman Foundation does not focus solely on supporting high-tech and life sciences activity in Kansas City.

One failed effort in Kansas City did try to focus on a region-wide support system for entrepreneurs. KCCatalyst (Anderson, 2004), formed from a membership-based organization called Silicon Prairie Technology Association, was established in 2001 to promote the growth of the information technology and life sciences sectors by facilitating collaboration, contributing to capital formation, and supporting the commercialization of new ideas. The organization was funded through grants from state government (both Missouri and Kansas), the Kauffman Foundation, the Greater Kansas City Chamber of Commerce, and other organizations. The effort was modelled after the San Diego CONNECT programme and the North Carolina Council for Entrepreneurial Development, and regional leaders hoped it would play an important role in regional economic development (Buckley, 2001). Unfortunately, KCCatalyst never achieved substantial success and was closed in early 2005. Interviewees and newspaper articles cited several reasons for its failure, such as the timing of the organization's formation during the downturn of the economy and the associated difficulty in raising risk capital, as well as mismanagement and failure to devise a clear strategy and niche (Marcusse interview, 2005; Anderson, 2004). Still, KCCatalyst had broad support from government leaders on both sides of the state line, as well as industry and academic representation, and its focus on providing support to high-growth entrepreneurs distinguished it from other organizations. Some interviewees – primarily the entrepreneurs – felt that there is still a need for such an organization in the region.

Networking among entrepreneurs and academic leaders facilitates information exchange and learning. In turn, such activity may contribute to a more resilient and sustainable industry cluster. Strong networks exist among former Marion Laboratories employees (Higuchi interview, 2005; Mitchell interview, 2005). An alumni organization and a newsletter (the Marion Phoenix) facilitate their interactions, and entrepreneurs who worked for Marion Laboratories can draw on the Marion alumni network for support in finding talented workers for their firm. But while the level of interaction among Marion alumni is rather strong (Herman interview, 2005), several interviewees indicated that overall networking among entrepreneurs in the region, and between local industry and universities, is generally underdeveloped (Garver interview, 2005; Boran interview, 2005). Networking events are sparse and some have only recently been established.

While efforts to create institutional networking, such as the Kansas

Table 6.4   Assessing Kansas City's innovation milieu

Innovation milieu component	Strength	Weakness
Specialized business support services	✓	
Strong and specialized labour market	✓	
Quality of life	✓	
Strong research infrastructure		✓
Capital formation		✓
Entrepreneurial environment and support system		✓
Active and supportive networking		✓

Source: Author's analysis of interview data.

City Area Life Sciences Institute, have been successful in making connections between academic institutions, they have not yet focused on making connections to industry. Also, the Stowers Institute has not yet developed relationships with the local life sciences industry; for example, local start-up firms are not yet working with researchers at the institute. It will be critical for the region to find ways to connect the already existing industrial strengths with the research capacities that are forming at the universities and research institutions in the region.

Table 6.4 reviews the strengths and weaknesses of Kansas City's innovation milieu, illustrating that while the region has strong business support services, a highly specialized labour market, and a good quality of life, it does not yet have a strong research infrastructure and it substantially lacks the entrepreneurship, commercialization, and networking functions that can translate innovation created at local firms and laboratories into real economic benefits.

WORKING TOWARDS ESTABLISHING A SECOND TIER LIFE SCIENCES REGION

Public policy leaders and business representatives in the Kansas City region have recognized the weaknesses in their regional economy, particularly as they relate to research and commercialization. In response they have developed public policy efforts that are aggressively supporting a budding life sciences industry. A myriad of state initiatives emerged over the last decade (Pew Centre on the States and National Governors Association, 2007). In 2001 the legislature passed the University Research and Development Act, which authorized about $130 million in bonds to finance various bioscience facilities at its universities. In 2004, then-Governor Kathleen Sebelius signed into law the Kansas Economic Growth Act (KEGA). In 2006 the legislature also appropriated $5 million for the University of Kansas Cancer Center which will be housed at the University of Kansas Medical Center (KUMC) in Kansas City.

The impetus for the Kansas Economic Growth Act was the establishment of the Stowers Institute in the late 1990s and it galvanized the business, higher education, and political communities in Kansas. When Stowers and KCALSI formed, the state's business and political leaders realized that they had to respond by contributing to the growth of the state's bioscience community. As a result, two legislators championed KEGA, and the Kansas Technology Enterprise Corporation, the state's technology-based economic development organization, played a pivotal role in conceptualizing it. KEGA set the stage for the state's investments in science and technology. In contrast to Idaho, Kansas has managed to set up a robust financial and institutional structure for investments in academic and industry research. The Act includes two initiatives: The Kansas Entrepreneurship Initiative ($3.5 million annually for ten years) and the Kansas Bioscience Initiative ($500 million over the next ten to 12 years).

KEGA also created the Kansas Bioscience Authority (KBA), an independent authority of the state which is charged with administering the state's bioscience investments (Kansas Technology Enterprise Corporation, 2005) and will oversee the implementation of the bioscience initiative. KEGA requires the KBA to be headquartered in the county with the highest number of bioscience employees, thereby guaranteeing physical proximity to the industry. The KBA is governed by an 11-member board, of which one member is an agricultural expert and the others are a mix of industry and academic representatives. Funding for the KBA comes from the Emerging Industry Investment Act, which authorizes the use of tax increment revenues generated from the growth of the employee base in bioscience companies and research institutions. The base year is 2004, and estimates used a compound annual growth rate of about 8.45 per cent. Lawmakers estimate the cumulative incremental revenue by 2015 to be $593.1 million. According to the KBA president and CEO (Thornton interview, 2007), tax increment revenues for 2005 and 2006 were about $30 million (exceeding the initial projection of $21.2 million for that period).

The Kansas Bioscience Authority uses the funding for a variety of programmes, each of which aims at increasing Kansas' standing in life sciences. Besides traditional economic development tools such as the attraction of companies and tax credits, the funds are also used to foster university-industry partnerships and the development of new types of collaborations and centres of innovation. The Kansas Bioscience R&D Voucher Program, for example, provides incentives for bioscience companies or entrepreneurs to do business in Kansas by providing them with vouchers to undertake R&D activities with bioscience research institutions and universities. The programme encourages collaboration between industry and academia and, according to interviewees, is very popular, well received, and highly regarded. Incentivizing university-industry collaboration through a voucher programme highlights the open innovation concept of searching outside a firm's boundary for new ideas. It also highlights the role of the state as an innovation investor. The other types of KBA programmes invest in collaborations between Kansas-based researchers and others in the nation. The Collaborative Biosecurity Research Initiative dedicates $2.5 million for inter-institutional research projects that examine animal-borne diseases that may infect humans. The initiative builds on the existing animal health industry in the state, which accounts for more than a third of the global animal health industry market (Animal Health Corridor, 2007). A similar initiative is aimed at investing in collaborative research in the area of cancer and builds on the investments the state has made in the University of Kansas Cancer Center. Lastly, KBA dedicates funding to various centres of innovation. These centres are intended to operate as collaborative projects among industry, higher education, and other research organizations and require strong private-sector involvement. One example is the Kansas Center for Biomaterials Innovation and Design, which received a $200000 planning grant and involves more than 20 private industry, research, and public institutions. These centres represent 'hubs of innovation' where the open innovation model is applied. Through these various centres, the state acts as an innovation investor and benefactor, as outlined by Chesbrough (2003b).

The Kansas Economic Growth Act is the landmark legislation in Kansas. However, it is not the only programme aimed at supporting R&D investments. Since about the mid-1980s, KTEC has supported centres of excellence at universities. According to KTEC, these university-based research centres 'conduct innovative research and provide technical assistance with the overlapping aims of creating new companies, strengthening existing companies, and serving as expert resources to other KTEC programs' (Kansas Technology Enterprise Corporation, 2008). There are currently five centres. One is the Advanced Manufacturing Institute, which is affiliated with Kansas State University and helps companies in Kansas with their product and process development. The institute provides services such as product design and engineering, manufacturing process development, technology development, and commercialization. Other centres are the Biotechnology Innovation and Optimization Center and the Information and Telecommunication Technology Center at the University of Kansas, the Kansas Polymer Research Center at Pittsburg

State University, and the National Institute for Aviation Research at Wichita State University. All these centres work closely with industry and provide a collaborative environment for idea creation and innovation.

Kansas exhibits an interesting evolutionary pattern regarding state R&D investments. During the 1980s, the state invested in the creation of centres of excellence. In recent years, however, the state's focus has shifted towards a strategy to support life sciences and, more specifically, towards fostering collaboration, commercialization, and technology transfer. By creating a unique funding mechanism in the form of tax increment financing, the state may shelter itself from unexpected political vagaries. Kansas' programmes are unique for their strong focus on collaboration among industry, research universities, and public organizations. The deliberate emphasis on creating inter-institutional research projects, centres of innovation, and R&D partnerships allows the state to leverage its existing strengths in certain sectors such as animal health, cancer research, and biosciences. The structure of these programmes and their eligibility requirements ensure partnerships among the various innovation actors. A drawback might be that the bulk of state investments is focused on the bioscience industry, while there are also other sectors that play an important role in Kansas' economy (such as, aerospace in Wichita and information technology and telecommunications in Kansas City).

CONCLUSIONS

The Kansas City region's economy is characterized by a strong firm legacy, significant industry strengths, and a resolute effort to build a research and commercialization infrastructure. Among second tier biotechnology regions that are trying to position themselves as the challengers to established regions such as Boston, San Francisco and Raleigh-Durham (North Carolina), Kansas City is in a very good position. However, the region faces one major challenge: the region's political and business leaders need to find ways to connect the region's advantages and to facilitate the commercialization of ideas and entrepreneurship. To the outside observer, Kansas City looks like a puzzle that needs to be finished. The pieces – a well-developed industrial base (Marion Laboratories and its successor firms and spin-offs), a research infrastructure that is beginning to show significant strengths (Stowers), and nascent efforts to commercialize ideas – are present, but have yet to be put together in a strategic way. The stakes are high: without a strategic plan for putting innovation-led, entrepreneurial development at the top of the region's economic development agenda, ideas and knowledge created within industry and academic laboratories will not be captured locally, and the economic benefits will materialize in other areas of the country, particularly the nation's already established biotech or high-tech centres (Fogarty and Sinha, 1999). In short, if Kansas City wants to further leverage the legacy of Marion Labs and exploit the presence of the Stowers Institute to keep ideas, innovation, and entrepreneurs in the region, then regional leaders need to continue to focus on building research capacity; strengthening linkages among universities, research institutions, and industry; and supporting an innovation milieu by building an entrepreneurial pipeline.

Over the past several years, the Stowers Institute has boosted Kansas City's reputation in life sciences research, but Stowers alone cannot fully meet the region's research needs. Without better local research capacity, firms and private laboratories that function as surrogate universities can only go so far in creating spillover effects for the Kansas City region. To fill this gap, regional leaders would need to match Stowers' investments by continuing to support research capacity at the region's public universities, particularly the University of Missouri-Kansas City (UMKC) and the University of Kansas Medical Center (KUMC). Such focus on academic research is necessary for two primary reasons. First, former Marion employees, Marion spin-off companies, and other firms in sectors as diverse as information technology and telecommunications need to be connected to academic research, because they can be the critical agents in commercializing academic discoveries. A stronger higher education infrastructure will provide the Stowers Institute, local hospitals, and industry with these viable academic partners. Second, a strong university presence is essential for attracting talent – students, professors, post-docs, and so on – to the region, who in turn can be employed in established firms and start-ups.

Building academic capacity is not enough. Kansas City needs to pay more attention to connecting its already established and vibrant industrial capacity with emerging academic institutions. While KCALSI has been successful in forming collaborations among Kansas City's research organizations, as yet there are no systematic efforts to connect them to industry. Both industry leaders and academics can benefit from increased interaction: firms could leverage academic resources for applied research, and researchers could partner with companies for the purpose of commercialization. These local connections need to be made if the region wants to keep innovative ideas and turn them into profitable ventures.

The Kansas City region is well-positioned to develop a vibrant second tier life sciences economy. While virtually every region in the country is aiming to foster knowledge-based industries, only a few will have the capacity to reap serious economic development benefits. In the case of Kansas City, the industrial capacity that originated with Marion Laboratories helped to attract and retain a highly skilled and specialized talent pool in the region, with seasoned managers and industry executives now running competitive and innovative spin-offs. This industrial capacity is augmented with basic research through the presence of the Stowers Institute. The key to Kansas City's continued and growing success is the ability of civic leaders to connect industry with research and to develop an environment in which the commercialization of ideas will flourish. Building an entrepreneurial pipeline is essential to ensuring that other regions do not reap all the benefits from the ideas created in Kansas City. The research for this case study has shown that a region can bootstrap its life sciences capacity, but organized civic leadership and sound public policy are necessary to push this burgeoning prowess to the next level.

NOTE

1. In addition, the telecommunications and information technology sectors provided additional new economy capacities with 25 471 employees and 12 498 employees, respectively.

7. Conclusion

'What "works" right now in this dynamic, regional, high-technology economy tells us little of how precisely Silicon Valley came to be just such a place, or how any such place comes into being. The potential disaster lies in the fact that these static, descriptive efforts culminate in policy recommendations and analytical tomes that resemble recipes or magic potions, such as: combine liberal amounts of technology entrepreneurs, capital, and sunshine. Add one (1) university. Stir vigorously.'

Moore and Davis (2004: 8)

IMPORTANT FEATURES OF HIGH-TECH DEVELOPMENT

Building a regional high-tech economy is nothing like mixing a magic potion or a tasty cocktail, and there is no simple recipe for how to create 'the next Silicon Valley'. In fact, efforts to replicate Silicon Valley in different places have failed because identifying the critical ingredients for the region's success is far easier than combining them into a working recipe for regional economic development (Leslie, 2001; Leslie and Kargon, 1996). As the case studies in this book show, the evolution of second tier high-tech regions follows very different models of regional development than studies of Silicon Valley would suggest. Portland, Boise, and Kansas City took alternative development paths. Their stories highlight mechanisms and dynamics that might be more applicable to a broader range of places, and their cases may therefore represent more realistic models of high-tech regional development. The research presented in this book provides strong support for the idea that world-class research universities are not necessary for building a thriving high-tech industry cluster. In the three study regions, firms acted as 'surrogate universities' and created spillover effects that contributed to high-tech industry growth. These firms functioned as entrepreneurial seedbeds and were critical in transforming their respective regions into entrepreneurial and innovative high-tech economies. In all three cases, entrepreneurial processes transformed the regional economy. New firms diversified the industrial structure and created opportunities. Local leaders reacted to the evolution of local high-tech economies with the creation of innovative public policies, especially as they relate to fostering university-industry partnerships. The theoretical implications of these cases point to the role of firms as anchor institutions in regional economies and to the importance of entrepreneurial processes as dynamics that build and maintain regional economic specialization.

Empirically, the cases of Portland, Boise, and Kansas City illustrate five important features of high-tech development that are likely to be relevant to other metropolitan areas: industry specialization, presence of anchor firms, entrepreneurship through spin-offs and other start-up firms, lagging public policy efforts, and lack of a world-class research university. First, while large, pioneering high-tech regions such as Silicon Valley and Boston have diverse high-tech economies, Portland, Kansas City, and Boise are specialized in particular kinds of high-tech industries. Portland focuses on high-tech manufacturing and has competencies in semiconductors, test and measurement instruments, display technology, and software. Boise is known for semiconductor manufacturing (particularly memory chip production) and computer peripherals (particularly printers). These specializations emerged, in part, because large, established firms relocated routine production operations to lower-cost locations. (For a theoretical treatment of this process, see Duranton and Puga, 2001). Kansas City, which specializes in life sciences, particularly drug development and testing and animal health, followed a different model. The Kansas City area was able to support an innovative life sciences economy because of its historical assets and strengths (primarily related to Marion Laboratories). In this metropolitan area, the life sciences economy grew out of institutions and capabilities that already existed.

Second, anchor firms helped each region's high-tech industry to develop – Tektronix and Intel in Portland, HP and Micron Technology in Boise, and Marion Laboratories in Kansas City. Some were started locally (Tektronix, Micron, and Marion), while others relocated from elsewhere as their industries matured (Intel and HP). Anchor firms employ a significant number of talented employees, are engaged in innovation, have strong market connections inside and outside the region, often dominate or play a strong role in their product markets, and generate spin-off companies. They have other characteristics that make them especially likely to influence regional high-tech growth. Being leaders in their specific markets, they play an important role in the local economy, supporting much of the area's employment and income and, directly or indirectly, creating business opportunities for locally based small- and medium-sized firms. Consequently, their growth and decline can have large impacts on the economies of their host regions.

Third, although anchor firms played an important role in planting the initial seeds of high-tech industry in Portland, Kansas City, and Boise, it is entrepreneurship that has led to its sustained growth there. The three high-tech centres grew because new firms spun off from existing ones, often as a result of corporate changes such as mergers and acquisitions, lay-offs, and corporate downsizing. In most cases, entrepreneurs stayed in the areas when starting their firms. In Portland and Kansas City, clusters of related and supporting firms evolved over time. Although the anchor firms in these regions initially located and grew in isolation from other firms, they gradually developed relationships with customers, suppliers, subcontractors, and research partners. Intel, for example, attracted many suppliers, subcontractors, and competitors.

Although Portland and Boise started as low-cost manufacturing sites for firms whose headquarters and R&D activities were located elsewhere (such as Silicon Valley), over time these firms moved some of their R&D and other innovative activities to the places where related production facilities were already located (Angel, 1994). In this way, Portland and Boise became locations for both R&D and production. In addition, suppliers, subcontractors, and customers, who are often co-located, have become important sources of innovation. As a result, regions that started out as mere branch plant locations are now part of an integrated innovation system.

Fourth, high-tech industry in Portland, Kansas City, and Boise evolved without the aid of explicit public policy. Although each region's roots in high-tech go back decades, little or none of their presence resulted from aggressive firm recruitment by governmental agencies. Proactive public policy, however, has become more important in recent years. As these high-tech firms prospered, their needs for highly skilled workers and sophisticated research grew. Consequently, they became more concerned with postsecondary education and university-based research and advocated public policies to support higher education. Grassroots efforts on behalf of entrepreneurs and local business representatives helped set up angel investor networks and other entrepreneurship support programmes. Civic leadership by entrepreneurs and high-tech firms followed, sometimes leading to changes in public policy. However, public policies differ substantially among the three regions, in part because of differences in political culture. In addition, regional high-tech development is a long-term endeavour. Policymakers should be aware that technology-based metropolitan economic development needs to be a long-term strategy.

Fifth, anchor firms in high-tech regions that lack a world-class research university can take on the role of 'surrogate universities', attracting and developing talent, investing in R&D, and spinning off entrepreneurial start-up firms (Mayer, 2005b). Each of the three study regions became a high-tech centre even though it lacked a strong higher education infrastructure. This indicates that universities are not necessary for high-tech development. However, once the firms became established, local universities became important partners, by helping to develop talent, providing opportunities for university-industry interactions and applied research, and supporting entrepreneurship through small business development centres, incubators, or prototyping facilities. Although technology licensing, patenting, and spin-offs are often a prominent focus of public policy directed toward universities in relation to high-tech industry, these activities seem to be less important in the three cases than informal interactions such as faculty consulting, student internships, and small business advice. In addition, corporate leaders and entrepreneurs in each region have been important supporters and advocates of the local post-secondary education system.

ANCHOR ORGANIZATIONS AND REGIONAL DEVELOPMENT

There is a common theme linking the three second tier high-tech regions analysed for this book: large, dominant firms catalysed cluster evolution through their ability to attract and develop talent, their emphasis on cutting edge R&D, and their impact on local entrepreneurship. In Portland, Tektronix and Intel influenced the evolution of the Silicon Forest and shaped the region's specialization in test and measurement instruments, computers, and semiconductors. In Boise, HP and Micron Technology shaped regional economic development and formed the basis for an emerging high-tech economy that specializes in printers and semiconductors. Marion Laboratories and the Stowers Institute shaped Kansas City's evolution as a second tier life sciences region. In all three cases, the firms held a dominant position in their respective markets, they were – at times, at least – technology and market leaders with international recognition, and they grew into attractive employers, lucrative business partners, and incubators for a large number of spin-off companies. The firms also influenced the local economy as employers, purchasers or contractors, workforce developers, and political actors that influenced public policy.

There is a small emerging literature that conceptualizes large dominant institutions such as firms, universities, hospitals, and so on as anchor institutions and analyses their role in shaping regional economies (Agrawal and Cockburn, 2003; Feldman, 2003; Lucas, et al., 2009). This literature conceptualizes the function of the anchor firm much like the function of the large department store as an anchor tenant in a retail shopping mall.

Agrawal and Cockburn define the anchor organization in a regional economy as a large, locally present firm that is engaged in R&D and has 'minor absorptive capacity in a particular technology area' (2003: 1229). Lucas et al. note that the anchor firm played a role in 'focusing resources on exploiting the commercial potential of new knowledge and technology' (2009: 196). And Feldman notes that 'an anchor, in the form of a large, established firm may create externalities that benefit agglomerations' (2003: 323). Menzel and Fornahl describe anchor firms as 'focal points' (2009: 209) around which clusters develop. Simmie (1998) describes them as intermediaries that connect the local and the global. Caniels and Romijn note that such firms are 'knowledge gatekeepers' (2003: 1256). Common to these definitions is the notion that a small number of dominant firms act as anchors around which a cluster of economic activity forms. They are major employers and they attract and develop a skilled talent base. Anchor firms can be important business partners to small- and medium-sized firms in the region. Anchor firms influence the provision of business services and factor inputs and shape the local economy through their demand. Anchor firms act as incubators for spin-off companies and as such they influence the evolution of the regional economy in important ways. The Portland case discussed in this book illustrates these roles: Tektronix's growth and evolution into the world's pre-eminent manufacturer of oscilloscopes turned the firm into an attractive employer. Tektronix grew rapidly and needed to hire the best and brightest. Due to the lack of an appropriate local higher education infrastructure, it developed in-house education and training capacities. It also built significant R&D and manufacturing expertise as a result of its strategy to vertically integrate many aspects of its production process. Tektronix employees experienced a supportive and nurturing work environment, in which they could hone both their technical and managerial skills. Over time, however, Tektronix restructured and, as a result, had to lay off employees, divest business units, and scale back its innovation efforts. These changes catalysed entrepreneurial activities by former Tektronix employees. Corporate changes and restructuring at Tektronix seeded the Silicon Forest through the development of many successful new firms that are leading the cluster even today.

Anchor firms typically attract superior employees interested in working for market leaders (Klepper, 2008). Each anchor firm in the three regions discussed in this book attracted talent from across the nation and even the world. Working for anchor firms offers employees many opportunities to gain skills, especially as they relate to organizing business processes, connections to business partners such as suppliers or competitors, and being able to work on innovative activities. Once these employees decide to turn to entrepreneurship and leave the anchor firms, they are well prepared to start their own businesses. Entrepreneurs leaving anchor firms may have highly specialized skills that they can use in their new ventures. They may also draw on important business contacts and networks that they have been able to develop through their work at the anchor firm. And they may be able to more quickly detect market niches, because the anchor firm may be in the lead in terms of developing new products and services. In Portland, Tektronix seeded the growth of a host of spin-offs that have become smaller anchor firms themselves. These spin-offs diversified the Silicon Forest into new technology areas such as display technology, computers, and software. Tektronix spin-offs like Planar Systems and Mentor Graphics exemplify this process.

The anchor firms were needed to seed the cluster because they created the necessary conditions for each region's evolution as a second tier high-tech region. Through their firm-building activities (such as creating a new skill base, offering business opportunities to small- and medium-sized firms through backward and forward linkages, familiarizing employees with production networks and innovative niches) and through their corporate change processes, anchor firms create positive externalities that small firms can leverage, providing the seedbeds for clusters to emerge. The anchor firm shapes the region's labour pool through its ability to attract talent from outside the region. Backward and forward linkages allow smaller firms to engage in business activities that might also introduce them to global markets. R&D activities may spill over to the region because employees might take the chance and leave the anchor firm to create entrepreneurial ventures. These externalities facilitate cluster growth because they lower the barriers to entry for smaller firms, and the anchor's demand for business services and other factors may exert a strong influence on the character and quality of these factor inputs. Anchors also attract high quality suppliers and competitors that stimulate the cluster environment. In Portland, for example, Intel attracted a range of specialized suppliers that helped create a competitive semiconductor cluster. In addition, Intel's expanding activities signalled to other semiconductor producers (especially foreign-owned firms) that Portland is a viable business location.

The role of anchor firms changes over time and throughout the cluster's evolution (Lucas, et al., 2009). Anchor firms are most critical in the initial phases of cluster emergence. The successful growth of an anchor firm, however, depends on conditions that are mostly external to the region. In the regions discussed in this book, Tektronix, Intel, HP, Micron Technology, and Marion Laboratories grew because they were able to cover a niche and take advantage of the exuberant growth trends in emerging industry sectors. Much like Perroux's growth pole theory suggests (Perroux, 1950), these firms grew within the realm of a propulsive industry. Their industries were characterized by their size, market power, high growth rates and intra-industry changes, such as the emergence of a flexibly specialized production system (Saxenian, 1994b). Tektronix took advantage of the emerging electronics industry and fulfilled the needs of many emerging markets such as military, radio, and television. Intel took advantage of inventions such as the transistor and attained a leadership position in the development of high-quality, mass-produced semiconductors. HP developed printers that helped revolutionize office work at a time when computers required the development of new peripherals. Marion Laboratories advanced the life sciences industries through its novel business and innovation model. During the phase in which clusters emerge, anchor firms are pivotal because they organize and focus resources in the region. During this phase the anchor firm typically is only one of a few firms that emerge in the region. The anchor firm might focus more externally than locally, and this might be apparent through the recruitment of national rather than local talent, the development of business partnerships with firms external to the region, and doing business with external markets. Over time, anchor firms start to develop local relationships, and this is the time when the emerging cluster transitions into a growing cluster. During this phase the anchor firms help the region develop a critical mass of related businesses. Most often the anchor firm contributes to this process as an incubator for spin-offs. The anchor may contract with spin-offs, it may turn to spin-offs for the supply of non-core business activities, it may fund spin-offs, and it may allow them to work in areas not directly relevant to the anchor's business niche. During the cluster's emergence, the anchor firm is pivotal because it implants resources into the region. The anchor turns into a facilitator of cluster growth primarily through its role as an entrepreneurial seedbed. During the maturation and specialization phase of a cluster, the anchor becomes less important. Ideally, regions will see the growth of second-generation spin-offs (this was most prominent in the case of Portland where second-generation spin-offs deepened the region's specialization in technology areas such as displays and semiconductors). Large anchor firms may also exert significant political power and shape the region's policies, primarily as they relate to workforce development, university education and research, and tax policies (Christopherson and Clark, 2007; Mayer, 2008). Anchors may cease to seed the cluster during the cluster's stagnation and decline phase. During this phase, it is important that the cluster develops new anchor firms that help seed subsequent cluster development and rejuvenation. These new anchor firms allow the cluster to draw on resources that are implanted from outside, thereby stimulating cluster development. If anchor firms exert too much control over the region's economic development, the cluster may also experience lock-in (Grabher, 1993) because smaller firms may be inhibited from growing out of the shadows of the large anchor firms.

POLICY IMPLICATIONS

This book makes an important contribution to regional economic policy. In particular, the case studies help develop a new understanding of the role of economic actors such as firms and universities. The analysis suggests that second tier high-tech regions can take different evolutionary paths depending on their initiating conditions. This is an important conclusion because policymakers, economic developers and higher education officials are often myopically focused on the role of the university as an engine of economic growth, due to the popularity of the Stanford/MIT model. The case studies also show that the development of a critical mass of knowledge-based industries in second tier high-tech regions takes a long time and that policymakers have to be patient. Portland's successful development of the Silicon Forest began in the 1930s, when the US Forest Service relocated its radio lab to Portland, and the 1940s, when Tektronix started to manufacture oscilloscopes. Boise's emergence as a second tier high-tech region started in the 1970s, when HP relocated its disk drive manufacturing operation from California. And Kansas City's ascendance as a second tier life sciences region began in the 1950s, when Ewing Marion Kauffman started to sell medical drugs out of the basement of his home, which was the genesis of Marion Laboratories. Having patience is not easy because the economic development profession is often more interested in quick fixes and early wins than in long-term structural changes and lasting economic success (Rubin, 1988).

Previous attempts to imitate Silicon Valley have failed miserably (Leslie, 2001; Leslie and Kargon, 1996). Yet the dominance of Silicon Valley in the scholarly and practitioner literature did not allow alternative models of regional high-tech development to emerge. Policymakers need to realize that it does not make sense to imitate Silicon Valley. More fitting might be the model presented here, whereby second tier regions leverage the growth of large, locally embedded, R&D-oriented firms as anchor institutions. In each region studied here, policymakers became proactive once regional high-tech development started to be more forceful, and they helped support entrepreneurship and university-industry linkages. The findings suggest that policymakers need to be more aware about their regional economies and the evolution of a region's clusters. They need to pay attention to whether a region hosts a set of anchor firms and whether the presence of these anchors could be leveraged.

These insights, however, may elicit false reactions from local policymakers because the most simple, but also misguided, policy advice would be that policymakers need to attract potential anchor firms. Such advice seems to recall traditional economic development practices whereby policymakers and practitioners hand out expensive tax breaks to attract firms. This practice is associated with the so-called first wave of economic development policies that was characterized by a strong emphasis on exogenously stimulated economic development through firm attraction strategies (Glasmeier, 2000). The success of this practice, however, is disputed. The benefits of attracting firms through tax breaks might be short-lived because often these firms do not become locally embedded, move away after a short while, and may not meet expectations of job creation and connections to the local economy. In addition, firms have become more footloose and now seek out locations across the world. Even though Intel and HP relocated to Portland and Boise, respectively, and therefore strengthened these US regions, relocations nowadays might take firms to far-flung places in Asia, Europe, or Latin America. Foreign direct investments, especially in the global economic triad (North America, Europe, and East and Southeast Asia) have increased considerably during the post-war period (Dicken, 2007). These investments are not only geared towards establishing a manufacturing presence; increasingly firms are turning to foreign locations for R&D. Boise's HP printer division opened a research facility in Shanghai, China, in 2006 (Spohn interview, 2007). Intel has a strong network of R&D labs across the world, including a site in Bangalore, India. These developments show that firms are increasingly interested in developing research capacities abroad, and policymakers cannot continue to count on the relocation of firms within the nation. Firms are building these global networks to tap into other regional knowledge bases (Zeller, 2010). These networks allow firms to tap into external knowledge and link regions at a global level, thereby allowing regional clusters to simultaneously build a local innovative environment and pipelines that connect the region to knowledge sources worldwide (Bathelt et al., 2004).

What should policymakers take away from these studies? The case studies illustrate that economic development policies are most critical during the growth and maturation phases of a high-tech industry cluster. Each region was able to create the necessary conditions for the emergence of the cluster without help from public policy. The anchor firms established themselves without government assistance. Tektronix and Micron Technology were locally grown firms because their founders wanted to live and work in the regions where they grew up. This location inertia of the founders is typical (Feldman, 2001), and cannot be influenced by policy. Intel and HP established branch operations in Portland and Boise without tax breaks or subsidies. However, in each region public policies became critical as the high-tech clusters grew and matured. Policies to support entrepreneurship and university-industry relationships were especially helpful to root the high-tech industry (see Figure 7.1). Portland's Oregon Nanoscience and Microtechnologies Institute (ONAMI) initiative leveraged the region's industrial strengths and connected universities with each other and with the corporate sector. Kansas City's efforts to build university assets in life sciences and bring together the various players may help leverage existing industrial strength in contract manufacturing and the growing scholarly activities based at research organizations like The Stowers Institute. Through these policies, each region has leveraged the growth and development of its anchor firms. Once the anchor firms created externalities, the regional economies diversified through the growth of entrepreneurial firms and the attraction of suppliers, competitors, and business service firms. Public policy plays a critical role when it comes to helping the cluster mature because public policy can help shape the provision of specialized inputs such as university research and training, entrepreneurial support services, infrastructure development, and quality of life. Anchor firms cease to exert their influence in these areas because they represent public goods and do not affect the firms' immediate bottom line. The ability of anchor firms to shape the regional economy can only go so far, and public policy needs to step in to take the cluster to the next level. Boise illustrates this well: public policy efforts have been less successful in Boise than in Portland and Kansas City. In Boise, the major proponents of government intervention to build university assets and increase entrepreneurship have been smaller firms. Large firms like Micron or HP show less interest in regional policy and do not advocate for change, primarily because the proposed policies would not immediately influence their local activities.

Each stage of the cluster life cycle requires a different policy approach (see also Figure 7.1). At the firm-building stage, economic development policies have to focus on building competitiveness and supporting firm-building activities. To do this, policymakers should link the region to global markets, attract and retain the talent necessary for corporate growth, and facilitate linkages to other regions to keep up with market developments. During the region's growth stage, policies need to look different. When a region starts to see entrepreneurial dynamics, it is important to support start-ups. This can be done through an emphasis on financing start-ups, providing small business support services and

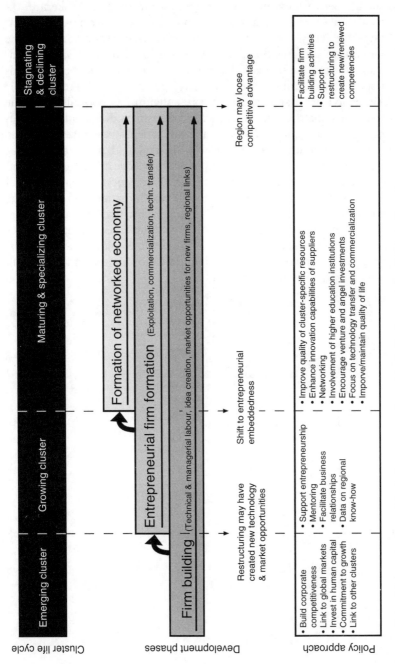

Cluster life cycle

| Emerging cluster | Growing cluster | Maturing & specializing cluster | Stagnating & declining cluster |

Development phases

Firm building (Technical & managerial labour, idea creation, market opportunities for new firms, regional links)

Entrepreneurial firm formation (Exploitation, commercialization, techn. transfer)

Formation of networked economy

Restructuring may have created new technology & market opportunities

Shift to entrepreneurial embeddedness

Region may loose competitive advantage

Policy approach

- Build corporate competitiveness
- Link to global markets
- Invest in human capital
- Commitment to growth
- Link to other clusters

- Support entrepreneurship
- Mentoring
- Facilitate business relationships
- Data on regional know-how

- Improve quality of cluster-specific resources
- Enhance innovation capabilities of suppliers
- Networking
- Involvement of higher education institutions
- Encourage venture and angel investments
- Focus on technology transfer and commercialization
- Imporve/maintain quality of life

- Facilitate firm building activities
- Support restructuring to create new/renewed competencies

Figure 7.1   Theoretical model of cluster growth and policies in emerging high-tech regions

213

assistance, networking and mentoring, and information brokerage. As a cluster is maturing and specializing, policymakers may have the greatest influence. They should improve cluster-specific resources such as the higher education infrastructure, as well as R&D investments, and infrastructure. During the stagnation and decline stage of a region, policy needs to support restructuring.

The second tier high-tech regions presented in this book illustrate the ways in which metropolitan areas need to transform. Regional economies are no longer autonomous hosts for a set of vertically integrated firms that combine manufacturing and R&D in-house. Today, these regional economies depend on the continuous creation of knowledge and innovation and they represent nodes within global production networks. Each region will follow its own path, and policymakers will have to understand the specific local circumstances of this transformation. Rather than trying to imitate Silicon Valley, the realistic and informed economic development planner will be more aware about distinct local economic development potentials, especially as they relate to the conditions that allow that region's high-tech industry cluster to grow and mature.

Appendix

METHODOLOGY

This study of the evolution and development of second tier high-tech regions used a variety of sources. I have tried to triangulate the phenomenon of high-tech growth in the US from multiple perspectives, using a variety of methods and a range of data sources. For the most part, the research was historical in nature, particularly when I tried to trace the history of the lead firms in each region. Through these historical accounts, I have been able to open the 'black box' of the firm and analyse in great detail how the firm's evolution influenced the region's growth. The research started with the work on my dissertation (Mayer, 2003), which I conducted from 2000 to 2003 at Portland State University in Portland, Oregon, and continued with detailed case studies of Boise and Kansas City throughout until 2011.

In addition to conducting more than 104 interviews, I employed a quantitative analysis and analysed high-tech employment, innovation and entrepreneurship dynamics in 360 metropolitan statistical areas in the US. In Portland and in Boise, data was also collected through an online business survey. Qualitative and quantitative data are complemented by research into secondary sources such as company histories, archival records, industry and trade press, local and national media reports, and a variety of public and private sources. In addition, I used a unique method to visualize the genealogy of spin-off firms and illustrate these dynamics in graphics presented for the case studies on Portland and Boise. The study on Kansas City's life sciences industry serves as an exploratory case through which ideas about second tier regions are tested and developed for the life sciences sector. Through this triangulation approach I hope to have developed an accurate account of high-tech development in second tier regions. The following outlines several important elements of the methodology.

DEFINING HIGH-TECH AND LIFE SCIENCES

Defining high-tech industries is not an easy task. Analysts typically distinguish between output and input-based definitions. Output-based definitions, such as the one used by the American Electronics Association (AeA), consider an industry high-tech if its products embody technologies (Hecker, 2005). The selection typically involves industry experts and can be quite labour intensive and subjective. A more common and less subjective approach is to define high-tech industries by the inputs needed to create innovative and technology-oriented products and processes. The two most common measures are employment of engineers, scientists and technicians and investments in R&D. Typically a threshold is defined at which an industry becomes high-tech.

For this study, I use an employment-based definition of high-tech industries and follow Hecker's approach (Hecker, 2005). Hecker selected eight technology-oriented occupations including engineers, technicians, life and physical scientists, engineering and natural science managers. He then used the Bureau of Labor Statistics' National Employment Matrix to compute the intensity of technology occupations in four-digit NAICS codes for 2002. The national average of technology-oriented occupations for all industries is 4.9 per cent. An industry is defined high-tech if its employment share in technology-oriented occupations is at least twice this national average. As a result, Hecker defined a total of 46 four-digit NAICS codes, which were further distinguished into three levels of high-tech (Level I to III).

For this study we only use those industry sectors that Hecker defined as so-called Level I high-tech industries. Fourteen NAICS-based sectors qualified as Level I because technology-oriented occupations accounted for 'a proportion that was at least five times the average or greater and constituted 24.7 per cent or more of industry employment' (Hecker, 2005: 59). In general, these 14 sectors group broadly into biotechnology, information technology, high-tech manufacturing, and high-tech services and R&D. We adjusted the NAICS codes to reflect the redefinition of the classification system that occurred in 2002 (see below for a complete list of the relevant NAICS codes).

CREATING A TYPOLOGY OF HIGH-TECH REGIONS

To examine the ways in which metropolitan areas differ in their high-tech development, we employ a principal component and model-based cluster analysis to create typologies of high-tech regions. The main idea behind a regional typology of US metropolitan areas is to cluster observations into groups that share similar features and then investigate the way in which the groups differ. Clustering methods are among the most widely used techniques to partition such data into meaningful sub-groups. However,

Table A1   High-tech NAICS-codes

NAICS	Industry description	High-tech level
3254	Pharmaceutical and medicine manufacturing	1
3341	Computer and peripheral equipment manufacturing	
3342	Communications equipment manufacturing	
3344	Semiconductor and other electronic component manufacturing	
3345	Navigational, measuring, electromedical, and control instruments manufacturing	
3364	Aerospace product and parts manufacturing	
5112	Software publishers	
5161	Internet publishing and broadcasting	
5179	Other telecommunications	
5181	Internet service providers and web search portals	
5182	Data processing, hosting, and related services	
5413	Architectural, engineering, and related services	
5415	Computer systems design and related services	
5417	Scientific research and development services	
1131	Timber tract operations	2
1132	Forest nurseries and gathering of forest products	
2111	Oil and gas extraction	
2211	Electric power generation, transmission and distribution	
3251	Basic chemical manufacturing	
3252	Resin, synthetic rubber, and artificial synthetic fibres and filaments manufacturing	
3332	Industrial machinery manufacturing	
3333	Commercial and service industry machinery manufacturing	
3343	Audio and video equipment manufacturing	
3346	Manufacturing and reproducing magnetic and optical media	
4234	Professional and commercial equipment and supplies merchant wholesalers	
5416	Management, scientific, and technical consulting services	
3241	Petroleum and coal products manufacturing	3
3253	Pesticide, fertilizer, and other agricultural chemical manufacturing	
3255	Paint, coating, and adhesive manufacturing	
3259	Other chemical product and preparation manufacturing	
3336	Engine, turbine, and power transmission equipment manufacturing	

Table A1   (continued)

NAICS	Industry description	High-tech level
3339	Other general purpose machinery manufacturing	
3353	Electrical equipment manufacturing	
3369	Other transportation equipment manufacturing	
4861	Pipeline transportation of crude oil	
4862	Pipeline transportation of natural gas	
4869	Other pipeline transportation	
5171	Wired telecommunications carriers	
5172	Wireless telecommunications carriers (except satellite)	
5173	Telecommunications resellers	
5174	Satellite telecommunications	
5211	Monetary authorities – central bank	
5232	Securities and commodity exchanges	
5511	Management of companies and enterprises	
5612	Facilities support services	
8112	Electronic and precision equipment repair and maintenance	

Source: Hecker (2005).

most clustering approaches are largely heuristic and lack the rigour usually associated with structural models. In order to address these issues, we use a procedure that adopts a statistical model to group the data. Specifically, we follow Fraley and Raftery (2002) who implement a cluster analysis based on parameterized Gaussian mixture models.

A distinctive advantage of a model-based clustering approach is that it permits the use of more objective model selection techniques (such as the Bayesian Information Criterion or BIC) to compare outcomes rather than the arbitrary choices of more popular clustering approaches such as k-means or hierarchical clustering. Model-based clustering thus provides us with a systematic means of selecting both the parameterization of the model and also the number of clusters. Baum et al. (2007) apply this approach of model-based clustering to develop a typology of socio-economic performance across Australia's non-metropolitan cities, towns and regions

In developing the typology, we use a wide range of data that reflect the MSAs' economic performance and their associated degrees of industrial specialization as well as input-based characteristics, such as quality of the labour force, R&D funding and employment concentration. The 20 individual variables used for the cluster analysis are listed below. The data can broadly be grouped into four thematic categories, namely, *economic performance*, *talent*, *innovation*, and *entrepreneurship*. Our empirical strategy can roughly be described in three steps:

1. We performed an exploratory investigation of spatial properties of the data.
2. Since cluster analysis data usually consists of independent multivariate observations, the dimensions of the data set are reduced by means of a principal component analysis (PCA) in order to derive independent key drivers.
3. The principal components formed the basis for the model-based cluster analysis with the aim to create different groups of MSAs.

From our total of 20 socio-economic variables, the principal component analysis identifies six factors with eigenvalues larger than unity which explain just over 75 per cent of the total variation in the data. We include a measure of natural amenities in order to control for the regional variation in the quality of life among MSAs. The model-based clustering procedure and the BIC outcome lead to the selection of five clusters of MSAs (BIC = − 8325.8) using the VVI parameterization (diagonal, varying volume, varying shape) for the component covariance matrix. Once we determined the five clusters (see Chapter 3), we illustrate dynamics of growth for each type (that is industry measures such as high-tech employment, number of establishments, GDP, as well as measures of innovation, talent, and entrepreneurship). These measures describe the five different regional types and were ultimately instrumental in providing a qualitative characterization of each cluster.

The main intuition behind this approach of constructing a typology of US metropolitan areas is twofold. First, metropolitan areas are clustered into groups that share similar features and, second, by examining the way in which these clusters vary, we obtain additional insights into the different economic dynamics that influence each region. In other words, this method allows us to group different metropolitan areas on the basis of similar characteristics. For example, high-tech challenger regions are generally more innovative and entrepreneurial than the metropolitan average. However, they differ from high-tech centres with regard to other measures, for instance their growth dynamics. Similarly, metropolitan areas fall into the hidden gem regions category, because as a group they show improving measures of high-tech specialization and growth in industry R&D funding. The method lets us identify those metropolitan areas that are similar to each other as measured by the variables that reflect of innovation, talent, and entrepreneurship.

Contrary to simply ranking MSAs by a small set of variables (such as the number of high-tech jobs, location quotients, or firms), we can use the additional information that is contained in our much broader set of variables by reducing the dimensionality of the data via Principal Component Analysis. This then permits us to form model-based clusters which – in contrast to other clustering or ranking techniques – are not based on arbitrary cut-off points. Since we are more interested in identifying emerging high-tech regions, we are able to go beyond the largest high-tech centres and examine other regions in more depth.

A simple ranking along two or three single measures typically produces very unstable rankings which tend to favour the largest high-tech regions without shedding light on smaller regions with similar growth dynamics. As a result, a metropolitan region which – if only measured by its location quotient or high-tech employment – appears as 'low-tech' might nonetheless be categorized as 'high-tech'. This is because all of its other characteristics are very similar to more obvious members of that cluster. The reverse is of course also true for prima facie 'high-tech' candidates that end up categorized in 'low-tech' clusters.

For example, although Gulfport-Biloxi, Mississippi, has a high-tech location quotient of 0.63 and high-tech employment stands at 2732, it is grouped among the high-tech centres. In contrast, nearby Mobile, Alabama, is listed as a region with no high-tech activity. Yet, Mobile has more employees (5709) and a slightly higher location quotient (0.74). The growth dynamics and high-tech potential in the two regions, however, differ in significant ways. While both MSAs enjoyed above average annual GDP growth of 3.9 per cent and 5.2 per cent from 2000 to 2005 respectively, the high-tech employment in Gulfport-Biloxi increased by almost two thirds as opposed to only one quarter in Mobile over the same time period. As a result, Gulfport-Biloxi's high-tech specialization more than doubled compared to a modest one-sixth increase in Mobile. This deepened specialization has also materialized in higher value creation in Gulfport-Biloxi as its GDP of $97 369 per job clearly exceeds the $80 815 per job in Mobile. Furthermore, the two MSAs also diverge fundamentally in terms of their potential for innovation and entrepreneurship: R&D employment in Gulfport-Biloxi accounts for 78 per cent of all high-tech employment, whereas a mere 2 per cent of high-tech employment in Mobile is focused on R&D. Similarly, cumulative industry R&D funding in Gulfport-Biloxi dwarfs that of Mobile by a factor of over 20, having more than quadrupled between 2000 and 2005, when funding barely grew by half in Mobile. Lastly, Gulfport-Biloxi's self-employment is almost 40 per cent higher than the same indicator for entrepreneurship in Mobile.

It is not sufficient to merely rank regions by the number of high-tech

Table A2   Data variables and description

Variable	Description	Sources
Employment in high-tech (2005)	Number of employees in high-tech industries as defined in Appendix E	County Business Patterns, (1998–2005)
Employment: percentage change (1998–2005)	Absolute percentage change of number of employees from 1998 to 2005	
Employment: pre-bubble compound annual growth (1998–2001)	Annualized compound percentage change of number of employees from 1998 to 2001. This includes the 2002 CBP data set which covers employment up to March 2002.	
Employment: post-bubble compound annual growth (2002–5)	Annualized compound percentage change of number of employees from 2002 to 2005	
High-tech establishments (2005)	Number of employees in high-tech industries as defined in Appendix E	
Share of R&D employment (2005)	MSA-share of employment in R&D-intensive industries (NAICS code 5471, also referred to as Scientific R&D Services).	
Business density	Number of establishments per 1000 inhabitants	
GDP from high-tech (2005)	Percentage of metropolitan GDP due to high-tech industries using 2-digit NAICS codes	Bureau of Economic Analysis, Regional Economic Accounts
Dispersion	Personal income as percentage of per-capita metropolitan GDP	
% creative employment (2000)	Creative class measure with percentage employed in creative class occupations and a metro/non-metro indicator for all counties, 1990 and 2000	US Department of Agriculture Economic Research Service, http://www.ers.usda.gov/data/creativeclasscodes/
% bohemian employment (2000)	Bohemian class measure with percentage employed in creative class occupations and a metro/non-metro indicator for all counties, 1990 and 2000	
% with bachelors degree (2000)	Population 25 years and over with Bachelor's degree as percentage of total population segment. (Series P037001, P037015, P037032)	2000 Decennial Current Population Survey, US Census Bureau

Table A2   (continued)

Variable	Description	Sources
% self-employed (2000)	Percentage of households with self-employment income (Series P052001 and P060002)	
Cumulative R&D funding (1998–2005)	Cumulative amount of non-university NSF funding in nominal dollars from 1998 to 2005. State level data attributed to MSA-level using the MSA-share of employment in R&D-intensive industries (NAICS code 5471, also referred to as Scientific R&D Services) as attribution key for state-level data. See also endnote 23.	US National Science Foundation, SRS Publications and Data, Federal Funds for R&D Series (1998–2005), http://www.nsf.gov/statistics/
Number of patents (1990–99)	Cumulative number of MSA-level patent registrations from 1990 to 1999	US Patent and Trademark Office
Firm births/deaths (1998–2004)	Ratio of cumulative number of firm births to firm deaths from 1998 to 2004	US Small Business Administration, Office of Technology (SBIR/STTR)
Small business innovation research grants (1998–2004)	Total number of state level data attributed to MSA-level using the MSA-share of employment in R&D-intensive industries (NAICS code 5471, also referred to as Scientific R&D. Services) as attribution key for state-level data.	US Small Business Administration, Office of Advocacy

jobs. We were interested in the dynamics that drive a region's capacity to be innovative and entrepreneurial. We first examined the size and performance of the regions' high-tech industries, as measured by high-tech employment, establishments, location quotients, and GDP. We then focused on the innovation capacities for each type of region, as measured by industry and university R&D funding, share of employment in R&D-intensive industries, small business innovation research grants, and patents. Talent was measured by the presence of research-intensive universities, educational attainment, and the percentage employed in creative class occupations. Lastly, entrepreneurial capacity was examined, as measured by the number of high-tech firm births and deaths, the percentage of the population that is self-employed, and the number of venture capital deals. Each cluster represents a specific type of high-tech region.

METROPOLITAN STATISTICAL AREAS

In contrast to other studies of high-tech growth which often focus only on the largest cities and regions, we examine the universe of all 360 metropolitan areas in the US (MSAs).[1] Such a comprehensive approach allows us to not only focus on the largest and most prominent high-tech regions but also on regions that may have been able to make inroads into the knowledge economy from a less advantageous position. We thereby avoid a bias towards the largest and most successful regions.

We collected data for all 360 MSAs across the contiguous US.[2] A focus on MSAs does not take into account that individual close-by metropolitan areas have important economic connections (through commuter ties, but also possibly through business networks such as supplier or buyer linkages). For example, the initial set of metropolitan areas shows Durham and Raleigh as separate Metropolitan Statistical Areas (MSAs). The conventional view, however, is that both are considered important parts of the Research Triangle region and we decided to combine these two regions (Luger and Goldstein, 1990).

Since 2005 is the most recent year for which County Business Pattern data is available, we use the December 2005 definition for MSAs with their respective county components. This yields a total of 363 MSAs for the 50 US states (we exclude Puerto Rico). Wherever possible, we use county-level data which is then aggregated at the MSA-level using the 2005 definition file, thus permitting consistent measure for comparison at the MSA-level. This means, for example, that county-level data from the 2000 Decennial Current Population Survey is aggregated into MSA-level data using the 2005 definition files of the Metropolitan and Micropolitan Statistical Areas and components. The definitions of metropolitan areas are provided by the Office of Management and Budget (OMB).

INTERVIEWS

In addition to the quantitative analysis of the metropolitan areas in the US, I conducted case study research. Data for each case study were collected through a variety of methods, including semi-structured key informant interviews. The following is a list of the 104 interviews that were conducted from 2001–7.

Interviews Conducted in Portland, Oregon

Andersen, Morgan (2001). Interview by author with Intel education manager, Hillsboro, OR, 16 November.

Battjes, Carl (2001). Interview by author with former Tektronix engineer, Portland, OR, 6 September.

Chew, Robert (2001). Interview by author with former Tektronix employee, Portland, OR, 20 August.

Crosby, Philip (2001). Interview by author with former Tektronix employee and Network Elements employees, Beaverton, OR, 20 August.

Cunningham, Ward and Sears, Richard (2001). Interview by author with FLIR system manager and employee, Portland, OR, 26 November.

Earnshaw, Aliza (2001). Interview by author with *Portland Business Journal* journalist, Portland, OR, 25 May.

Fahey, Les (2001). Interview by author with venture capitalist, Portland, OR, 16 August.

Gibson, Scott (2001). Interview by author with co-founder of Sequent, Lake Oswego, OR, 19 July.

Gill, Frank (2001). Interview by author with former Intel manager, Portland, OR, 13 November.

Guilami, Dave (2001). Interview by author with Intel patent attorney, Portland, OR, 21 August.

Hallen, Thor (2001). Interview by author with retired Tektronix engineer, Beaverton, OR, 21 August.

Henry, Suzy (2002). Interview by author with Intel human resource manager, Hillsboro, OR, 2 February.

Huffman, Lois (2001). Interview by author with patent attorney and former Tektronix employee, Portland, OR, 21 August.

Huntzicker, Jim (2002). Interview by author with former Tektronix education manager, Beaverton, OR, 12 June.

Hurt, Jack (2001). Interview by author with Tektronix engineer, Beaverton, OR, 8 August.

Johnson, Jim (2001). Interview by author with former Intel Oregon manager, Portland, OR, 1 June.

Kendall, Abbie (2001). Interview by author with founder of Armstrong Kendall, Portland, OR, 30 August.

King, Chris (2001). Interview by author with Planar executive, Beaverton, OR, 7 July.

Laird, Michelle (2001). Interview by author with business services firm representative, Portland, OR, 12 July.

Lattin, Bill (2001). Interview by author with former Intel manager, Portland, OR, 13 November.

London, Ralph (2001). Interview by author with former Tektronix employee, Portland, OR, 30 August.

Long, Tom (2003). Interview by author with Tektronix engineer, Beaverton, OR, 19 May.

Mackworth, Hugh (2001). Interview by author with venture capitalists of Smart Forest Ventures, Portland, OR, 14 November.

McGeady, Steven (2001). Interview by author with former Intel engineer, Portland, OR, 20 September.

McLaughlin, Glenn (2001). Interview by author with former Forest Service Radio Laboratory employee, Portland, OR, 16 August.

Nelson, Joe (2001). Interview by author with former Tektronix employee and founder of Chemtrix, Portland, OR, 22 August.

Newman, Bill and Hoffman, Gordon (2001). Interview by author with venture capitalists, Portland, OR, 19 November.

Preston, David (2001). Interview by author with Intel Capital manager, Portland, OR, 2 November.

Shaw, Ralph (2001). Interview by author with venture capitalist, Portland, OR, 27 August.

Sickinger, Ted (2001). Interview by author with *The Oregonian* journalist, Portland, OR, 18 July.

Squire, Dave (2001). Interview by author with former Tektronix employee and Planar employee, Beaverton, OR, 17 August.

Strain, Doug (2001). Interview by author with founder of Electro Scientific Industries, Portland, OR, 20 August.

Taylor, Mike (2001). Interview by author with Silicon Forest entrepreneur, Portland, Oregon, 27 August.

TenZeldam, Paul (2001). Interview by author with Tektronix manager, Beaverton, OR, 20 November.

Thomson, Keith (2001). Interview by author with first Intel Oregon manager, Portland, OR, 15 October.

Visveswarian, Venky (2001). Interview by author with former Tektronix and Mentor Graphics engineer, Portland, OR, 18 August.

Walker, Bill (2001). Interview by author with former Tektronix manager, Beaverton, OR, 15 August.

Wills, Rick (2003). Interview by author with Tektronix CEO, Beaverton, OR, 14 May.

Winningstad, Norm (2001). Interview by author with founder of Floating Point System, Portland, OR, 25 September.

Woodward, Steve (2001). Interview by author with *The Oregonian* journalist, Portland, OR, 15 June.

Interviews Conducted in Boise, Idaho

Bedard, Kip (2007). Interview by author with Vice President at Micron Technology, Boise, ID, 8 May.

Benedict, Kevin (2007). Interview by author with CEO of MobileDataforce, Boise, ID, 4 May.

Boyce, Shril (2007). Interview by author with member of Boise Metro Chamber of Commerce, Boise, ID, 4 May.

Bradley, Phil (2007). Interview by author with former CEO of ProClarity and angel investor, Boise, ID, 30 April.

Caleb, John (2007). Interview by author with founder of Ugobe, Boise, ID, 8 May.

Codd, Todd (2007). Interview and tour through HP printer museum, Boise Division, Boise ID, 7 May.

Crawforth, Jason (2007). Interview by author with founder of Treetop Technologies, Boise, ID, 2 May.

Glen, Roy (2007). Telephone interview by author with Associate Professor, College of Business at Boise State University, 30 January.

Glerum, John (2007). Interview by author with Director of TECenter at Boise State University, Boise, ID, 2 May.

Haney, Tim (2007). Interview by author with former HP engineer, Boise, ID, 4 May.

Hodges, Steve (2007). Interview by author with founder of M2M Communications, Boise, ID, 7 May.

Howard, Julie (2007). Interview by author with former journalist and manager at Idaho Department of Commerce, Boise, ID, 4 May.

Howard, Julie (2007). Telephone interview by author with former journalist and manager at the Idaho Department of Commerce, 10 January.

Learned, Kevin (2007). Interview by author with founding member of Boise Angel Fund and Associate Business Consultant with SBDC Idaho, Boise, ID, 7 May.

Lundt, Holmes (2007). Interview by author with former president of Kestrelink, Boise, ID, 1 May.

Moeser, Jeff (2007). Interview by author with founder of Dedicated Devices, Boise, ID, 3 May.

Parkinson, Ward (2007). Interview by author with co-founder of Micron Technology, Boise, ID, 3 May.

Reed, Phil (2007). Interview by author with Co-Founder and Managing Partner of Highway 12 Ventures, Boise, ID, 2 May.

Riskey, Frank (2007). Interview by author with founder of TenXsys, Boise, ID, 8 May.

Ritter, Rick (2007). Interview by author with CEO and President of Idaho TechConnect, Boise, ID, 2 May.

Sasso, Ray (2007). Telephone interview by author with former Chief Strategy Officer with J.R. Simplot Company, 30 January.

Schrader, Cheryl (2007). Interview by author with Dean of College of Engineering at Boise State University, Boise, ID, 2 May.

Sewall, Pat (2007). Interview by author with CEO and founder of CradlePoint, Boise, ID, 2 May.

Simplot, Scott (2007). Interview by author with son of JR Simplot, Boise, ID, 3 May.

Simpson, Steve (2007). Interview by author with former president/CEO of Extended Systems, Boise, ID, 1 May.

Smelek, Ray (2007). Telephone interview by author with former General Manager of HP Boise Division, 5 November.

Solon, Mark (2007). Interview by author with General Partner of Highway 12 Ventures, Boise, ID, 2 May.

Sosoka, John (2007). Interview by author with co-founder and Chief Technology Officer of Ugobe, Boise, ID, 8 May.

Spohn, Nor Rae (2007). Interview by author with HP General Manager of Boise Division, Boise, ID, 7 May.

Tueller, Karl (2007). Telephone interview by author with Executive Director, Office of Science & Technology, Department of Labor, 6 February.

Volk, Chris (2007). Interview by author with president and board member of Kickstand, Boise, ID, 7 May.

Wrigley, Krissa (2007). Interview by author with VP of Research and Evaluation of Idaho TechConnect, Boise, ID, 2 May.

Interviews Conducted in Kansas City, Kansas-Missouri

Boran, Diarmuid (2005). Interview by author with Entrepreneur in Residents at the Kansas Technology Enterprise Corporation, Kansas City, KS-MO, 24 October.

Brown, Richard (2005). Interview by author with Co-Chariman of the Board of The Stowers Institute, Kansas City, KS-MO, 18 August.

Byrnes, James (2005). Interview by author with Executive Vice President at airPharma, Kansas City, KS-MO, 17 August.

Cowden, Tim (2005). Interview by author with Senior VP for Business Development of the KC Area Development Council, Kansas City, KS-MO, 16 August.

Dispensa, Stephen (2005). Interview by author with Chief Technology Officer of Positive Networks, Kansas City, KS-MO, 15 August.

Duncan, Bill (2005). Interview by author with President of the Kansas City Life Sciences Institute, Kansas City, KS-MO, 17 August and 25 October.

Duncan, Bill (2007). Telephone interview with President of the Kansas City Area Life Sciences Institute, 19 January.

Franano, Nicholas (2005). Telephone interview by author with President and CEO of Proteon Therapeutics, 23 August.

Garver, Steve (2005). Interview by author with Chief Executive Officers of SoftVu, Kansas City, KS-MO, 24 October.

Herman, Mike (2005). Interview by author with former CFO of Marion Laboratories, Kansas City, KS-MO, 18 August.

Higuchi, Peter (2005). Interview by author with Vice President for Corporate Development at airPharma, Kansas City, KS-MO, 17 August.

Hockaday, Irvine (2005). Interview by author with Lead Independent Director at Sprint, Kansas City, KS-MO, 4 August.

Illig, Cliff (2005). Interview by author with Vice Chairman and Co-Founder of Cerner, Kansas City, KS-MO, 26 October.

Jackson, Brian (2005). Interview by author with business development manager at Medi-Flex, Kansas City, KS-MO, 26 October.

Jacob, Larry (2005). Interview with Vice President for Community Investment at the Greater Kansas City Community Foundation, Kansas City, KS-MO, 27 October.

Kelly, Steve (2007). Interview with Deputy Secretary of the Kansas Department of Commerce, 31 January.

Kessinger, Joe (2005). Interview by author with founder of Innovia Medical, Kansas City, KS-MO, 15 August.

Laufenberg, Jim (2005). Interview by author with President and CEO of ImmunoGenetix Therapeutics, Kansas City, KS-MO, 25 October.

Lenk, Frank (2005). Interview by author with Director of Research at the Mid-America Regional Council, Kansas City, KS-MO, 18 August.

Marcusse, Robert (2005). Interview by author with President and CEO of the KC Area Development Council, Kansas City, KS-MO, 16 August.

McHug, Michael (2005). Interview by author with Business Development manager at Teva Neuroscience, Kansas City, KS-MO, 25 October.

Meyers, Maria (2005). Interview by author with Network Builder and Managing Director of KCSourceLink, Kansas City, KS-MO, 15 August.

Mitchell, Lesa (2005). Interview by author with the Vice President for Advancing Innovation at the Kauffman Foundation, Kansas City, KS-MO, 19 August.

Mitchum, Jim (2005). Interview by author with President of Medi-Flex, Kansas City, KS-MO, 26 October.

Scott, Jewel (2005). Interview by author with President of Civic Council, Kansas City, KS-MO, 14 August.

Slaughter, Michie (2005). Interview by author with retired VP for Human Resources at Marion Laboratories, Kansas City, KS-MO, 25 October.

Song, Michael (2005). Telephone interview by author with Professor at the University of Missouri, Kansas City, KS-MO, 22 August.

Strohmeier, Karl (2005). Telephone interview by author with Director of Business Development at Pharmion Corporation, 22 August.

Taylor, Tracy (2005). Interview by author with President of the Kansas Technology Enterprise Corp., Kansas City, KS-MO, 19 August.

Thornton, Tom (2007). Telephone interview with President of the Kansas Bioscience Authority, 19 January.

Vranicar, David (2005). Interview with author with former employee of Marion Laboratories, Kansas City, KS-MO, 26 October.

Warm, David (2005). Interview by author with President of the Mid-America Regional Council, Kansas City, KS-MO, 18 August.

NOTES

1. Most studies examine only a subset of the officially defined Metropolitan Statistical Areas. Typically, the authors examine the 50 largest metropolitan areas or economically successful regions (as measured by job growth). For examples, see Chapple et al. (2004), Cortright and Mayer (2002), amd Gittell and Sohl (2005).
2. The 2005 Office of Budget Management (OMB) defines a total of 363 Metropolitan Statistical Areas (MSA) for the 50 US states. Our analysis encompasses only the 360 MSAs located in the contiguous 48 states. We excluded the MSAs of Fairbanks and Anchorage in Alaska and Honolulu in Hawaii. We also combined the Raleigh and the Durham metropolitan statistical areas and called it the Research Triangle metropolitan region.

References

Abbott, C. (1981), *The New Urban America: Growth and Politics in Sunbelt Cities*, Chapel Hill, NC: University of North Carolina Press.

Abbott, C. (1983), *Portland: Planning, Politics, and Growth in a Twentieth-century City*, Lincoln, NE: University of Nebraska Press.

Abbott, C. (2000), 'The capital of good planning: metropolitan Portland since 1970', in R. Fishman (ed.), *American Planning Tradition*, Washington, DC: Woodrow Wilson Centre Press.

Abbott, C. (2001), *Greater Portland: Urban Life and Landscape in the Pacific Northwest*, Philadelphia, PA: University of Pennsylvania Press.

Abbott, C., D.A. Howe and S. Adler (1994), *Planning the Oregon Way: A Twenty-year Evaluation*, Corvallis, OR: Oregon State University Press.

Adams, S.B. (2005), 'Stanford and Silicon Valley: lessons from becoming a high-tech region', *California Management Review*, **48**(1): 29–51.

Agrawal, A. and I. Cockburn (2003), 'The anchor tenant hypothesis: exploring the role of large, local, R&D intensive firms in regional innovation systems', *International Journal of Industrial Organization*, **21**: 1227–53.

Aldrich, H. and M.A. Martinez (2001), 'Many are called, but few are chosen: an evolutionary perspective for the study of entrepreneurship', *Entrepreneurship Theory and Practice*, **25**(4): 41–56.

Amin, A. (1994), *Post-Fordism: A Reader*, Oxford: Blackwell.

Amin, A. and N. Thrift (1992), 'Neo-Marshallian nodes in global networks', *International Journal of Urban and Regional Research*, **16**, 571–87.

Anderson, C. (2004), 'Frankland quits at KCCatalyst', accessed 23 March 2011 at www.bizjournals.com/kansascity/stories/2004/07/19/story1.html.

Angel, D. (1994), *Restructuring for Innovation: The Remaking of the US Semiconductor Industry*, New York: Guilford.

Angel, D. (2000), 'High-tech agglomeration and the labor market: the case of Silicon Valley', in M. Kenney (ed.), *Understanding Silicon Valley: The Anatomy of an Entrepreneurial Region*, Stanford, CA: Stanford University Press.

Animal Health Corridor (2007), KC Animal Health Corridor, website data, accessed 30 August at www.kcanimalhealth.com/.

Arita, T. and P. McCann (2007), 'The industrial structure and location behavior of the US, European, and Asian semiconductor industries', in P. Pellenbarg and E. Wever (eds), *International Business Geography: Case Studies of Corporate Firms*, London: Routledge, pp. 139–68.

Armstrong-Hough, M. (2006), 'A good fit: North Carolina's place in the biotechnology value chain', accessed 5 April 2009, from www.soc.duke.edu/NC_GlobalEconomy/pdfs/paper/armstrong_hough_1.pdf.

Arthur, B. (1996), 'Increasing returns and the two worlds of business', *Harvard Business Review*, July-August, 1996.

Arthur, W.B. (1987), 'Competing technologies, increasing returns and lock-in by historical events', *Economic Journal*, **99**: 116–31.

Attebery, L. (2000), *JR Simplot: A Billion the Hard Way*, Caldwell, ID: Caxton Press.

Audretsch, D. and M. Feldmann (1996), 'R&D spillovers and the geography of innovation and production', *American Economic Review*, **86**(1): 630–40.

Audretsch, D. and E. Lehmann (2005), 'Does the knowledge spillover theory of entrepreneurship hold for regions?', *Research Policy*, **34**: 1191–202.

Bagchi-Sen, S., H. Lawton Smith and L. Hall (2004), 'The US biotechnology industry: industry dynamics and policy', *Environment and Planning C*, **22**: 199–216.

Banatao, D.P. and K.A. Fong (2000), 'The valley of deals: how venture capital helped shape the region', in C.-M. Lee, W.F. Miller, M.G. Hancock and H.S. Rowen (eds), *The Silicon Valley Edge: A Habitat for Innovation and Entrepreneurship*, Stanford, CA: Stanford University Press, pp. 295–313.

Barnett, J. (1994), 'Tek spinoff prospers on its own: Merix is a growing business, manufacturing circuit boards in a factory at Forest Grove', *The Oregonian*, 7 July, p. B1.

Barnett, J. (1995), 'Intel's chip comes', *The Oregonian,* 1 November, p. D01.

Barry, F. (2006), 'The emergence of Ireland's ICT clusters: the role of foreign direct investment', in M. Feldman and P. Braunerhjelm (eds), *Cluster Genesis: Technology-Based Industrial Development*, Oxford: Oxford University Press, pp. 148–71.

Bathelt, H., A. Malmberg and P. Maskell (2004), 'Clusters and knowledge: local buzz, global pipelines and the process of knowledge creation', *Progress in Human Geography,* **28**(1): 31–56.

Baum, S., M. Haynes Y. van Gellecum and J.H. Han (2007), 'Considering regional socio-economic outcomes in nonmetropolitan Australia: a typology building approach', *Papers in Regional Science,* **86**(2): 261–86.

Beaudry, C. and S. Breschi (2003), 'Are firms in clusters really more innovative', *Economics of Innovation and New Technology,* **12**(4): 325–42.

Beebe, P. (1988), 'Hewlett-Packard reorganizes peripherals group', *The Idaho Statesman,* 5 May, pp. 8-B.

Benneworth, P. (2004), 'In what sense "regional development?": entrepreneurship, underdevelopment and strong tradition in the periphery', *Entrepreneurship & Regional Development,* **16**, 439–58.

Berger, S. (2005), *How We Compete: What Companies Around the World Are Doing to Make it in Today's Global Economy*, New York: Currency Doubleday.

Berlin, L. (2001), 'Robert Noyce and Fairchild Semiconductor, 1957–1968', *Business History Review,* **75**(1): 63–101.

Berlin, L. (2005), *The Man Behind the Microchip: Robert Noyce and the Invention of Silicon Valley*, New York: Oxford University Press.

Bhide, A. (2000), *The Origin and Evolution of New Businesses*, Oxford and New York: Oxford University Press.

Birch, K. (2008), 'Alliance-driven governance: applying a global commodity chains approach to the UK biotechnology industry, *Economic Geography,* **84**(1): 83–103.

Blanchard, C. (2005), 'This urban Idaho', *Idaho Issues Online*, accessed 4 November 2007 at www.boisestate.edu/history/issuesonline/spring2006 _issues/5f_numbers_06spr.html#.

Boschma, R.A. and J.G. Lambooy (1999), 'Evolutionary economics and economic geography', *Journal of Evolutionary Economics,* **9**: 411–29.

Boschma, R.A. and G.A. van der Knaap (1999), 'New high-tech industries and windows of locational opportunity: the role of labour markets and knowledge institutions during the industrial era', *Geografiska Annaler,* **81**(B): 73–89.

Brandt, R., O. Port and R. Hof (1988), 'Intel: the next revolution', *Businessweek*, 26 September.

Braunerhjelm, P. and M. Feldmann (2006), *Cluster Genesis: Technology-based Industrial Development*, Oxford: Oxford University Press.

Brenner, T. (2004), *Local Industrial Clusters: Existence, Emergence and Evolution*, London: Routledge.

Breshnahan, T. and A. Gambardella (2004), *Building High-Tech Clusters: Silicon Valley and Beyond*, Cambridge: Cambridge University Press.

Bresnahan, T., A. Gambardella and A. Saxenian (2001), '"Old economy" inputs for "new economy" outcomes: cluster formation in the new Silicon Valleys', *Industrial and Corporate Change,* **10**(4): 835–60.

Brittain, J. and J. Freeman (1986), 'Entrepreneurship in the semiconductor industry', unpublished manuscript.

Bruno, A. and T. Tyebjee (1982), 'The environment for entrepreneurship', *Encyclopedia of Entrepreneurship* Englewood Cliffs, NJ: Prentice-Hall, pp. 288–315.

Buckley, M. (2001), 'Conditions right for KCCatalyst to make play for tech businesses', *Kansas City Business Journal,* 1 June.

Burress, D., J. Rosenbloom and S. Manzoor (2004), '*The Kansas City Economy: Performance, Innovation, and Resources for Future Economic Progress*', Lawrence, KS: University of Kansas, Policy Research Institute.

Caniels, M. and H. Romijn (2003), 'Firm-level knowledge accumulation and regional dynamics', *Industrial and Corporate Change,* **12**(6): 1253–78.

Carroll, G.R. and O.M. Khessina (2005), 'The ecology of entrepreneurship', in S.A. Alvarez, R. Agarwal and O. Sorenson (eds), *Handbook of Entrepreneurship Research: Disciplinary Perspectives*, Heidelberg, Germany: Springer, pp. 167–200.

Ceh, B. and J. Gatrell (2006), 'R&D production in the United States: rethinking the Snowbelt-Sunbelt shift', *The Social Science Journal,* **43**: 529–51.

Ceruzzi, P. (2000), *A History of Modern Computing*, Cambridge, MA: The MIT Press.

Chandler, A. (1990), *Scale and Scope*, Cambridge, MA: The Belknap Press.

Chapple, K., A. Markusen, G. Schrock, D. Yamamoto and P. Yu (2004), 'Gauging metropolitan "high-tech" and "I-tech" activity', *Economic Development Quarterly,* **18**(1): 10–29.

Chesbrough, H. (2001), 'The Intel lookout', *Technology Review, 2002,* 9 October.

Chesbrough, H. (2002), 'Graceful exits and missed opportunities: Xerox's management of its technology spin-off organizations', *Business History Review,* **76**(4): 803–37.

Chesbrough, H. (2003a), 'The era of open innovation', *MIT Sloan Management Review,* **44**(3): 35–41.

Chesbrough, H. (2003b), *Open Innovation: The New Imperative for Creating and Profiting from Technology*, Boston, MA: Harvard Business School Press.

Chico State University (2000), 'Mueter's leaving signals the end of an era', *Inside Chico State,* **30**.

Christensen, C. (1997), *The Innovator's Dilemma: When New Technologies Cause Great Firms to Fail*, Boston, MA: Harvard Business School Press.

Christopherson, S. and J. Clark (2007), *Remaking Regional Economies: Power, Labor, and Firm Strategies in the Knowledge Economy*, London, New York: Routledge.

Colby, R. (1992), 'Tek: looking for a turnaround', *The Oregonian*, 19 July.

Colby, R. (1993), 'Tektronix plans to become even more trim', *The Oregonian*, 25 June.

Cooke, P. (2001), 'New economy innovation systems: biotechnology in Europe and the USA', *Industry and Innovation*, **8**(3): 267–89.

Cooper, A. (1971), *The Founding of Technologically-based Firms*, Milwaukee, WI: The Centre for Venture Management.

Cooper, A. (1985), 'The role of incubator organizations in founding growth-oriented firms', *Journal of Business Venturing*, **1**: 75–86.

Cortright, J. and H. Mayer (2001), *High Tech Specialization: A Comparison of High Technology Centers*, Survey Series, Washington DC: The Brookings Institution.

Cortright, J. and H. Mayer (2002), *Signs of Life: The Growth of Biotechnology Centers in the US*, Washington DC: The Brookings Institution.

Cortright, J. and H. Mayer (2004), 'Increasingly rank: the use and misuse of rankings in economic development', *Economic Development Quarterly,* **18**(1): 34–43.

Crevoisier, O. and D. Maillat (1991), 'Milieu, industrial organizaton and territorial production system: towards a new theory of spatial development', in R. Camagni (ed.), *Innovation Networks: Spatial Perspectives*, London: Belhaven Press, pp. 13–34.

De Figueiredo, J. and D. Teece (1996), 'Mitigating procurement hazards in the context of innovation', *Industrial and Corporate Change*, **5**(2): 537–59.

deFigueiredo, J. and M. Kyle (2006), 'Surviving the gales of creative destruction: the determinants of product turnover', *Strategic Management Journal*, **27**: 241–64.

Dicken, P. (2007), *Global Shift: Mapping the Changing Countours of the World Economy*, New York: The Guilford Press.

Dodds, G. and C. Wollner (1991), *Thriving on Change: A History of Mentor Graphics, 1981–1991*, Wilsonville, OR: Mentor Graphics.

Dodds, G.B. and C.E. Wollner (1990), *The Silicon Forest: High Tech in the Portland Area*. Portland, OR: The Oregon Historical Society.

Duranton, G. and D. Puga (2001), 'Nursery cities: urban diversity, process innovation, and the life cycle of products', *American Economic Review*, **91**(5): 1454–77.

ECONorthwest (1998), 'Economic impacts of Intel's Oregon operations', Portland, OR: Intel Corporation.

Ernst & Young (2008), 'Beyond borders: global biotechnology report 2008'.

Etkin, J. (1979), 'Marion asks to market Ulcer drug', *The Kansas City Star,* 3 July, p. 5c:1.

Etzkowitz, H. (2001), 'The entrepreneurial university and the emergence of democratic corporatism', in H. Etzkowitz and L. Leydesdorff (eds), *Universities and the Global Knowledge Economy: A Triple Helix of University-Industry-Government Relations*, New York: Continuum, pp. 141–52.

Feldman, M. (1994), 'The university and economic development: the case of Johns Hopkins University and Baltimore', *Economic Development Quarterly,* **8**(1): 67–76.

Feldman, M. (2001), 'The entrepreneurial event revisited: firm formation in a regional context', *Industrial and Corporate Change*, **10**(4): 861–91.

Feldman, M. (2003), 'The locational dynamics of the US biotech industry: knowledge externalities and the anchor hypothesis', *Industry and Innovation*, **10**(3): 311–28.

Feldman, M. and P. Braunerhjelm (2006), 'The genesis of industrial clusters', in M. Feldmann and P. Braunerhjelm (eds), *Cluster genesis: Technology-based Industrial Development*, Oxford: Oxford University Press, pp. 1–13.

Feldman M. and J. Francis (2001), 'Entrepreneurs and the formation of industrial clusters', unpublished paper.

Feldman, M. and J. Francis (2003), 'Fortune favors the prepared region: the case of entrepreneurship and the capitol region biotechnology cluster', *European Planning Studies*, **11**(7): 765–88.

Feldman, M., J. Francis and J. Bercovitz (2005), 'Creating a cluster while building a firm: entrepreneurs and the formation of industrial clusters', *Regional Studies*, **39**(1): 129–41.

Feldmann, M. and P. Braunerhjelm (2006), 'The genesis of industrial clusters', in M. Feldmann and P. Braunerhjelm (eds), *Cluster Genesis: Technology-based Industrial Development*, Oxford: Oxford University Press, pp. 1–13.

Feser, E.J. (1998), 'Enterprises, external economies and economic development', *Journal of Planning Literature*, **12**(3): 283–302.

Florida, R. (2002a), 'The rise of the creative class', *Washington Monthly*.

Florida, R. (2002b), '*The Rise of the Creative Class and How it's Transforming Work, Leisure, Community and Everyday Life*', New York: Basic Books.

Florida, R. and M. Kenney (1990a), *The Breakthrough Illusion: Corporate America's Failure to Move from Innovation to Mass Production*, New York: BasicBooks.

Florida, R. and M. Kenney (1990b), 'Silicon Valley and Route 128 won't save us', *California Management Review*, **33**: 68–88.

Florida, R. and M. Samber (1999), 'Capital and creative destruction. Venture capital and regional growth in US industrialization', in T. Barnes and M. Gertler (eds), *The New Industrial Geography*, London: Routledge, pp. 265–291.

Fogarty, M.S. and A.K. Sinha (1999), 'Why older regions can't generalize from Route 128 and Silicon Valley: university-industry relationships and regional innovation systems', in L.M. Branscomb, F. Kodama and R. Florida (eds), *Industrializing Knowledge: University-Industry Linkages in Japan and the United States*, Cambridge, MA: MIT Press.

Fornahl, D., S. Henn and M.-P. Menzel (2010), *Emerging Clusters: Theoretical, Empirical and Political Perspectives on the Inital Stage of Cluster Evolution*, Cheltenham, UK and Northampton, MA, USA: Edward Elgar.

Fraley, C. and A.E. Raftery (2002), 'Model-based clustering, discriminant analysis and density estimation', *Journal of the American Statistical Association*, **97**(2): 611–31.

Francis, M. (1995), 'Who owns "Silicon Forest"?', *The Oregonian*, 3 December, p. G01.

Freeman, C. and L. Soete (1999), *The Economics of Industrial Innovation*, Cambridge, MA: The MIT Press.

Friend, J. (1986), 'Printer jets H-P to top of line', *The Idaho Statesman*, 4 February, p. 6B.

Gibbons, J. (2000), 'The role of Stanford University: a dean's reflection', in C.-M. Lee, W. Miller, M.G. Hancock and H. Rowen (eds), *The Silicon Valley Edge: A Habitat for Innovation and Entrepreneurship*, Stanford, CA: Stanford University Press.

Gittell, R. and J. Sohl (2005), 'Technology centres during the economic downturn: what have we learned?', *Entrepreneurship & Regional Development*, **17**(4): 293–312.

Giuliani, E. (2005), 'Cluster absorptive capacity: why do some clusters forge ahead and others lag behind?', *European Urban and Regional Studies*, **12**(3): 269–88.

Glasmeier, A. (1988), 'Factors governing the development of high-tech industry agglomerations: a tale of three cities', *Regional Studies*, **22**: 287–301.

Glasmeier, A. (2000), 'Economic geography in practice: local economic development policy', in G.L. Clark, M. Feldman and M.S. Gertler (eds), *The Oxford Handbook of Economic Geography*, Oxford: Oxford University Press, pp. 559–79.

Goldstone, J.A. (2009), 'Engineering culture, innovation, modern wealth creation', in C. Karlsson, R. Stough and B. Johansson (eds), *Entrepreneurship and Innovations in Functional Regions*, Cheltenham, UK, and Northampton, MA, USA: Edwardd Elgar, pp. 21–47.

Gompers, P., J. Lerner and D. Scharfstein (2003), *Entrepreneurial Spawning: Public Corporations and the Genesis of New Ventures, 1986–1999*, Cambridge, MA: National Bureau of Economic Research.

Grabher, G. (1993), 'The weakness of strong ties: the lock-in of regional development in the Ruhr area', in G. Grabher (ed.), *The Embedded Firm: On the Socio-economics of Industrial Networks*, London: Routledge.

Gray, G.C. (1982), *Radio for the Fireline: A History of Electronic Communication in the Forest Service 1905–1975*, Washington DC: US Department of Agriculture, Forest Service.

Gray, M. (2006), 'Studying the new economy: an activity specific approach to the high-tech firm', in M. Taylor and P. Oinas (eds), *Understanding the Firm: Spatial and Organizational Dimensions*, Oxford: Oxford University Press, pp. 191–213.

Gray, M., E. Golob and A. Markusen (1996), Big firms, long arms, wide shoulders: the 'hub-and-spoke' industrial district in the Seattle region, *Regional Studies*, **30**(7): 651(616).

Gray, M., E. Golob and A. Markusen (1999), 'Seattle: a classic hub-and-spoke region', in A. Markusen, Y.-S. Lee and S. DiGiovanna (eds), *Second Tier Cities: Rapid Growth Beyond the Metropolis*, Minneapolis, MN: University of Minnesota, pp. 287–90.

Gray, M., E. Golob, A.R. Markusen and S. Ock Park (1999), 'The four faces of Silicon Valley', in A. Markusen, Y.-S. Lee and S. DiGiovanna (eds), *Second Tier Cities. Rapid Growth Beyond the Metropolis*, Minneapolis, MN: University of Minnesota Press, pp. 291–310.

Gray, M. and A. Markusen (1999), 'Colorado Springs: a military-anchored city in transition', in A. Markusen, Y.-S. Lee and S. DiGiovanna (eds), *Second Tier Cities: Rapid Growth Beyond the Metropolis*, Minneapolis, MN: University of Minnesota.

Greater Kansas City Community Foundation (2005), *Time to Get it Right: A Strategy for Higher Education in Kansas City*, Kansas City, MO: Greater Kansas City Community Foundation.

Greater Kansas City Community Foundation (2010), *Time to Get it Right: staying Competitive in the New Economy. The View from Year Five*, Kansas City, MO: Greater Kansas City Community Foundation.

Guerber, S. (1973), 'Question of why Hewlett-Packard chose Boise gets nebulous reply', *The Idaho Statesman*, 14 June.

Harrison, B. (1992), 'Industrial districts: old wine in new bottles?', *Regional Studies*, 26(5): 469–83.

Harrison, B. (1994), *Lean and Mean: The Changing Landscape of Corporate Power in the Age of Flexibility*, New York: Basic Books.

Heaster, R. (1989), 'Marion Labs will remain in KC', *The Kansas City Star*, 18 July, p. A1:4.

Hecker, D. (2005), 'High-technology employment: a NAICS-based update', *Monthly Labor Review*, July.

Hellmann, T. (2000), 'Venture capitalists: the coaches of Silicon Valley', in C.-M. Lee, W.F. Miller, M.G. Hancock and H.S. Rowen (eds), *The Silicon Valley Edge: A Habitat for Innovation and Entrepreneurship*, Stanford, CA: Stanford University Press, pp. 276–94.

Herbig, P. and J. Golden (1993), 'Analysis note: the fall of innovative hot spots Silicon Valley and Route 128', *International Marketing Review*, **10**(6): 13–29.

Herrigel, G. (2000), 'Large firms and industrial districts in Europe: deregionalization, re-regionalization, and the transformation of manufacturing flexibility', in J. Dunning (ed.), *Regions, Globalization, and the Knowledge-based Economy*, Oxford: Oxford University Press, pp. 286–302.

Herrigel, G. (2004), 'Large firms and regions: new forms of commitment', in J. Lears and J.V. Scherpenberg (eds), *Cultures of Economy – Economics of Culture*, Heidelberg, Germany: Winter, pp. 97–108.

Hewlett-Packard (2007), Company history, accessed 2 November at www.hp.com/hpinfo/abouthp/histnfacts/index.html.

Howard, J. (2003), 'Hewlett-Packard 30 years in Boise: coming to Boise', *The Idaho Statesman*, 11 November, p. 1S.

HP Computer Museum (2010), Boise, accessed 9 September at www.hpmuseum.net/divisions.php?did=9#

Iammarino, S. and P. McCann (2006), 'The structure and evolution of industrial clusters: transactions, technology and knowledge spillovers', *Research Policy*, **35**: 1018–36.

Idaho Department of Commerce (2011), Science and Technology Advisory Council, accessed 21 March at http://commerce.idaho.gov/about-us/innovation/innovation-council/.

Intel (2002), Intel oral histories archives, Santa Clara, CA.

Intel (2008), 'Intel in your community: key Oregon data', accessed 10 November at www.intel.com/community/oregon/campus/key.htm.

Intel (1993), Defining Intel: 25 years/25 events, accessed 29 March 2011, at www.intel.com/Assets/PDF/General/25yrs.pdf.

Kansas City Area Life Sciences Institute (2011), 'About KCALSI', accessed 23 March at www.kclifesciences.org/about/about.php.

Kansas Technology Enterprise Corporation (2005), 'Statewide Bioscience

Initiative: Kansas Economic Growth Act', accessed 15 September at www.ktec.com/sec_bioscience/section/kega.htm.

Kansas Technology Enterprise Corporation (2008), 'Centres of Excellence', accessed 21 October at www.ktec.com/sec_research/section/centers.htm.

Karash, J. (1999), 'Drug firm's pullout costs KC 900 jobs. Hoechst Marion headquarters going to NJ', *The Kansas City Star*, 15 October, p. A1.

KCSourceLink (2011), 'Who we are', accessed 23 March at www.kcsource-link.com/.

Keeble, D., C. Lawson, B. Moore and F. Wilkinson (1999), 'Collective learning processes, networking and the "institutional thickness" in the Cambridge region', *Regional Studies*, **33**(4): 319–32.

Keenan, J. (1985), 'Marion Labs attributes soaring success to its staff', *The Kansas City Star*, 13 August, p. D1:1.

Keltz, M. (1981), 'H-P unveils line of disc memories designed in Boise', *The Idaho Statesman*, 3 November, pp. B-1.

Kenney, M. and R. Florida (2000), 'Venture capital in Silicon Valley: fueling new firm formation', in M. Kenney (ed.), *Understanding Silicon Valley: The Anatomy of an Entrepreneurial Region*, Stanford, CA: Stanford University Press.

Kenney, M.E. (ed.) (2000), *Understanding Silicon Valley: The Anatomy of an Entrepreneurial Region*, Stanford, CA: Stanford University Press.

Ketelhöhn, N. (2006), 'The role of clusters as sources of dynamic externalities in the US semiconductor industry', *Journal of Economic Geography*, **6**: 679–99.

Klepper, S. (1996), 'Entry, exit, growth, and innovation over the product life cycle', *The American Economic Review*, **86**(3): 562–83.

Klepper, S. (2001a), 'Employee startups in high-tech industries', *Industrial and Corporate Change*, **10**(3): 639–73.

Klepper, S. (2001b), 'The evolution of the US automobile industry and Detroit as its capital', accessed 11 November 2008, at www.druid.dk/conferences/winter2002/gallery/klepper.pdf.

Klepper, S. (2008), 'Silicon Valley – a Chip off the Old Detroit Bloc', paper presented at the 25th DRUID conference on Entrepeneurship and Innovation: Organizations, Institutions, Systems and Regions.

Klepper, S. and S. Sleeper (2005), 'Entry by spinoffs', *Management Science*, **51**(8): 1291–306.

Klepper, S. and P. Thompson (2005), 'Spinoff entry in high-tech industries: motives and consequences', accessed 29 January 2009, at www2.fiu.edu/~thompsop/current/adobe/spinoff.pdf.

Kochut, B. and J. Humphreys (2007), 'Shaping infinity: the Georgia life sciences industry analysis 2007', accessed 5 April 2009 at www.georgiabiosciences.com/MediaDocuments/Shaping%20Infinity%202007.pdf.

Kogut, B. and U. Zander (2003), Knowledge of the firm and the evolutionary theory of the multinational corporation, *Journal of International Business Studies,* **34**: 516–29.

Kovsky, E. (2007), 'Otter recommendations disappoint tech council', *Idaho Business Review*, 22 January.

KTEC (2011), 'About' accessed 23 March at http://kansaspipeline.org/s/1300/index.aspx?sid=1300&gid=1&pgid=304.

Langlois, R. (1992), 'External economies and economic progress: the case of the microcomputer industry', *Business History Review,* **66**(1): 1–50.

Lazerson, M. and G. Lorenzoni (1999), 'The firms that feed industrial districts: a return to the Italian source', *Industrial and Corporate Change,* **8**(2): 235–66.

Lazonick, W. (2009), *Sustainable Prosperity in the New Economy*, Kalamazoo, MI: W.E. Upjohn Institute of Employment Research.

Leachman, R. and C. Leachman (2004), 'Globalization of semiconductors: do real men have fabs, or virtual fabs?', in M. Kenney and R. Florida (eds), *Locating Global Advantage: Industry Dynamics in the International Economy*, Stanford, CA: Stanford University Press, pp. 203–31.

Lecuyer, C. (2000), 'Fairchild Semiconductor and its influence', in C.-M. Lee, W. Miller, M.G. Hancock and H. Rowen (eds), *The Silicon Valley Edge: A Habitat for Innovation and Entrepreneurship*, Stanford, CA: Stanford University Press.

Lecuyer, C. (2003), 'High-tech corporatism: management–employee relations in US electronics firms, 1920s–1960s', *Enterprise & Society,* **4**(3): 502–20.

Lecuyer, C. (2005), *Making Silicon Valley: Innovation and the Growth of High Tech, 1930–1970*, Cambridge, MA: The MIT Press.

Lee, M.M. (1986), *Winning with People: The First 40 Years of Tektronix*, Portland, OR: Tektronix, Inc.

Leslie, S.W. (1993), *The Cold War and American Science: The Military-Industrial-Academic Complex at MIT and Stanford*, New York: Columbia University Press.

Leslie, S.W. (2000), 'The biggest "angel" of them all: the military and the making of Silicon Valley', in M. Kenney (ed.), *Understanding Silicon Valley: The Anatomy of an Entrepreneurial Region*, Stanford, CA: Stanford University Press.

Leslie, S.W. (2001), 'Regional disadvantage: replicating Silicon Valley in New York's capital region', *Technology and Culture,* **42**(2): 236–64.

Leslie, S.W. and R.H. Kargon (1996), 'Selling Silicon Valley: Frederick Terman's model for regional advantage', *Business History Review,* **70**: 435–72.

Levin, H.M., D.W. Jeong and D. Ou (2006), 'What is a world class university?', accessed 17 March 2011 at www.tc.columbia.edu/centers/coce/pdf_files/c12.pdf.

Longhi, C. (1999), 'Networks, collective learning and technology development in innovative high technology regions: the case of Sophia-Antipolis', *Regional Studies,* **33**(4): 333–42.

Lorenzen, M. (2005), 'Why do clusters change?', *European Urban and Regional Studies,* **12**(3): 203–8.

Lowe, N. (2007), 'Job creation and the knowledge economy: lessons from North Carolina's life science manufacturing initiative', *Economic Development Quarterly,* **21**(4): 339–53.

Lucas, M., A. Sands and D.A. Wolfe (2009), 'Regional clusters in a global industry: ICT clusters in Canada', *European Planning Studies,* **17**(2): 189–209.

Luger, M. and H. Goldstein (1990), *Technology in the Garden,* Chapel Hill, NC: University of North Carolina Press.

Lyons, D. (1995), 'Agglomeration economies among high technology firms in advanced production areas: the case of Denver/Boulder', *Regional Studies,* **29**(3): 265–78.

Lyons, D. (2000), 'Embeddedness, milieu, and innovation among high-technology firms: a Richardson, Texas, case study', *Environment and Planning A,* **32**: 891–908.

Markoff, J. (1998), 'Inside Intel, the future is riding on a new chip', *The New York Times,* 5 April.

Markusen, A. (1994), 'Studying regions by studying firms', *Professional Geographer,* **46**(4): 477–90.

Markusen, A., P. Hall, S. Campbell and S. Deitrick (1991), *The Rise of the Gunbelt: The Military Remapping of Industrial America,* New York: Oxford University Press.

Markusen, A.R., Y.-S. Lee and S. DiGiovanna (1999), *Second Tier Cities: Rapid Growth Beyond the Metropolis* (vol 3), Minneapolis, MN: University of Minnesota Press.

Marshall, A. (1920), *Principles of Economics,* London: Macmillan.

Martin, R. and P. Sunley (2003), 'Deconstructing clusters: chaotic concept or policy panacea?', *Journal of Economic Geography,* **3**: 5–35.

Martin, R. and P. Sunley (2006), 'Path dependence and regional economic evolution', *Journal of Economic Geography,* **6**: 395–437.

Martin, S. (2008), 'Understanding the ONAMI experience: success factors and transferability', accessed 9 October 2010 at www.pdx.edu/sites/www.pdx.edu.ims/files/media_assets/onamifinal.pdf.

Martinelli, F. and E. Schoenberger (1991), 'Oligopoly is alive and well: notes for a broader discussion of flexible accumulation', in G. Benko and M. Dunford (eds), *Industrial Change and Regional Development: The Transformation of New Industrial Spaces*, London: Belhaven Press.

Maskell, P. (2001), 'The firm in economic geography', *Economic Geography,* **77**(4): 329–44.

Mayer, H. (2003), 'Taking root in the Silicon Forest: the role of high technology firms as surrogate universities in Portland, Oregon', unpublished dissertation, Portland State University, Portland, OR.

Mayer, H. (2005a), 'Planting high technology seeds: Tektronix role in the creation of Portland's Silicon Forest', *Oregon Historical Quarterly,* **106**(4): 568–93.

Mayer, H. (2005b), 'Taking root in the Silicon Forest: the role of high technology firms as surrogate universities in Portland, Oregon', *Journal of the American Planning Association,* **71**(3): 318–33.

Mayer, H. (2006), 'Completing the puzzle: creating a high-tech and life science economy in Kansas City', accessed 23 June 2011 at www.brook ings.edu/metro/pubs/20061101_kansasmayer.pdf.

Mayer, H. (2007), 'What is the role of the university in creating a high-technology region?', *Journal of Urban Technology,* **14**(3): 33–58.

Mayer, H. (2008), 'Competition for high-tech jobs in second-tier regions: the case of Portland, Oregon', in D.J. Watson and J.C. Morris (eds), *Building the Local Economy: Cases in Economic Development*, Carl Vinson Institute of Government, The University of Georgia, pp. 61–78.

Mayer, H. (2009a), *Bootstrapping High-tech: Evidence from Three Emerging High Technology Metropolitan Areas*, Washington DC: The Brookings Institution.

Mayer, H. (2009b), 'Constructing competitive advantage: the evolution of state R&D investment funds in the United States', in K. Benesch and M. Zwingenberger (eds), *Scientific Cultures – Technological Challenges: A Transatlantic Perspective*, Heidelberg, Germany: Universitätsverlag Winter.

Mayer, H. and J. Provo (2004), 'The Portland edge in context', in C. Ozawa (ed.), *The Portland Edge*, Washington DC: Island Press, pp. 9–34.

McCann, P. and T. Arita (2006), 'Clusters and regional development: some cautionary observations from the semiconductor industry', *Information Economics and Policy,* **18**: 157–80.

McDonald, C. (1998), 'The evolution of Intel's Copy EXACTLY! technology transfer method', *Intel Technology Journal,* **4**.

McKendrick, D.G., R.F. Doner and S. Haggard (2000), *From Silicon Valley to Singapore: Location and Competitive Advantage in the Hard Disk Drive Industry*, Stanford, CA: Stanford University Press.

Menzel, M.-P. (2005), 'Networks and technologies in an emerging cluster:

the case of bioinstruments in Jena', in C. Karlsson, B. Johansson and R. Stough (eds), *Industrial Clusters and Inter-Firm Networks*, Cheltenham, UK, and Northampton, MA, USA: Edward Elgar Publishing, pp. 413–49.

Menzel, M.-P. and D. Fornahl (2007), 'Cluster life cycles: dimensions and rationales of cluster development', accessed 6 September 2008 at http://zs.thulb.uni-jena.de/servlets/MCRFileNodeServlet/jportal_deriva te_00079989/wp_2007_076.pdf.

Menzel, M.-P. and D. Fornahl (2009), 'Cluster life cycles – dimensions and rationales of cluster development', *Industrial and Corporate Change*, **19**(1): 205–38.

Miller, R. and M. Cote (1985), 'Growing the next Silicon Valley', *Harvard Business Review,* **63**(July-August): 114–23.

Mitton, D. (1990), 'Bring on the clones: a longitudinal study of the proliferation, development, and growth of the biotech industry in San Diego', *Frontiers of Entrepreneurship Research*, Proceedings of the Tenth Annual Babson College Entrepreneurial Research Conference, Center for Entrepreneurial Studies/Babson College, 344–58.

Moore, G. and K. Davis (2004), 'Learning the Silicon Valley way', in T. Bresnahan and A. Gambardella (eds), *Building High-tech Clusters: Silicon Valley and Beyond*, Cambridge: Cambridge University Press, pp. 7–39.

Morgan, A. (1995), *Prescription for Success: The Life and Values of Ewing Marion Kauffman*, Kansas City, MO: Andrews and McMeel.

Mpoyi, R. (2000), 'Changing corporate strategies: restoring competitive advantage through vertical disintegration', *Advances in Competitiveness Research,* **8**(1): 71–80.

Muro, M. (2010), 'Reclaiming prosperity in the Treasure Valley: designing a sustainable future in the new West', accessed 2 September at www.brookings.edu/~/media/Files/rc/speeches/2010/0604_idaho_ muro/0604_idaho_muro_speech.pdf.

Muro, M., E. Istrate and J. Rothwell (2010), 'Export West: how mountain west metros can lead national export growth and boost competitiveness', accessed 2 September www.brookings.edu/~/media/Files/rc/ reports/2010/0726_exports/0726_mountain_exports_muro.pdf.

Neck, H., D.G. Meyer, B. Cohen and A. Corbett (2004), 'An entrepreneurial system view of new venture creation', *Journal of Small Business Management,* **42**(2): 190–208.

Nelson, R. and S. Winter (1982), *An Evolutionary Theory of Economic Change*, Cambridge, MA: Harvard University Press.

New Economy Strategies (2004), *The Greater Kansas City Health Care Innovation Scenario: A Road Map for Life Sciences & Convergent Technologies*, Washington DC: New Economy Strategies.

Noble, D. (1977), *America by Design: Science, Technology, and the Rise of Corporate Capitalism*, Oxford: Oxford University Press.

Northeast Parallel Architecture Centre (2002), BiiN, accessed 3 June 2009, at www.npac.syr.edu/nse/hpccsurvey/orgs/biin/biin.html.

O'Malley, E. and C. O'Gorman (2001), 'Competitive advantage in the Irish indigenous software industry and the role of inward foreign direct investment', *European Planning Studies*, **9**(3): 303–21.

O'Mara, M.P. (2005), *Cities of Knowledge: Cold War Science and the Search for the Next Silicon Valley*, Princeton, NJ: Princeton University Press.

O'Connor, A.C., D.W. Wood and H.J. Walls (2008), 'Economic impact assessment of the Oregon Nanoscience and Microtechnology Institute (ONAMI)', accessed 9 October 2010 at http://blog.oregonlive.com/sili conforest/2008/11/ONAMI%20Report.pdf.

Oden, M. (1997), 'From assembly to innovation the evolution and current structure of Austin's high-tech economy', *Planning Forum*, 3: 14–30.

Office of Science and Technology (2004), 'S&T strategy update and action plan 2004. Moving forward: accelerating Idaho's innovation economy (executive summary)', accessed 16 November 2006 at http://technology. idaho.gov/Portals/33/documents/ExecutiveSummary.pdf.

Office of Science and Technology, & Idaho Commerce and Labor (2004), 'Moving forward: accelerating Idaho's innovation economy', accessed 10 October 2008 at http://commerce.idaho.gov/assets/content/docs/ ExecutiveSummary.pdf.

Oregon Council for Knowledge and Economic Development (2002), *Renewing Oregon's Economy: Growing Jobs and Industries through Innovation. A Report from the Oregon Council for Knowledge and Economic Development*, Portland, OR: Publishing.

Otter, C.L.B. (2007), 2007 State of the State/State Budget Message, accessed 20 October 2008 at www.gov.idaho.gov/mediacenter/speeches/ sp_2007/sp_stateaddress.html.

Packard, D. (1995), *The HP Way*, New York: HarperCollins.

Penrose, E.T. (1959), *The Theory of the Growth of the Firm*, New York: Wiley.

Perroux, F. (1950), 'Economic space: theory and application', *Quarterly Journal of Economics*, **64**: 89–104.

Pew Centre on the States and National Governors Association (2007), 'Investing in innovation', accessed 23 August at www.nga.org/Files/ pdf/0707INNOVATIONINVEST.PDF.

Pewitt, J. (1988), 'Hewlett-Packard hikes printer production', *The Idaho Statesman*, 8 December, pp. 8-B.

Piore, M. and C. Sabel (1984), *The Second Industrial Divide: Possibilities for Prosperity*, New York: Basic Books.

Pisano, G.P. (2006), *Science Business: The Promise, the Reality, and the Future of Biotech*, Boston, MA: Harvard Business School Press.

Pollard, J and M. Storper (1996), 'A tale of twelve cities: metropolitan employment change in dynamic industries in the 1980s', *Economic Geography*, **72**: 1–22.

Porter, M. (2000a), 'Location, competition, and economic development: local clusters in a global economy', *Economic Development Quarterly*, **14**(1): 15–34.

Porter, M. (2000b), 'Locations, clusters, and company strategy', in G.L. Clark, M. Feldmann and M.S. Gertler (eds), *The Oxford Handbook of Economy Geography*, Oxford: Oxford University Press, pp. 253–74.

Porter, M.E. (1990), *The Competitive Advantage of Nations*, New York: Free Press.

Porter, M.E. (1998), 'Clusters and the new economics of competition', *Harvard Business Review*, November-December, 77–90.

Portland Business Journal (2008), *The Book of Lists 2008*, Portland, OR: Portland Business Journal.

Portland Chamber of Commerce (1950), *Highlights of the Industrial Economy of Oregon With Particular Emphasis on the Portland Metropolitan Area*, Portland, OR: Portland Chamber of Commerce.

Powell, W., K. Koput, J. Bowie and L. Smith-Doerr (2002), 'The spatial clustering of science and capital: accounting for biotech firm-venture capital relationships', *Regional Studies*, **36**(3): 291–305.

PricewaterhouseCoopers (2009), PricewaterhouseCoopers/Thomson Reuters/NVCA Moneytree Venture Capital Profiles, accessed 5 May at http://vx.thomsonib.com/VxComponent/static/stats/2008q4/0MAIN MENU.html.

PricewaterhouseCoopers and National Venture Capital Association (2007), 'Money tree report', accessed 3 January 2008 at www. pwcmoneytree.com/MTPublic/ns/moneytree/filesource/exhibits/Q307_ Money%20Tree_Report_Final.pdf.

Rogers, E.M. and J.K. Larsen (1984), *Silicon Valley Fever: Growth of High Technology Culture*, New York: Basic Books.

Rogoway, M. (2005), 'Linus Torvalds, incognito inventor', accessed 19 March 2011 at www.oregonlive.com/business/index.ssf/2005/06/linus_ torvalds_incognito_inven.html.

Romanelli, E. and C.B. Schoonhoven (2001), 'The local origins of new firms', in C.B. Schoonhoven and E. Romanelli (eds), *The Entrepreneurship Dynamic: Origins of Entrepreneurship and the Evolution of Industries*, Stanford, CA: Stanford University Press, pp. 40–67.

Rosenbloom, J., D. Burress and P. Oslund (2004), *The Bioscience Industry in Douglas County: An Analysis of Economic Impacts Opportunities and Challenges*, Lawrence, KS: The Lawrence Chamber of Commerce.

Rubin, H. (1988), 'Shoot anything that flies; claim anything that falls', *Economic Development Quarterly*, **2**(3): 236–51.

Saxenian, A. (1994a), 'Lessons from Silicon Valley', *Technology Review*, **97**: 42–51.

Saxenian, A. (1994b), *Regional Advantage: Culture and Competition in Silicon Valley and Route 128*, Cambridge, MA: Harvard University Press.

Saxenian, A. (2000), 'The origins and dynamics of production networks in Silicon Valley', in M. Kenney (ed.), *Understanting Silicon Valley: The Anatomy of an Entrepreneurial Region*, Stanford, CA: Stanford University Press, pp. 141–62.

Schachtel, M., Y. Bi and M. Kuklick (2004), 'The genealogy of Maryland information technology company founders: bioinformatics, medical informatics, health informatics', accessed 25 October 2007 at www. marylandtedco.org/_media/pdf/publications/Reportehealth_medicine.pdf.

Scott, A. (2008), 'Resurgent metropolis: economy, society and urbanization in an interconnected world', *International Journal of Urban and Regional Research*, **32**(3): 548–64.

Scott, A.J. (2004), 'Flexible production systems and regional development: the rise of new industrial spaces in North America and Europe', in T. Barnes, J. Peck, E. Sheppard and A. Tickell (eds), *Reading Economic Geography*, Malden, MA: Blackwell Publishing, pp. 125–36.

Segal, N. (1985), *The Cambridge Phenomenon: The Growth of High Technology Industry in a University Town*, Cambridge: Segal Quince Wicksteed.

Shane, S. (2003), *A General Theory of Entrepreneurship: The Individual-Opportunity Nexus*, Cheltenham, UK, and Northampton, MA, USA: Edward Elgar.

Simmie, J. (1998), 'Reasons for development of "islands of innovation": evidence from Hertfordshire', *Urban Studies*, **35**(8): 1261–89.

Skodack, D. (1992), 'Ciba-Geigy executive to lead Marion Merrell research', *The Kansas City Star*, 15 January, p. B1:2.Smilor, R.W., G.B. Dietrich and D.V. Gibson (1993), 'The entrepreneurial university: the role of higher education in the United States in technology commercialization and economic development', *International Social Science Journal*, **45**(1): 1–11.

Smilor, R.W., D.V. Gibson and G. Kozmetsky (1989), 'Creating the technopolis: high-technology development in Austin, Texas', *Journal of Business Venturing*, **4**: 49–67.

Smith, D. and R. Alexander (1988), *Fumbling the Future: How Xerox Invented, then Ignored the First Personal Computer*, New York: William Morrow.

Soher, H. (1962), *Oregon Today and Tomorrow. An Economic Study of the Quality State for Pacific Power & Light Company*, Portland, OR: Pacific Power & Light Company.

Sorenson, O. and P.G. Audia (2000), 'The social structure of entrepreneurial activity: geographic concentration of footwear production in the United States, 1940–1989', *American Journal of Sociology*, **106**(2): 424–61.

Staber, U. (2005), 'Entrepreneurship as a source of path dependency', in G. Fuchs and P. Shapira (eds), *Rethinking Regional Innovation and Change: Path Dependency or Regional Breakthrough*, New York: Springer.

Stafford, D. (2001), 'Smooth moves – Aventis assists workers in transition', *The Kansas City Star*, 3 April, p. D1.

Storper, M. and S. Christopherson (1987), 'Flexible specialization and regional industrial agglomerations: the case of the US motion picture industry', *Annals of the Association of American Geographers*, **77**(1): 104–17.

Storper, M. and R. Walker (1989), *The Capitalist Imperative: Territory, Technology, and Industrial Growth*, Oxford and New York: Blackwell Publishing.

Sturgeon, T. (2000), 'How Silicon Valley came to be', in M. Kenney (ed.), *Understanding Silicon Valley*, Stanford, CA: Stanford University Press.

Tappi, D. (2005), 'Clusters, adaption and extroversion: a cognitive and entrepreneurial analysis of the Marche music cluster', *European Urban and Regional Studies*, **12**(3): 289–307.

Taylor, J. (2006), 'What makes a region entrepreneurial?', Cleveland, DH: Centre for Economic Development, Maxine Goodman Levin College of Urban Affairs, Cleveland State University.

Taylor, M. (2006), 'Fragments and gaps: exploring the theory of the firm', in M. Taylor and P. Oinas (eds), *Understanding the Firm: Spatial and Organizational Dimensions*, Oxford: Oxford University Press, pp. 3–31.

Taylor, M. and P. Oinas (2006), *Understanding the Firm: Spatial and Organizational Dimensions*, Oxford; New York: Oxford University Press.

Tekweek (1974), 'Fall term student body stands at 2,200', *Tekweek*, *5*, 4 October.

Tekweek (1979), 'Earl Wantland answers questions on state of Tek', *Tekweek, 9,* 16 February.

ter Wal, A. and R.A. Boschma (2007), 'Co-evolution of firms, industries and networks in space', accessed 6 September 2008 at http://econ.geo. uu.nl/peeg/peeg0707.pdf.

The Business Journal (2004), *22nd Annual Book of Lists, 2003–2004*, vol 23, Kansas City, MO: The Business Journal.

The Idaho Statesman (1976), 'H-P unit to mean 400 jobs', *The Idaho Statesman*, 2 September, pp. B-1.

The Idaho Statesman (1984), 'H-P introduces Boise-developed printer', *The Idaho Statesman*, 24 May, pp. 7-B.

The Stowers Institute for Medical Research (2011), 'About the institute', accessed 5 January.

Thomas Miller and Associates (2003), 'Greater Kansas City Life Sciences Industry Survey', report prepared for the Kansas City Life Sciences Institute and Kansas City Area Development Council.

Thornton, P. (1999), 'The sociology of entrepreneurship', *Annual Review of Sociology*, **25**: 19–46.

Trippl, M. and F. Toedtling (2007), 'Developing biotechnology clusters in non-high technology regions – the case of Austria', *Industry and Innovation*, **14**(1): 47–67.

Vey, J.S. (2006), *Organizing for Success: A Call to Action for the Kansas City Region*, Washington DC: Brookings Institution.

Waits, M.J. (1998), 'Economic development strategies in the American states', in K. Liou (ed.), *The Handbook of Economic Development*, New York: Marcel Dekker Inc.

Walcott, S. (1998), 'The Indianapolis "Fortune 500": Lilly and regional renaissance', *Environment and Planning A*, **30**(10): 1723–41.

Walcott, S. (2001), 'Growing global: learning locations in the life sciences', *Growth and Change*, **32**(4): 511–32.

Walcott, S.M. (2002), 'Analyzing an innovative environment: San Diego as a bioscience beachhead', *Economic Development Quarterly*, **16**(2): 99–114.

West, J. and C. Simard (2006), 'Balancing intrapreneurial innovation vs. entrepreneurial spinoffs during periods of technological ferment', paper presented at the Babson College Entrepreneurship Research Conference.

Wicksteed, B. (2000a), *The Cambridge Phenomenon Revisted Part One*, Cambridge: Seagal Quince Wicksteed.

Wicksteed, B. (2000b), *The Cambridge Phenomenon Revisted Part Two*, Cambridge: Seagal Quince Wicksteed.

Wolfe, T. (1983, December 1983), 'The tinkerings of Robert Noyce. How the sun rose on the Silicon Valley', *Esquire*, December, pp. 346–73.

Yu, A. (1998), *Creating the Digital Future: The Secrets of Consistent Innovation*, New York: The Free Press.

Zeller, C. (2010), 'The pharma-biotech complex and interconnected regional innovation arenas', *Urban Studies*, **47**(3): 2867–94.

Zhang, J. (2003), 'High-tech start-ups and industry dynamics in Silicon Valley', accessed 23 June 2011 at www.ppic.org/content/pubs/report/R_703JZR.pdf.

Zucker, L.G. and M.R. Darby (1996), 'Star scientists and institutional transformation: patterns of invention and innovation in the formation of the biotechnology industry', *Proceedings of the National Academy of Sciences*, **93**(23): 12709–16.

Zucker, L.G., M.R. Darby and M.B. Brewer (1998), 'Intellectual human capital and the birth of US biotechnology enterprises', *The American Economic Review*, **88**(1): 290–306.

Index